# Three Minutes a Day

VOLUME 49

# THREE MINUTES A DAY
## VOLUME 49

**Tony Rossi**
*Editor-in-Chief*

**Gerald M. Costello**
*Contributing Editor*

**The Christophers**
**5 Hanover Square**
**New York, NY 10004**

**www.christophers.org**

Scriptural quotations in this publication are from the Revised Standard Version Bible, Catholic Edition, copyright 1965 and 1966 by the Division of Christian Education of the National Council of Churches of Christ in the U.S.A. and the New Revised Standard Version Bible, Catholic Edition, copyright 1989 by the Division of Christian Education of the National Council of Churches of Christ in the U.S.A. and used by permission.

Lord, make me an instrument of Your peace.
Where there is hatred, let me sow love;
where there is injury, pardon;
where there is doubt, faith;
where there is despair, hope;
where there is darkness, light;
and where there is sadness, joy.

O Divine Master, grant that I may not so much seek
to be consoled as to console;
to be understood as to understand;
to be loved as to love.
For it is in giving that we receive;
it is in pardoning that we are pardoned;
and it is in dying that we are born to eternal life.
Amen.

PRAYER OF ST. FRANCIS
(ADOPTED AS THE PRAYER OF THE CHRISTOPHERS)

The Christophers warmly thank
all our friends, sponsors and supporters
who have made this 49th volume of
*Three Minutes a Day* possible.

## Contributing Writers

Tony Rossi

Gerald M. Costello

Sarah E. Holinski

Joan Bromfield

# Dear Christopher Friend,

We hope you will enjoy Volume 49 of our *Three Minutes a Day* book. Our founder, Maryknoll Father James Keller, believed that everyone has a unique purpose in life, and the stories contained within these pages demonstrate this truth. Taken together, these readings explore the full range of human emotions through real-life stories and situations that help us to better understand people in their suffering and their joy.

This book is intended as a daily reminder that there is good in the human heart—and that amazing things can happen when we have faith and use our talents in service to others. These stories can make us laugh and cry and root for good to come out of the most difficult situations. When we do that for just a few minutes every day we become better people, able to face the world with a spirit of compassion and hope.

This year of 2015 marks The Christophers' 70th anniversary. We have accomplished so much with help from those who have supported our mission throughout the years. There have been many blessings along the way, but the greatest is found in knowing that we have touched people's hearts and souls, and influenced lives for the better. The most important support we receive is from people like you who live by our motto, "It's better to light one candle than to curse the darkness." Thank you for inspiring us and keeping our mission alive within your heart.

*Mary Ellen Robinson, Vice President*
*Father Jonathan Morris*
*Father Dennis W. Cleary, M.M.*

## 'I'm Not a Victim'

When TV host Mike Rowe met retired Army Staff Sergeant Travis Mills at the Science and Engineering Festival in Washington, D.C., he was astonished at the condition of the man standing in front of him. It wasn't just the fact that Mills was a quadruple amputee with two prosthetic arms and two prosthetic legs, but also that his spirit was shockingly upbeat.

When Rowe inquired what happened to him, Mills said an IED in Afghanistan had destroyed his limbs. Despite that, Mills said, "I'm not a victim, Mike, and I refuse to be portrayed that way." Instead, Mills focuses on his wife, his child, and on helping wounded veterans adjust to life with their injuries.

On Facebook, Rowe wrote, "Travis is missing more than a few original parts; he's missing all traces of self-pity. And that presents a challenge for mortals like me...[to] listen to a guy with no arms or legs tell me how lucky he is, and how much he appreciates all my hard work. That's called a gut-check, and I could use one from time to time."

**Be strong, and let us be courageous.**
**(2 Samuel 10:12)**

*Instead of dwelling on misfortune, Father, inspire me to be a blessing to others.*

## Thank You for Listening, Young Lady

While working as a Spanish translator for a meditation class at Mercy Center in the Bronx, New York, Angelica Perez encountered a woman in her late fifties who opened up about her lifetime of physical and emotional pain. Though Perez realized this woman needed professional treatment for depression, she listened sympathetically as she talked for over an hour.

Before leaving to see a social worker to get the help she needed, the woman hugged Perez and said, "Thank you for listening to my story... No one has ever sat with me and listened for such a long time. Thank you, young lady."

Recalling that experience on the Mercy Volunteer Corps blog, Perez wrote, "Did I really say the magical words to get this lady to feel better and cure her depression? Not quite; all I did was listen with compassion and respond gently. I was reminded on this day that the simplest acts of kindness can make a big difference; even when we think we're not making a difference, we may be doing more than we give ourselves credit for."

**Speak, for Your servant is listening.
(1 Samuel 3:10)**

*Give me the patience and compassion to listen to the lost and lonely, Savior.*

## Listen to Your Mother...Usually

You should always follow your mother's advice. Well, almost always. Consider this story that actor and comedian Tim Conway shared as a guest on *Christopher Closeup* while promoting his memoir *What's So Funny?*

During his third year starring in the 1960s hit sitcom *McHale's Navy*, Tim got a call from his mother, Sophia, in Chagrin Falls, Ohio. She told him, "Ken Shutts down at the hardware store is taking on new help. You know him rather well, so you should apply."

A little surprised, Tim responded, "Ma, have you been watching television in the last couple of years?"

Sophia answered, "I saw it, but that junk isn't going to last. You got a chance to get a good steady job. You should take it."

Thankfully, Tim didn't pursue the hardware store job, which freed him up to eventually make it onto *The Carol Burnett Show*, where he cemented his legacy as a comedy great. But the down-to-earth attitudes he learned from his parents stay with him to this day. And he's a better (and funnier) man for it.

**A cheerful heart is a good medicine.
(Proverbs 17:22)**

*May laughter lift my spirits, Heavenly Father.*

## A Labor of Love and Faith

Twenty-nine-year-old Daniel Andrade suffers from a severe type of cerebral palsy, rendering him unable to walk, talk, or move since birth. Yet thanks to the singular efforts of his loving mother, Irma, he is able to attend Mass once a week.

Every Sunday, 56-year-old Irma Gomes-Andrade washes, dresses and carries her son down the stairs of their second-floor apartment to his wheelchair waiting in the driveway below. The pair then walk the three blocks to St. John the Baptist Church, located in their hometown of Pawtucket, Rhode Island.

Irma has gone through some especially rough periods in her life. Daniel's birth father left her after learning their son was disabled, and it took years to get Daniel to hold up his own head. Even today, he still requires constant everyday care. But Irma is grateful to God for the gift of Daniel's life—and her own.

"I opened my arms and I trusted God that He would give me the strength to raise him the best I can," Irma told the *Rhode Island Catholic*. "I thank God for everything He has given me."

**God, the Lord, is my strength. (Isaiah 40:31)**

*Christ, may we always lean upon Your ineffable strength.*

## 'What Is Needed Is Trust'

After graduating college, Michigan resident Jim Ziolkowski hitchhiked around the world, spending time in developing countries like India and Nepal, where he felt overwhelmed by the poverty he witnessed. One day, he passed through a village where they were celebrating the opening of a school. Ziolkowski realized how powerful education can be.

When he returned to the U.S. in 1990, he got a job in corporate finance at GE. But after 15 months, he quit that job to start the nonprofit buildOn. Their initial mission was to build three schools in poor areas of three different continents, using inner-city youth from America to help do it.

Beyond good intentions, though, Ziolkowski had no idea how to accomplish that task. He felt paralyzed by fear, until one night he opened his Bible and read Jesus's words from Mark's gospel: "Fear is useless. What is needed is trust."

Ziolkowski got the courage to call up the CFO of GE Capital, and ask for financial help. His pitch worked, and the project came together. Today, buildOn has built 618 schools in developing countries.

**My heart shall not fear. (Psalm 27:3)**

*Strengthen my belief in Your loving providence, Lord.*

## Addicts Challenge Atheist's Unbelief

When photographer Chris Arnade started taking pictures of homeless drug addicts in New York's South Bronx, he expected to find a group of people who, like himself, were atheists. After all, how could individuals living desperate lives on the streets believe there was a loving God who cares for everyone?

Arnade was shocked that the exact opposite view prevailed. Michael, a crack addict, always carries a rosary with him. Heroin addicts Sonya and Eric count a picture of the Last Supper as their most valued possession. Takeesha, a prostitute, describes herself as "a child of God."

Arnade's hard shell of disbelief cracked. He wrote in *The Guardian,* "In Biblical terms, we are all sinners. On the streets the addicts, with their daily battles and proximity to death, have come to understand this viscerally. Many successful people don't. Their sense of entitlement and emotional distance has numbed their understanding of our fallibility."

Arnade now sees his own fallibility, and admires the addicts whose faith offers them a source of hope.

**He instructs sinners in the way. (Psalm 25:8)**

*Lord, guide all people who search for You to a better life.*

# A Millionaire's Dream Job

When Jon Kitna hung up his cleats in 2011 after 15 years as an NFL quarterback, he not only went back to school but he went there to teach—at Lincoln High School, the same one he'd attended while growing up in Tacoma, Washington.

Lincoln is in a high-poverty area these days, and many of the students are potential dropouts. That didn't trouble Kitna. "Give me your toughest students," he said. And he certainly got them.

Kitna didn't turn to teaching because he needed the money. His football career brought him over $20 million, $2.3 million of it in his final year with the Dallas Cowboys. He did it for love of the profession, a feeling he doesn't attempt to hide. "This is my dream job," he says.

His "dream job" includes teaching three algebra classes, and he loves seeing students go from outright failure straight to the honor roll.

"To see lives changed," he said. "That's something!"

**Jesus said to him, "If you wish to be perfect, go, sell your possessions, and give the money to the poor." (Matthew 19:21)**

*Lord, bless teachers who bring wisdom to young people.*

# A Brain Surgeon's Snowy Trek

When a major snowstorm paralyzed Birmingham, Alabama, in 2014, most residents just stayed inside. But not 62-year-old neurosurgeon Dr. Zenko Hrynkiw.

While assisting another brain surgeon at Brookwood Medical Center, he received the CT scans of a patient at Trinity Medical Center on his phone. Dr. Hrynkiw believed the patient had a 90 percent chance of dying, so he decided to walk six miles in his scrubs to Trinity to perform emergency surgery.

As reported by the Alabama Media Group, Dr. Hrynkiw's journey "included stops to help push stranded motorists stuck in the roadway due to the snowstorm—and a stop to sit in an ambulance to warm up from the below 20-degree weather."

Dr. Hrynkiw insisted, "I walk a lot so it wasn't that big a deal." But in light of the patient's good prognosis, Trinity CEO Keith Granger disagreed with the humble physician, saying, "It's a remarkable physical and mental feat. We have an individual alive today who wouldn't be here if not for his efforts."

**The Lord has made my journey successful. (Genesis 24:56)**

*Guide my steps during difficult journeys, Divine Savior.*

## Making Life Harder than It Has to Be

Writer Tim Hoch believes that many of us are making life harder than it has to be. He points out some ways in which we do this—and how we can move past them to find happiness.

- "Another driver cut you off. Your friend never texted you back. Your co-worker went to lunch without you. Everyone can find a reason to be offended on a steady basis. So what caused you to be offended? You assigned bad intent to these otherwise innocuous actions. You took it as a personal affront. Happy people don't ascribe intent to the unintentional actions of others."

- "I have a bad habit of fast forwarding everything to its worst possible outcome and being pleasantly surprised when the result is marginally better than utter disaster. My mind unnecessarily wrestles with events that aren't remotely likely, [such as] my lost driver's license fell into the hands of an al-Qaeda operative who will wipe out my savings account. Negativity only breeds more negativity. It is a happiness riptide. It will carry you away from shore and if you don't swim away from it, will pull you under."

**Can any of you by worrying add a single hour to your span of life? (Luke 12:25)**

*Help me to nurture a positive outlook on life, Creator.*

## Moving On and Letting Go

Today, a few more ideas from writer Tim Hoch on ways that you can make your life easier and happier.

- "Do you need to forgive someone, turn your back on a failed relationship, or come to terms with the death of a loved one? Closure is a word for people who have never really suffered. There's no such thing. Just try to 'manage' your loss. Put it in perspective. You will always have some regret and doubt about your loss. You're not alone. Find someone who understands and talk to that person. Reach out for support."

- "One way to deal with loss is to immerse yourself in doing good. Volunteer. Get involved in life. It doesn't even have to be a big, structured thing. Say a kind word. Encourage someone. Pay a visit to someone who is alone. Get away from your self-absorption. When it comes down to it, there are two types of people in this world. There are givers and there are takers. Givers are happy. Takers are miserable. What are you?"

**The measure you give will be the measure you get back. (Luke 6:38)**

*Guide me in moving beyond behaviors that stand in the way of my own happiness, Divine Redeemer.*

## A Prayer to the Holy Family

Every family can use a little spiritual guidance from above. Who better to ask than the Holy Family: Jesus, Mary and Joseph? *Catholic Digest* offers this prayer for intercession:

"Jesus, Mary and Joseph, like you we are members of the Father's family. We pray that our family love may reflect His love in its openness to all people. May we forgive even when not forgiven, and be patient with others' weaknesses.

"Jesus, give us peace, unity and strength to meet the difficulties of daily living. May we use our family resources to improve the quality of life for ourselves and all people. Let us show joy in serving, for whatever we do for others, we do for You.

"Mary, inspire us, that our love may be strong but not possessive. Let our willingness to give depend on the needs of others rather than on the cost of giving.

"Joseph, help us to be attentive to the Father's will. Let us be ready, as you were, to act whenever He calls us. Amen."

**The prayer of the humble pierces the clouds, and it will not rest until it reaches its goal. (Sirach 35:21)**

*Guide and bless the members of my family, Holy Trinity.*

## The $90,125 Pay Cut

Raymond Burse, the interim president at Kentucky State University, remembers the minimum-wage jobs he held during his high school and college years—and he empathizes with workers in similar jobs who struggle to make ends meet today.

Actually, he does more than empathize with them. He has taken a step to make their lives a little bit easier, by taking a 25 percent cut in his own salary—equaling $90,125—in order to boost their wages.

As reported by the *Washington Post*, the 24 employees at KSU ("including custodial staff, groundskeepers and lower end clerical workers") who make below $10.25 an hour will now be bumped up to that baseline. Burse says he believes in raising wages, but didn't want to put the financial burden on the school, so he lived up to his own principles in a unique way.

He said, "I didn't have any examples of it having been done out there and I didn't do it to be an example to anyone else. I did it to do right by the employees here."

**The laborer deserves to be paid.**
**(Leviticus 19:14)**

*Bless those struggling financially, Lord, with bosses who are willing and able to improve their lives.*

## Marriage is Like Chicken Soup

During what he calls his "extended bachelorhood," Joel Schmidt learned to cook, and eventually used his culinary skills to win over his wife Lisa. When she came down with a nasty cold during their first year of marriage, he found a recipe online for Italian Chicken Soup, which includes fennel seeds that are good for respiratory infections.

In the years since then, that soup has become a staple in the Schmidt house because it's "practical, comforting, and economical." The recipe has also changed a bit over time. Joel now throws in peppers and zucchini from the family vegetable garden, and also adds flour to thicken up the chicken broth (something Lisa never does when she cooks it).

In addition, Joel has come to see the soup as a great analogy for marriage. He says, "It has changed over the years, but by making adjustments and working through conflicts, it has continued to improve. Rather than getting old, staying the same, and losing interest, it instead remains ever fresh and new, always satisfying and fulfilling."

**He who loves his wife loves himself. (Ephesians 5:28)**

*Lord, help married couples grow in love for each other.*

## Ella's Doodles

Nine-year-old Ella Frech hasn't had an easy life. For two years, she's endured painful injections to treat juvenile rheumatoid arthritis. While that is now under control, she's been burdened with a mysterious new ailment that has weakened her legs so much that she needs a wheelchair.

Despite all this, the little girl who used to take ballet classes hasn't let her struggles overcome her. As family friend Calah Alexander noted on her Patheos.com blog, Ella has faced her challenges with so much "grace and courage" that she decided to channel her energies into a new activity she could do while seated: drawing.

Ella had never shown a particular aptitude for art, but six months into her new hobby, she has sketched and colored beautiful pictures of her favorite Disney characters and even some religious drawings of St. Joseph and the Virgin Mary. Her mother posts her drawings on EllasDoodles.blogspot.com to share her work with others—and hopefully to attract a few prayers for a little girl who could use a break from her suffering.

**O Lord, heal me. (Psalm 6:2)**

*Relieve the burdens of suffering children, Divine Healer.*

## The Fastest Nun in the West

Billy the Kid was a notorious Old West outlaw who normally wouldn't shy away from a fight. Unless it was with a nun—or at least, with Sister Blandina Segale, the Italian-born Sister of Charity of Cincinnati whose life is being investigated by the Archdiocese of Santa Fe for possible sainthood.

The *Associated Press* reported that she came to the U.S. in 1877, "co-founded public and Catholic schools...and worked with the poor, the sick, and immigrants." So many stories spread about her encounters with outlaws that the TV series *Death Valley Days* did an episode about her: *The Fastest Nun in the West*. Even more legendary were her run-ins with Billy the Kid.

In one story, Segale nursed Billy's friend back to health after a gunshot wound because four doctors refused to treat him. Billy came to town to thank Sister Segale, but also to kill the doctors. She asked him to abandon his murderous plans—and he agreed. In another story, Billy was going to rob a covered wagon until he looked inside and saw Segale. Then, he simply tipped his hat and left. The lesson: even outlaws don't mess with nuns.

**You are citizens with the saints.**
**(Ephesians 2:19)**

*Help me to follow the saintly example of good people, Lord.*

## Keith Urban Takes Strength in Faith

"As an observer, I would say his faith is his strength." That's how Father Ed Steiner from Nashville's Cathedral of the Incarnation described his parishioner, Grammy Award-winning singer Keith Urban.

During an interview with the website Celebuzz in 2013, Father Steiner discussed the role that faith plays in the lives of Urban—who has struggled with drug and alcohol addiction in his past—and his wife, actress Nicole Kidman. Though the couple travel a lot, they attend church when they're home in Nashville. The priest said, "They both take their faith very seriously."

In addition, Father Steiner describes Urban as an attentive father to his two daughters with Kidman: "When they've had to take their daughter to the church nursery, Keith is not the type of father who just drops his daughter off. He visits with all our sitters, he visits with the Religious Ed teachers. He interacts with other people's children in a very positive way. What I've really experienced from him is what a loving father he is."

**Be open to the love of your Father in heaven. See what love the Father has given us. (1 John 3:1)**

*May my faith in Your love be my rock, Father.*

## Dude, Your House is on Fire!

Ben Carroll is used to delivering *The Columbus Dispatch* newspaper to the community of Hilltop, Ohio, every morning at 5 a.m. But in 2013, he added an extra duty to his usual routine: saving lives.

The 28-year-old smelled smoke and saw flames coming from the side of a two-story house on Midland Avenue. He immediately called the fire department and started banging on the door. When no one answered, he peered through the window and saw a child, so he frantically banged even more.

A resident finally came to the door, but thought he was being pranked. Carroll insisted, "Dude, your house is on fire!" When the resident saw the flames himself, he rushed to wake up the other four adults and six children in the house, who all ran to safety and thanked their conscientious newspaper carrier.

Though Carroll downplayed his actions, his girlfriend noted, "He's a hero whether he wants to believe it or not."

In other words—Dude, you're a hero!

**In Your righteousness deliver me and rescue me; incline Your ear to me and save me. (Psalm 71:2)**

*Savior, help me to think and act fast in times of trouble.*

## Infinitely Loved by God

Priest, professor, and author Henri Nouwen once wrote the following words about the power of God's unconditional love:

"How do we know that we are infinitely loved by God when our immediate surroundings keep telling us that we'd better prove our right to exist?

"The knowledge of being loved in an unconditional way, before the world presents us with its conditions, cannot come from books, lectures, television programs, or workshops. This spiritual knowledge comes from people who witness to God's love for us through their words and deeds. These people can be close to us but they can also live far away or may even have lived long ago. Their witness announces the truth of God's love and calls us to act in accordance with it."

Are you living in accordance with the truth of God's love? He's offering it to you. All you have to do is accept.

**God, who is rich in mercy, out of the great love with which He loved us...made us alive together with Christ. (Ephesians 2:4-5)**

*Father, there are times when I feel alone and unloved. Remind me that Your unconditional love is ever-present.*

## A Carousel's Place in History

A small marker has been mounted on a carousel that now stands on the National Mall in Washington, D.C., a merry-go-round with an unbreakable connection to Dr. Martin Luther King's memorable "I Have a Dream" speech of Aug. 28, 1963. For it was on that same day that the carousel, then located in Baltimore, was first opened to white and black children. In Baltimore at that time, it was a truly historic event.

A civil rights protest, complete with counter-protests from a mob of segregationists, led to the decision—that the carousel, previously open to only whites, would instead be open to all. It set off an uproar, but the decision stood...and for years, both black children and white children rode its silent steeds.

Eventually the carousel found its way to Washington—near the site where Dr. King delivered his stirring speech. That's more than fitting. Not only did both events share the same day, but the opening of the carousel to all caused one of Dr. King's dreams—that black and white children would some day play side by side—to come true.

**Have unity of spirit. (1 Peter 3:8)**

*Move us past superficial divisions, Lord.*

## Don't Forget...

Father William Byrne, a gifted speaker, is pastor of St. Peter's Parish on Capitol Hill in Washington, D.C. He also livens the pages of the *Catholic Standard*, the archdiocesan newspaper, with his regular column—as he did with his thoughts on "Five Things We Shouldn't Forget to Do."

- **Call An Old Friend.** "An e-mail, a note or a call is not as awkward as it may seem. If they don't write back, it's good that you tried."

- **Lie on the Ground and Look at the Clouds.** "God is an amazing artist. Not only can He paint the sky, He can change it constantly."

- **Be Quiet.** "This is the hardest of all because we have such noise in our worlds...The quietest place of all is a church in the middle of the day. Pay a visit. No need to say anything; God knows it already."

- **Do a Divine Two-Step.** "Pray to be free enough to please God and to not worry about what others think."

- **Smell the Roses.** "No, literally stop and smell some roses."

> **Be careful not to forget the covenant that the Lord your God made with you.**
> **(Deuteronomy 4:23)**

*Keep me mindful of life's beauty, Divine Creator.*

## No Dibs

On snowy days in the Chicago neighborhood of Humboldt Park, residents who shovel out their cars put chairs in their parking spaces as a way of calling "dibs" on the spot when they return home. That leads to arguing over minimal parking spaces, so Jamie Lynn Ferguson decided to do something about it.

After a January 2014 snowstorm, the 29-year-old took the day off from her job at Breakthrough Urban Ministries and after-school program to dig out every car on her block. She told the *Chicago Sun Times,* "Forget about dibs, and I'll just do it for you. I think it's a better way for us to live as a community: as people who look out for each other instead of fighting for spots."

Ferguson started at 9 a.m., sharing her progress on Twitter. Elderly ladies came out to thank her, while others said she deserved a medal and wished that God would bless her. By 5 p.m., she completed her exhausting task, but felt it was worth it.

She said, "To me, it's a simple thing to do for your neighbors, but the look of awe on their faces is so rewarding."

**Assist your neighbor to the best of your ability. (Sirach 29:20)**

*When the world is cold, Father, create in me a warm heart.*

## Light Up Life

Molly Anne Dutton wasn't supposed to be born.

Twenty-two years ago, her mother was raped and became pregnant. Resisting pressure to have an abortion, she found support at the Birmingham, Alabama-based adoption agency Lifeline Children's Services, so she could have the baby. Peggy Dutton and her husband, who served on Lifeline's board of directors, decided to adopt the child themselves.

That baby was Molly who, 22 years later as a college student at Auburn University, decided to run for homecoming queen on the platform "Light Up Life," which was dedicated to sharing her personal story and promoting the light that adoption can bring into a dark situation.

Molly's story resonated with her fellow students—and even spread around the world. She was elected Auburn's 2013 Homecoming Queen. Said her adoptive mom Peggy, "Her joy spreads wherever she is, and this could only be the Lord."

**You have delivered my soul from death...so that I may walk before God in the light of life. (Psalm 56:13)**

*May we believe in the potential of all human life, Lord.*

## Family Makes Victory Sweeter

At the 2006 Olympics in Torino, Italy, Noelle Pikus-Pace was ready to compete in the women's skeleton competition (a sledding event) when a four-man bobsled team ran into her, breaking her leg. At the 2010 Vancouver Olympics, she would have earned a bronze medal if not for one maneuver that took her two inches too far to the right, earning her only fourth place.

After that, Pikus-Pace decided to retire because she and her husband wanted to start a family and her training wasn't conducive to that. They had a son and a daughter and then conceived a third child. But that pregnancy ended in an emotionally devastating miscarriage. With the desire to focus on something positive, Pikus-Pace turned to the Olympics again.

Her husband Janson quit his job and, with their kids in tow, accompanied his wife through all her training and finally, to the 2014 Sochi Olympics where she won a silver medal. As much as she wanted to win in the past, this victory felt sweeter because her whole family was there. As she told Today.com, "It's never been only me crossing the finish line. It's always been us."

**May we shout for joy over your victory. (Psalm 20:5)**

*Give me loved ones with whom I can share my joys, Father.*

## 'Can I Trust You?'

Forty-five-year-old Merrie Harris put her faith and American Express Platinum card into the hands of Jay Valentine, an unemployed homeless man in Manhattan. "I asked her for change and told her I wasn't working," Valentine told the *New York Post*. "She said she only had a card. She said, 'Can I trust you?' I said, 'I'm honest, yes.'"

Harris said she had no reservations about letting Jay borrow her card to buy some essentials. Valentine himself added that it never occurred to him to betray Harris's trust. "I wasn't tempted at all," added the 32-year-old former real estate agent. "She trusted me, and I didn't want to violate that trust."

Valentine's purchases totaled approximately $25, and included deodorant and Vitamin Water. He is also dependent on the kindness of strangers for his sleeping situation: the staff of a New York City internet café allows him to spend nights in their establishment. "It sets a good example that people in need—like I am or worse—can and should be trusted," Valentine concluded.

**Happy are those who make the Lord their trust. (Psalm 40:4)**

*Jesus, may we always give others the benefit of the doubt.*

## Like Feathers in the Wind

A Jewish man known for spreading gossip had ruined the reputation of many in his town. He went to see a rabbi because he felt guilty about his actions, but wasn't sure he could stop his deep-seated habit.

The rabbi told the man to get a pillow full of feathers, take it to the top of a high building, cut it open, and let the feathers fly. The man did as asked, then returned to the rabbi for more instructions. The rabbi told him to gather all the feathers, which represented all the rumors he had spread about others. Horrified at the impossible nature of this task, the man returned home determined not to gossip anymore.

Reflecting on this story for the website IgnatianSpirituality.com, Marina McCoy offers feather-free advice on avoiding the temptation to gossip. First, she suggests meditating on our own shortcomings before we put down other people. Also, focus on a "good character trait of the person we are tempted to malign. Gratitude for others' good gifts is a natural antidote to criticism and gossip."

**Let no evil come out of your mouths. (Ephesians 4:29)**

*May I always speak well of others, Eternal Word.*

## Life According to Sam

Sam Berns was born in 1996 with the rapid aging disease progeria, which usually results in death by age 13. But his physician parents, Dr. Scott Berns and Dr. Leslie Gordon, were not prepared to give up their son without a fight.

They founded the Progeria Research Foundation, through which Dr. Gordon embarked on a research project to discover the gene responsible for progeria and then develop a treatment.

The Christopher Award-winning documentary *Life According to Sam* chronicles her rigorous clinical study—and the roadblocks she faces trying to bring a measure of healing to the 250 children afflicted with the disease worldwide.

The film also introduces viewers to Sam, a Lego-loving, aspiring inventor whose joyful spirit and mature soul defy the danger of his condition. Without a trace of self-pity, he teaches us all to embrace each of our days on this earth, and fill them with happiness, kindness and love. Sam Berns unfortunately passed away at age 17 in January 2014. His parents' battle to help others with progeria continues, in memory of their son.

**He heals the brokenhearted. (Psalm 147:3)**

*Grant us the grace to comfort the sick, Divine Healer.*

## Beyond Left and Right

Pope Francis has had a remarkable impact on everyone in the world, Catholic and non-Catholic alike, with his frugal style of living, his humility and his strong emphasis on the teachings of Jesus. How best to understand him? Greg Burke, the U.S.-born Vatican media adviser, has some tips in that direction via *Catholic News Service,* and here are a few of them:

"Pope Francis is not a politically correct pope," Burke said, but rather "a loyal son of the church" who presents the hard truths with a heavy dose of mercy. He added that the pope "wants to get beyond left and right" by getting people to focus on the Gospels, on God and His truth and mercy.

Further, he said, the pope is not advocating a "feel good" religion, but talks about the truth of the Gospels—a truth "that will walk with them to the Lord."

"The pope's picture should have one of those warning labels," he concluded—one that says, "Danger: This man could change your life."

**You are righteous, O Lord...All Your ways are mercy and truth. (Tobit 3:2)**

*Help me follow Your ways, Lord, not the world's ways.*

## The Prison Angel

A woman who gave up her life just to live with prisoners? It sounds a little unreal, but that's just what happened to Mary Clarke, who grew up in a comfortable home in Beverly Hills, California, and raised a family there. She died in 2013, at the age of 86, as Mother Antonia Brenner (a.k.a. The Prison Angel) in Tijuana, Mexico—where she had lived among and ministered to prisoners at La Mesa Penitentiary.

She began her prison ministry in 1965 when she accompanied a priest as he delivered medicine and other supplies to the prison's infirmary. In 1977, with her children grown, she moved into the prison, sleeping in a cell in the women's wing—and chose to spend the rest of her life there. Eventually she established a religious order, the Eudist Sisters of the 11th Hour, for older women, which was approved by the bishop of Tijuana.

"In 30 years there," Mother Antonia said a few years ago, "I haven't met anyone that wasn't worth everything I could give to them—even my life. I see the image and likeness of God in each and every one of them."

**When he was in prison she did not leave him. (Wisdom 10:14)**

*May I see Your image in all people, Divine Creator.*

## The Teacher with Down Syndrome

People with Down syndrome are often perceived as having limitations. But perceptions aren't always true. Consider 22-year-old Columbia, South Carolina resident Bryann Burgess, who has combined hard work and a positive attitude in her quest to become a teacher.

Currently a junior living on campus at the University of South Carolina, Burgess is studying music and theater, while assistant teaching at a program called Kindermusik, which seeks to "instill a lifelong love of music and a foundation for learning in children," as stated on its website.

Burgess told *WLTX-TV* that she's always wanted to express herself in music, and this opportunity has given her the chance. Eventually, she wants to teach full-time.

Regarding her challenges, Burgess offers insights that can benefit anyone: "I always tried hard, and I always did my best. No matter what happens, I just keep on going and dust myself off."

**But you, take courage...for your work shall be rewarded. (2 Chronicles 15:7)**

*Help me face challenges with a positive attitude, Lord.*

## A Prayer for Generosity

Here's an excerpt from a prayer for generosity written by Father Jonathan Morris:

"Heavenly Father, today I am reminded of Jesus's parable of the rich landowner who, confident in his wealth, decides to build larger warehouses to store his earthly possessions. But God replies, 'You fool, this night your life will be demanded of you; and the things you have prepared, to whom will they belong?' Thus will it be for all who store up treasure for themselves but are not rich in what matters to God.

"Lord, at times, I have been like this man—holding onto my possessions and striving for more—instead of being mindful of others or of what matters to You. I haven't always given You all that You deserve. Forgive me for this.

"Lord God, You have been so generous to me, in so many ways. Help me to heed the lesson in Jesus's words. Grant me Your wisdom and perspective in dealing with not only the money I earn, but also my time, talents, and other possessions. All of these should be, and can be, used to help others and to glorify You. Amen."

**I treasure Your word in my heart.**
**(Psalm 119:11)**

*Help me choose to be generous today, Jesus.*

## They Would Have Killed the Kid

Jihad Abed didn't like what he was seeing.

A veteran New York City bus driver, he was guiding his vehicle on its run through the central Bronx and when he came to one of his usual stops, a gang of a dozen older teens boarded and made a beeline for a boy who was already a passenger. Seemingly determined to settle some kind of beef, they cornered the young passenger and began kicking and punching him.

"They were really beating him and nobody was doing anything," Abed said. "I couldn't take it. It was the father in me."

Abed pulled his bus to a halt and swung into action, finally ejecting all the attackers after a lengthy struggle. They banged on the bus door as it drove away, but to no avail.

And who happened to be on the bus? A union official named Derick Echevarria, recovering from recent surgery, who saw all the action unfold—and put Abed in for a special commendation. "If the bus driver wasn't there," he said, "they would have killed the kid."

**Be to me a rock of refuge, a strong fortress, to save me. (Psalm 71:3)**

*Give me courage to stand up for the persecuted, Savior.*

## The Roots of Black History Month

For those who don't know much about the origins of Black History Month, Professor Patricia Gloster-Coates of Pace University is instructive. During an *amNewYork* newspaper interview, Gloster-Coates, the history department chair, says the event was incorporated in 1976 but claims older roots.

"Carter G. Woodson, a historian who started the *Journal of Negro History* in 1916, later came up with the idea of celebrating Negro History Week on the Sunday closest to Abraham Lincoln and Frederick Douglass' birthdays," she says.

Originally, the remembrance was meant to highlight the cultural achievements of African-Americans. But a fixed annual event continues to be important, Gloster-Coates says, so "people can get together, reminisce and share facts and history."

Look into the history of your family or culture. It will help you celebrate accomplishments, learn from mistakes, honor ancestors, and better understand others.

**For whatever was written in former days was written for our instruction. (Romans 15:4)**

*Help us, Lord, to appreciate the human bonds that link all of Your children.*

## God Turns Gloom to Gratitude

C.S. Lewis once wrote, "I pray because I can't help myself. I pray because I'm helpless. I pray because the need flows out of me all the time—waking and sleeping. It doesn't change God—it changes me."

*Catholic New York* reporter Juliann DosSantos recalled that quote one day when she was feeling particularly gloomy. She admits in her book, *Footprints on the Journey*, that no matter how hard she tried, she couldn't lift herself out of her "rotten mood." Then she decided to let God do the lifting—and the results were far different.

DosSantos writes, "As soon as I opened my heart to say a little prayer to ask for help, I found I had resources right in front of me. I let God lead me—and He led me to the laughter, love, and kindness that come from friends and family. Before I knew it, my mood was starting to lift...There was a time in my life where I felt like I had to do everything on my own. But that is not a good way to live. I needed God and still do."

**She was deeply distressed and prayed to the Lord. (1 Samuel 1:10)**

*In my distress, hear my cry and heal me, Divine Redeemer.*

## You Had Your Baby Where?

A 20-year-old sales associate had gotten used to seeing everything in New York City, but this was one for the books: a woman giving birth to a baby in broad daylight at 68th Street and Third Avenue in Manhattan. Without thinking of the cold weather (this was in February of 2014), Isabel Williams turned into a Good Samaritan in a split second. She tore off her sweater and coat and used them to cover mother and young daughter as they awaited an ambulance.

Mom Polly McCourt explained that she'd been waiting for a taxi when the baby—named Ila Isabelle, in part after her Good Samaritan benefactor—decided the time had come. When they got to the hospital, both mother and daughter were doing fine. So was the father, Cian, who nearly missed all the excitement.

Williams was reunited with the whole McCourt family, including two more young children, a few days later. "I don't know how to express how touched I am," she said. Holding her little namesake, she said, "She's absolutely perfect."

**Do to others as you would have them do to you. (Luke 6:31)**

*Lord, inspire me to help someone at a moment's notice.*

## What's Next For You?

"In my mid-30s, I was 200 pounds," said Betty Smith. She smoked, didn't exercise, and couldn't even play tag with her daughter. "I had to get off that path," she realized.

Now a trim marathoner, Smith, 71, exemplifies how change is possible, according to AARP and its collaborators in the Life Reimagined project, which offers signposts for your new path:

- **Reflect.** What goals and values have motivated you? What future possibilities would you like to pursue?
- **Connect.** By retirement age you may have lost some earlier friends due to changed circumstances. Create a new mutually helpful support system.
- **Explore.** Leave your comfort zone. If you always read sports pages, try the food section. Or vice versa.
- **Narrow Choices.** Focus in on a few new paths.
- **Act.** Take your first steps in a new direction.

**In all your ways acknowledge Him, and He will make straight your paths. (Proverbs 3:6)**

*Holy Spirit, guide our steps as we travel throughout life.*

## No TYME Like the Present

At 23 years old, Elaine Newkirk found herself a foster mother of five kids—her 14-year-old sister and two friends, and two infants given up for adoption by their young mother. Now, two years later, Newkirk is not only the proud mother of five teenagers, but she is also the head of TYME (Teach Youth, Motivate and Empower) Ministries, a program in rural Pennsylvania meant to inspire youth and help the less fortunate through volunteer services.

Their ministries have expanded to include a nonprofit thrift store, a bakery and a youth center. Newkirk has taken on a daunting load, but one of the most important lessons she has learned is that she does not need to carry it alone.

"I think the biggest thing that I've learned is that even though I have a 'save the world' mentality, I can't save the world on my own," Newkirk told *Daily Good* writer Audrey Lin. "It takes the help of a community."

May we all be inspired by Newkirk's example to make a difference one organization, one volunteer project at a time.

**Bear one another's burdens. (Galatians 6:2)**

*God, motivate communities to work together for the sake of the greater good.*

## Compromise Is Not a Dirty Word

A frequent source of conflict in marriage is the very thing that's designed to avoid conflict: compromise. Some spouses think that by doing things differently than they always have, they're giving up their identity. Marriage counselor Dr. Greg Popcak offers a different perspective, though.

It's true that each partner needs to take the other into account when making decisions. But a little self-denial is good for the soul, and actually increases your sense of identity in the long run.

During an interview on *Christopher Closeup*, Dr. Popcak explained, "Our Catholic faith teaches us that we find ourselves by making a gift of ourselves. And the reason I bring that up is because a lot of couples are afraid of losing themselves to the marriage: 'If I make too many changes, maybe I won't be me anymore.' The reality is, we find ourselves by making those changes, we find ourselves in the generosity and the humility and the genuine love that making those changes really takes."

**Husbands, love your wives, just as Christ loved the church and gave Himself up for her. (Ephesians 5:25)**

*Help me love my spouse selflessly, King of Kings.*

## Becoming a Priest at Age 71

David Link was convinced he had the ideal job—until, at the age of 71, he was ordained a priest. He had finally found real happiness. Not that the job he used to have was insignificant.

For 24 years, until 1999, he was dean of Notre Dame's law school, imparting a love for the law to more than 4,000 students. Then, as his career was winding down, he reluctantly followed the suggestion of his wife, Barbara, and began teaching prisoners the fine points of the law. To his amazement he loved the work, impressed by his students' eagerness to learn.

When Barbara died in 2003, Link threw himself even more into his volunteer work with prisoners, catching the attention of many with his enthusiasm. Among those impressed was Bishop Dale J. Melczek of Gary, Indiana, who invited Link to become a priest. After seminary studies Father Link was ordained in 2008. In charge of the diocese's prison ministry program, Father Link couldn't be happier. "I need to bring my prisoners hope, and knowledge of eternal life," he said. "And I love that."

**He chose blameless priests devoted to the law. (1 Maccabees 4:42)**

*Help me bring hope to those who need it, Jesus.*

## Don't Overcomplicate Kindness

During the semi-finals in cross-country skiing at the 2014 Sochi Olympics, Russian skier Anton Gafarov fell and broke one of his skis. As he got up and attempted to finish the race on one ski, Team Canada's cross-country coach Justin Wadsworth quickly brought him a new ski and even dropped to his knees to affix it to Gafarov's boot.

Though the Russian finished last, news of this example of good sportsmanship spread around the world. It also led writer Cindy Keating to ask, "Can an Olympic moment change the way we've complicated kindness?" Keating notes that we sometimes hesitate when an impulse toward kindness strikes us. She says, "We don't want to intrude. We don't want to be rejected, or look silly. We end up talking ourselves out of something good."

If Coach Wadsworth had reacted that way, Gafarov and the world would have been denied a beautiful moment. Keating concludes, "The world needs people who will respond...people not afraid to get down on their knees and serve. Why? Because we all need help to finish the race we were put on earth to ski."

**I have kept the faith. (2 Timothy 4:7)**

*Instill me with the courage to act on kind impulses, Lord.*

## A Subway Hero

Tara Lewis couldn't believe her eyes.

A conductor in the New York subway system, she's used to seeing passengers either exit or board her train when it's stopped in a station and the doors are open. But here was one man, standing on the platform as the train approached, as if to board when it stopped. Instead he waited while the doors were opened, and once the train had started up again he hurled himself between cars and disappeared from sight.

Horrified, Lewis pulled the emergency brake cord and the subway train ground to a halt. It was an action that probably saved the man's life. Somehow he ended up on the landing between cars, opened the door and tried to blend in with regular passengers. Lewis would have none of it. She quickly contacted the police, who took the man to a hospital for evaluation.

"I believe he would have lost his life if I didn't see him and pull the emergency cord," she told Pete Donohue of the *Daily News*. Her supervisor agreed, putting her in for a "hero" award. And she went home, ready to start another day the next morning.

**You save me from violence. (2 Samuel 22:3)**

*May I be a help to others when needed, Jesus.*

## How to Be a Better Man

Comedian Jim Gaffigan is known for lovingly poking fun at the fact that he has five children. Yet he acknowledges that marriage and fatherhood have made him a less selfish person.

In his best-selling book *Dad Is Fat,* Gaffigan explains, "I watch the faces of single people in their 20s after I bring up that I 'have children.' I imagine them taking a small step backward as if to avoid contagion...Like I naively volunteered to contract leprosy, forever quarantining myself from having fun."

So why does Gaffigan have such a large family? He writes, "The reasons against having more children always seem uninspiring and superficial. What exactly am I missing out on? Money? A few more hours of sleep? A more peaceful meal? More hair? These are nothing compared to what I get from these five monsters who rule my life. I believe each of my five children has made me a better man...Each one of them has been a pump of light into my shriveled black heart. I would trade money, sleep, or hair for a smile from one of my children in a heartbeat. Well, it depends on how much hair."

**Their children become a blessing.
(Psalm 37:26)**

*Help me become a better, more selfless person, Father.*

## 'I Wish Everyone Had a Collette'

Steele Devitto can't say enough about Collette, which is understandable. Collette is his older sister, and every night when he was in high school and college, she'd talk to him on the phone, encouraging him while he pursued a career in pro football. There's something else about Collette. She also has Down syndrome, a fact which is perfectly fine with Steele.

"I wouldn't trade her for the world," he told Jeff Roberts of *The Record*, a New Jersey newspaper.

Steele Devitto has since gained all the credentials to make it into the pros. A linebacker, the Connecticut native played first for Don Bosco High School, a perennial New Jersey powerhouse, and then started for three years at Boston College. But talented as Devitto is, he knows he would never have gotten this far without Collette.

She attacks every day with a smile on her face, he says, and she's selfless and unflinchingly honest. "I wish everyone had a Collette," he declares, and when he says it, it's every bit as honest as his big sister.

**Therefore...build up each other.**
**(1 Thessalonians 5:1)**

*Jesus, may we always seek to support our fellow man.*

## A Different Side of Lincoln

Compassion and gentleness dominate the popular image of Abraham Lincoln, but he could be firm when circumstances required. For instance, his stepbrother John D. Johnston—whom Lincoln described as "not lazy," but an "idler"—often borrowed money from the lanky lawyer to tide him over rough spots. Finally, in December 1848, he asked once too often.

"You are now in need of some ready money," Lincoln wrote, "and what I propose is, that you shall go to work...You say if I furnish you the money you will deed me the land, and if you don't pay the money back, you will deliver possession. Nonsense! If you can't now live *with* the land, how will you then live *without* it?"

Lincoln also offered, however, to match dollar for dollar any money Johnston earned during the next five months.

There are moments when we all need compassion. But at other times, there is no substitute for hard-headed realism. Try, with God's help, to maintain a healthy balance between the two.

**We hear that some of you are living in idleness. (2 Thessalonians 3:11)**

*Lord, may I take advantage of good opportunities each day.*

## Valentines for Veterans

Valentine's Day is the perfect day to show the ones you love how much you appreciate them. Unfortunately, soldiers who are stationed in bases across the U.S. or fighting overseas do not always have the luxury of spending Valentine's Day with their family and friends.

In 2014, to honor the sacrifice and bravery of those who work to protect our nation, a few San Antonio groups under the Catholic Charities organization—including its After School and Summer Youth Program—decided to make and deliver more than 300 valentines to active-duty soldiers, veterans, and wounded warriors in and around Fort Sam Houston.

"It feels good to receive something on Valentine's Day from someone who loves you," Felicia Travieso, director of Volunteer Services, notes in *Today's Catholic,* the newspaper of the San Antonio Archdiocese. "But imagine how it feels to be surprised by a stranger knocking on your door, thanking you? Surprising a soldier on Valentine's Day with goodies and thanks is something I've never done before but will never forget."

**Everyone who loves is born of God. (1 John 4:7)**

*Father, bless all soldiers, guiding them in Your love.*

## Marriage is Bigger than a Wedding

On the occasion of her 10th wedding anniversary, singer-songwriter Brooke White recalled the day she married "Dave Ray, CPA" (as she jokingly calls her husband).

Though their wedding wasn't as big and fancy as the ones she sees in magazines nowadays, White said on Facebook that she wouldn't change a thing. Her dress was simple and the reception was held in her parents' backyard, but a lot of love went into the event and, more importantly, the relationship.

"The truth is," explained White, "that a wedding, as big and exciting and beautiful as it all is, is just one day. But marriage! That's every day. It's real life without DJs and chocolate fountains and fancy dresses. Nothing can truly prepare you; it's a leap of faith. There are no guarantees, but if two people decide to keep choosing each other every day, I believe it can go on forever. Ten years is a good long time [with] a lot of learning, changing, forgiving, letting go, hanging on, growing, building, and loving. But it's hardly a particle of dust in the scheme of eternity. It's all so much more. It's sacred."

**Let marriage be held in honor by all.
(Hebrews 13:4)**

*Help married couples choose each other anew each day, Lord.*

## Gifted with Blindness

To 75-year-old Father Patrick Martin, blindness has been as much of a gift as his very life. At age nine, he survived a battle with meningitis, which left him mostly blind, though he could read by putting words together "letter by letter." From the time he became an altar boy at age 10, he felt a persistent calling to the priesthood—yet his pastor told him it wouldn't be possible due to his blindness.

Instead, Patrick joined the Brothers of Christian Instruction. He never gave up on his dream, however, so—with the Brothers' blessing—he became a diocesan priest at age 35 while working in Norwich, Connecticut. In addition, Father Martin founded the ministry "People are Gifts" to help those with disabilities serve the church. He recently relocated to Texas to be closer to his sister.

Father Martin told *Today's Catholic*, the newspaper of the Archdiocese of San Antonio, "When we die, if the world isn't a better place because of our disabilities, then we've failed. Every one of us is here to make a difference."

**Suffering produces endurance, and endurance produces character. (Romans 5:3)**

*Abba, may our weaknesses serve to bring us closer to You.*

## Notes from George Washington's Childhood

School boys in George Washington's day copied inspirational sentences into their notebooks. Here are a few found in our first president's exercise books:

- "Speak not when you should hold your peace."
- "Show not yourself glad at the misfortune of another though he were your enemy."
- "Let your discourse with men of business be short and comprehensive."
- "Labor to keep alive in your breast that little spark of Celestial fire called conscience."
- "When you speak of God and His attributes, let it be seriously and with reverence."

We'll never know how much these kinds of maxims influenced the Father of our country. But we do know that the early years are a critical period in personality development. Pray and work for homes and schools that encourage children to give the best that is in them.

**I have said this to you, so that in Me you may have peace. (John 16:33)**

*Father, teach us to impart sound values to our children.*

## Hero Nanny Saves Boy from House Fire

Live-in nanny Alyson Myatt, 22, awoke in her bedroom in Louisville, Kentucky, at 6 a.m. to a loud boom. A faulty ventilation fan had fallen down in the bathroom, setting fire to the door and the entire hallway outside the bedroom of her five-year-old charge, Aden Hawes.

Heedless of the roaring flames before her, Alyson charged barefoot through the fire to retrieve the frightened Aden. She sustained third-degree burns on both her feet and one of her hands. But she wouldn't have had it any other way.

"I didn't even think about me getting hurt," Myatt told *Today* show correspondent Ann Curry. "I was just yelling for Aden."

Single parent J.B. Hawes, Aden's father, was away on business and as soon as he rushed home that same day, he went to the Louisville Hospital, where Alyson was recovering. "There's no words to put how grateful I am to have Alyson in our world," an emotional Hawes concluded. "God brought her into our world, that's for sure."

**Let us love...in truth and action. (1 John 3:18)**

*Father, grant us the courage to protect our loved ones.*

## Mercy in the City

Lent's focus on giving something up or adopting a new spiritual practice is one of the reasons Kerry Weber is fond of the season. She's grateful it lacks commercial aspects so she doesn't have to ask herself, "What do I get everyone for Lent?"

One Lent a few years ago, Weber decided to live out each of the Corporal Works of Mercy (feed the hungry, give drink to the thirsty, clothe the naked, shelter the homeless, visit the sick, visit the imprisoned, and bury the dead), an experience which became the basis for her book *Mercy in the City*. It led her from the St. Francis Breadline in New York City to San Quentin State Prison in California. Why did she set her sights so high?

Weber said, "I think that being Catholic [involves] trying to deal with people in the margins and include them in the body of Christ and the larger Christian community. Going to places where I've never been before are ways to bring them in…The Gospel calls us to be a little bit uncomfortable sometimes, so we have to challenge ourselves to move beyond our comfort zones."

**Reach out and give to them as much as you can. (Sirach 14:13)**

*Holy Spirit, help me choose my Lenten disciplines wisely.*

## Gary Sinise Puts Soldiers First

Actor Gary Sinise's dedication to helping members of the U.S. military was sparked at age 25 when he saw a play called *Tracers*. It was written by Vietnam veterans about their experiences during and after the war, experiences which often involved them being hated here in the U.S. Sinise felt bad that these men were being abused by their fellow citizens, so he befriended many of them and advocated on their behalf.

After the wars in Afghanistan and Iraq began, Sinise started visiting troops in hospitals. Though he felt awkward at first, he gained new perspective at Germany's Landstuhl Medical Center.

Sinise said, "I met a lot of folks that had been blown up, shot up and burned up. That was a difficult day. But when I left, I knew that my being there had helped some people, so you forget about your own reaction to what you're seeing, and it becomes about them. It's not about you. From that point on, I knew that even though it's difficult to see some of these injuries, my presence there helps them and their families."

**Humble yourselves before the Lord.
(James 4:10)**

*Make me humble enough to put the needs of others ahead of my own discomfort, Lord.*

## The Church as Field Hospital

In an interview with *America* magazine, Pope Francis shared his view of the best way to evangelize a culture that's often hostile to faith: "I see the church as a field hospital after battle. It is useless to ask a seriously injured person if he has high cholesterol and about the level of his blood sugars! You have to heal his wounds. Then we can talk about everything else."

The pope is basically saying that Christians need to meet people where they are. He's not saying to leave them where they are—or, using his own example, to ignore their high cholesterol and blood sugar. Rather, there's an order to follow. Treat the sucking chest wound before you encourage a low-fat diet.

In the same way, you can't expect to reach people who are unchurched or who have been poorly evangelized and catechized to understand where the Church is coming from if they don't have a solid foundation of experience and understanding. It's really about doing your best to become a personal example of holiness, and seeing that example bear fruit in relation to others.

**Let us set an example for our kindred.
(Judith 8:24)**

*Lord, help me to be a messenger of strength, truth, and love for others, especially those who don't believe in You.*

## Core Behaviors for Positive Leaders

Success coach Kathy Caprino has met people from all walks of life and circumstances who love their work and use their influence to "change the world for the better." She noted in *Forbes* magazine that there are several "core behaviors" these types of people share:

- **They dedicate themselves to what gives their life meaning and purpose.** "They have found that there is a purpose to their life, and that purpose usually involves some aspect of turning their 'mess into a message,' or using what they've learned as a means of being of service to others."

- **They commit to continually bettering themselves.** "Innovators who positively shape the world [have] an openness to see, learn, and experience new things."

- **They invest time and energy not in what is, but what can be.** "When they see something that agitates and disturbs them, they strive to know more, get to the root of the issue...and arrive at new solutions."

We'll share more "core behaviors" tomorrow.

**The Lord will fulfill His purpose for me. (Psalm 138:8)**

*Instill me with purpose and possibility, Father.*

## More Core Behaviors for Positive Leaders

Today, we share more of success coach Kathy Caprino's "core behaviors of people who positively impact the world:"

- **They embrace critique.** "The most powerful positive influencers don't need or want to be 'right'—they want to grow and be more effective...They know how to integrate constructive feedback to strengthen their work and ideas."

- **They uplift others as they ascend.** "These positive influencers want others to grow. They walk away from 'success-building' opportunities that will be hurtful and damaging to others. They know that those unethical, demeaning, or destructive approaches go against the very meaning and purpose they're committed to."

- **They use their power and influence well.** "Those who impact the world for the better are careful and judicious with their words, actions, and behaviors. They take [leadership] seriously, as a special honor and responsibility not to be flaunted or misused. They understand their special role, and accept it with grace, compassion, and care."

**Leaders of the congregation, pay heed!
(Sirach 33:19)**

*Help me follow Your example of leadership, Jesus.*

## When I Was Hungry...

"More people than ever are being brought out of poverty, and malnutrition is being conquered at an amazing rate," writes Patheos blogger and anti-hunger activist Billy Kangas about efforts to eradicate hunger around the world.

Kangas feels encouraged by how his fellow Catholics are responding to this mission, and he lists 50 ways they are working to end hunger today. Here are just a few:

- "Paulist brothers in Boston launched the annual 'Walk for Hunger' which has raised more than $40 million for hungry people in Massachusetts."
- "The St. Anthony of Padua farming collective in Tonga is providing micro-loans to farmers to help build economically sustainable farms."
- "Capuchin Brother Dave Schwab sends groups of volunteers to serve hungry people in Nicaragua as well as in communities in need across the country. [Other] Catholic volunteer programs...include the Jesuit Volunteer Corps, the Ignatian Volunteer Corps, and the Benedictine Volunteer Corps."

**Give some of your food to the hungry. (Tobit 4:16)**

*Inspire me to do my part to end hunger, Creator.*

## Gaining By Losing

"I struggled mightily," said Bob Groves, shocked at losing his job and the sense of identity it had fostered. "Suddenly, I was no longer 'The Man' I had been at work, the one people came to, and I had to figure out how to fulfill myself."

Then, the 66-year-old former executive set out to find a new path and discovered his calling as a teacher at the Osher Lifelong Learning Institute at Temple University in Philadelphia.

Groves now instructs a class of older adults in a human-rights course; he teaches English to a woman from Nepal; and he finds time each week to be with his toddler granddaughter.

People draw strength from the oft-expressed sentiment that when God closes a door He opens a window. If you're dealing with a loss of some kind, use creativity and courage to help you cope. And remember that a new reality might require stepping outside of your comfort zone and setting new goals.

**The Lord your God is with you wherever you go. (Joshua 1:9)**

*God, may we find the window of opportunity You have opened for us.*

## Blondes Didn't Have More Fun

Many years ago, a Maryland junior high school taught its students a lesson about discrimination by conducting a unique experiment. Though black students had endured segregation for many years in the school system, this effort—held during Brotherhood Week—singled out blonde young people.

They voluntarily agreed to use different rest rooms, stairways, and water fountains; endure snubs from brunettes; and sit at separate cafeteria and library tables. "You would be astounded at how many of these kids didn't know what prejudice and discrimination were," commented one faculty member.

Protests from parents, which forced the school to discontinue the program, received little sympathy from the student volunteers. They regretted that the experiment had ended just as it was "beginning to mean something."

Our rights are often accepted light-heartedly until we are deprived of them. If we are helped by education or experience to cherish freedom, we are in a better position to take a stand for others. God plays no favorites—and neither should we.

**Live in harmony with one another. (Romans 15:5)**

*Help me, Father, to respect the rights of all people.*

## A Goalie's Good Heart

What could a high school soccer goalie do to help send sick children to Disney World? He could make his saves in goal count for something extra, that's what. And Joseph Pigot, of Park Ridge High School in New Jersey, decided to do just that.

Captain of the school's varsity soccer team, Pigot launched Joey's Saves, which collected donations for each save he made.

In turn he saw to it that the proceeds went to Baking Memories 4 Kids, a local charity which sends ailing children and their families on all-expense-paid trips to Florida.

"It motivates me in tough games when I'm tired and I want to give up," he said. "You don't give up because you're fighting for something bigger than yourself."

Mary Diduch told Pigot's story in *The Record*, a leading northern New Jersey newspaper, alerting readers as to how they could join the project. As for Pigot, he envisions a lasting impact, hoping that future Park Ridge goalies follow in his footsteps.

**Do not hesitate to visit the sick, because for such deeds you will be loved. (Sirach 7:35)**

*Help me set a selfless example for others, Father of Light.*

## Finding God at the Oscars

The annual Academy Awards ceremony may not be a show where you expect to hear winners talk about God, but that was the case in 2014. The first reference came from singer Darlene Love, who was profiled in the Best Documentary Feature winner *20 Feet from Stardom*.

After the producers finished talking, Love came to the microphone to say, "Lord God, I praise You," then sang the last few lines of the Christian hymn "His Eye is on the Sparrow," bringing the audience to their feet.

The other God reference came from Best Actor winner Matthew McConaughey, whose reputation as a wild man seems to have mellowed now that he is a husband and father. He began his acceptance speech by saying, "I want to thank God because that's who I look up to. He has graced my life with opportunities that I know are not of my hand or any other human hand."

You don't have to stand in front of a microphone to thank God for your blessings. Just tell Him every day in your heart.

**With gratitude in your hearts, sing psalms, hymns, and spiritual songs to God. (Colossians 3:16)**

*Thank You, Lord, for the blessings in my life.*

## A Divine Mercy

The last words that 17-year-old Claire Davis spoke were "Oh my gosh, Karl, what are you doing?" Then Karl Pierson, 18, pulled the trigger and a shotgun blast ended up costing her life. She was the only murder victim that day in Arapahoe High School in Colorado, which came to a close when Pierson killed himself. And yet Claire's parents, through their tears, found the strength to forgive her killer.

Michael and Desiree Davis, speaking at a memorial service for their daughter that thousands of people attended, said that Pierson "was so blinded by his emotions he didn't know what he was doing." Pierson had walked into the school that day intending to shoot the debate coach he thought cost him the chance to join the Air Force, yet shot Davis—who succumbed to her wounds eight days later.

"My wife and I forgive Karl Pierson for what he did," Michael Davis said during the service. "We would ask all of you here and all of you watching to forgive Karl Pierson."

**Then the Lord said, "I do forgive, just as you have asked." (Numbers 14:20)**

*Free our hearts from revenge and hatred, Prince of Peace.*

## House Calls to the Homeless

"Pittsburgh's Dr. Jim Withers operates his practice with a simple idea: the best way to care for the homeless is to treat them where they live. Nightly, he takes to the streets with a man who once was homeless, to care for those no one else cares for."

So writes Deacon Greg Kandra on his Patheos blog about a physician living out the corporal works of mercy.

Dr. Withers began his ministry, called Operation Safety Net, 22 years ago after meeting Mike Sallows, a man who'd been homeless for seven years and was now giving out blankets and food to those who needed them. Withers offered to go along to provide free basic medical care. As stated in a video by the digital media company NationSwell, "Withers estimates he's treated over 1,200 homeless a year since 1992."

His influence extends beyond his Pennsylvania hometown as well. Dr. Withers said, "We have helped create organizations like ours—street medicine programs—in over 85 communities throughout the world. I'd love to see it become a point of pride, a jewel in the crown, for communities everywhere."

**Honor physicians for their services. (Sirach 38:1)**

*Teach me to care for society's outcasts, Father.*

## Keep Practicing Until You Get It Right

When someone asked Grammy award-winning singer Harry Connick Jr. if he was a practicing Catholic, he responded, "Yeah, and I'm gonna keep practicing until I get it right!"

Connick grew up in New Orleans with a Jewish mother and Catholic father who let him choose his own religious path. At age 14, he decided to become Catholic. He told *Christianity Today*, "The church manifests itself in my life through the people who have set the best examples for me, like my dad. My mother knew more about the Catholic Church than 99 percent of the Catholics I know. And her actions were Christian actions."

Connick also notes that his faith and family keep him grounded when he's traveling the world as an entertainer. He said on the *Busted Halo* radio show, "Somebody famous asked me one time, 'Don't you ever get tempted to cheat on your wife because there's a lot of beautiful women out there?' For me, [because of] my faith and my family, I know where my home is. It's the people that don't have that who may have a harder time separating those two worlds. They're clearly separated for me."

**The house of the righteous will stand. (Proverbs 12:7)**

*Help me grow stronger in my faith, Jesus.*

## What You Can Do

Many years ago, former Director of The Christophers Richard Armstrong shared the following thoughts on our power to make a positive difference in the world:

"Maybe you can't feed hungry millions around the globe. But you can see to it that the undernourished in your neighborhood or town get enough to eat.

"Maybe you can't provide jobs for the hardcore unemployed. But you can examine your attitude toward sharing your knowledge and skill with someone who has neither.

"Maybe you can't be a delegate at international peace talks. But you can be a peacemaker in your own family—and pray and work for peaceful communication between people of different racial, ethnic, or religious backgrounds.

"Maybe what you do is just a drop in the bucket. But you can keep in mind that God has given you a mission in life that He has given no other. Millions of drops can fill the bucket."

**I can do all things through Him who strengthens me. (Philippians 4:13)**

*I offer You my small acts of kindness and justice to do with as You will, Father.*

## Loving the Pursuit of Truth

For 25-year-old singer-songwriter Tori Harris, attending a Baptist university was the best thing that ever happened to her Catholic faith.

Though she grew up attending Catholic schools and seeing her parents as models of the faith, Harris acknowledged on *Christopher Closeup* that she embraced Catholicism more intentionally in college because of the challenging questions posed by her professors. She confronted the rationality of her belief in God, and found that the worldview presented by Christianity—and Catholicism in particular—seemed the most truthful and consistent.

Reflecting on her college years, Harris said, "It was a boon to my friends, too. The discussions that we had were really fruitful, though we don't all agree theologically on which expression of Christianity that we identify with. My closest friends are Southern Baptists, so there's definitely disagreement there. But we've never had more respect for each other. There's a great love and devotion on both sides for the pursuit of truth."

**All Your ways are mercy and truth. (Tobit 3:2)**

*Help me respect those whose beliefs differ from mine, Lord.*

# Life Lessons at Sunflower Bakery

The Sunflower Bakery in Gaithersburg, Maryland, doesn't just provide sweets to its customers; it's made life sweeter for some of its bakers as well. That's because the non-profit kosher Jewish bakery's staff includes adults with intellectual disabilities, such as autism and attention deficit hyperactivity disorder.

Founded in the kitchen of Beth Sholom synagogue, Sunflower not only teaches its students how to bake, but also instructs them about basic life skills, like being on time for work and speaking up for themselves. As reported by *Religion News Service*, 24 students to date have graduated and found work "at area restaurants, bakeries, and supermarkets."

Thirty-nine-year-old Zeke Koster, who is unable to read, learned to make *hamentaschen* for Purim celebrations in 2014. His mother Marilyn feels elated at what he's been able to accomplish: "He's always had menial jobs, so he's never had a positive feeling about what he's doing. At Sunflower, he feels so good about himself and what the potential down the road is. He's like a flower opening up."

**Bake what you want to bake. (Exodus 16:23)**

*Lead all people to discover their talents, Divine Creator.*

## It's Time to Leave the Pity Party

Julie and Rusty Bulloch make sure that the troubled teens and young adults they've been welcoming into their Lakeland, Florida home for the last 15 years don't fall into the trap of feeling sorry for themselves.

During a *Christopher Closeup* interview, Rusty explained his approach to helping these young people move past hardships: "We make sure they understand what's done is done. You can tell me about it and we'll pray through it and figure things out. But if you want to use bad things in your past to be a crutch for you not being a success, I'll say, 'Get real!'"

Julie added, "He's the tough one; I'm the tender one. I will sit there and cry along with them. Through all that, my response is, 'I can't explain why this happened to you. Did God make this happen? No. Was it allowed? Yes. Now, what are you going to do with it? Are you going to let it destroy you—or are you going to let it make you stronger? Life is a choice every day. And at the end of the day, it's on your shoulders.'"

**He encourages those who are losing hope. (Sirach 17:24)**

*With Your help, Lord, I will move toward a brighter future.*

## Faith and Free Lemonade

For many children, a lemonade stand serves as the ideal business prototype, where they can literally see the profits of their hard work grow before their eyes. For the children of St. Peter's Parish in Plymouth, Massachusetts, however, setting up a lemonade stand had a deeper purpose. They didn't charge for drinks, but instead informed passersby that voluntary donations would be given to the Missionary Childhood Association.

In exchange for their customers' generosity, the children told them about the tenets and importance of their Catholic faith. The kids of St. Peter's were motivated to lead this type of fundraising effort by a recent visit from a representative of the Pontifical Mission Society.

"The greatest commandment is to 'love one another,' and [the children] took it literally," said Kathy Liolios, director of religious education at St. Peter's, to *The Pilot,* Boston's archdiocesan newspaper. "They wanted to put their faith in action."

**Go into all nations and proclaim the good news. (Mark 16:15)**

*Abba, may we always be proud messengers of our faith.*

## What's It Like to be Pope?

What's it like to be pope? Members of a Rome parish got an unexpected chance to find out firsthand when Pope Francis paid a visit and opened the meeting to questions from the floor. As expected, the first question was about whether he ever thought he'd be the pope. Not at all, he replied—not even when he arrived for the conclave that would elect him the pontiff.

Following his election, did he feel stage fright when he addressed the throng? "Was I anxious? A little, yes, but everyone was nice," Pope Francis answered. "But it's true; having a lot of people in front of you is a bit scary!"

How do you serve as a good example to others? "Pray all the time, don't speak badly of others because gossip destroys friendships, and always greet people nicely, always with a smile."

The pope even managed to work in some humor as he said he decided to become a priest after going to confession with a priest he'd never met. They're the best confessors, he added with a smile—priests you don't know, and those who are deaf.

**Humility goes before honor. (Proverbs 15:33)**

*Help me deal with the unexpected, God of surprises.*

## From Chicago to Uganda

Six pregnant women about to give birth lay on a cold cement floor, shivering due to fever and malaria. That was the sight that greeted Chicago doctor Kevin Hunt during his first-ever trip to Northern Uganda in 2007. He had traveled there at the request of Father Sam Okori, an African priest working in his parish while in the United States taking pre-med classes.

The big-hearted doctor consequently found a poverty-stricken population that desperately needed help. During an interview on *Christopher Closeup,* he recalled the pivotal moment of seeing those pregnant women on the floor. Filled with compassion, he drove 50 miles to get them beds and mattresses, then returned the next morning. "Everybody was so happy that they could at least have some comfort," he said. "That's when I decided to do something about it when I got back home."

Dr. Hunt and Father Sam started a foundation called Medical Aid to Northern Uganda to provide financial aid for improved medical facilities, equipment, and medicines—along with mission trips, as well. Their ongoing work is saving lives.

**Be doers of the word. (James 1:22)**

*Convert my compassion into action, Divine Savior.*

## A TV Show Changes Lives

If you think watching TV is a waste of time, consider the story of Wisconsin pharmacists Jeanine Krueger and Nicole Schreiner. They saw Dr. Kevin Hunt and Father Sam Okori (featured in yesterday's entry) talking about their Medical Aid to Northern Uganda project on *The Bonnie Hunt Show* (Bonnie is Dr. Hunt's sister). The two of them felt inspired by the idea of helping and took the leap of faith to get involved with the organization, eventually becoming board members and traveling to Africa.

For Schreiner, that choice stemmed from a long habit of selflessness. She said on *Christopher Closeup,* "I did a lot of things locally here: teaching religion class at my church, playing Bingo with elderly folks in the area, making meals for people in need. It's always been something that brings me great joy and something that I wanted to teach my children…After being able to travel to Uganda, it fired up something more inside of me."

Consider taking the initiative to help someone in need. It may fire something up inside of you that will lead you down an unexpected yet fulfilling road.

**Faith…if it has no works, is dead. (James 2:17)**

*Inspire me, Holy Spirit, to act with courage.*

## Owen and Haatchi: Friends for Life

There is nothing like the love between a boy and his dog. Consider seven-year-old Owen Howkins and his three-legged Anatolian shepherd, Haatchi. Owen was born with a rare muscle disorder, which leaves his muscles in a constant state of tension. Haatchi, a two-time rescue dog, was found tied to a train track in North London. He was first rescued by the RSPCA (Royal Service for the Prevention of Animal Cruelty), and later by Ross McCarthy, who offered him to Owen's stepmother, Colleen.

"There was an immediate bond [between Owen and Haatchi]," Colleen explained in a 10-minute documentary entitled *A Boy and His Dog*. "It was like they both knew each other was different, and there was an instant acceptance of those differences, and that they were going to work as a team."

Owen and Haatchi also won the Crufts dog show 2013 Friends for Life award, given to a dog whose companionship to his or her owner is exemplary. Owen says Haatchi changed his life for the better. "He does look after me, and he's special," Owen concludes.

**A friend loves at all times. (Proverbs 17:7)**

*Father, bless all pets, companions and healers of us all.*

## Tackling Trauma

Catherine Woodiwiss, Associate Web Editor at Sojourners in Washington, D.C., managed to "skate by" without experiencing any traumas in her life for a long time. But after being hit by a car and enduring a long, painful recovery, she learned, "Trauma upends everything we took for granted."

She shared this and other lessons in *Sojourners* magazine:

- Presence is better than distance. Unless someone really wants "space," be with them.

- Healing can take a long time.

- Surviving trauma takes "firefighters" and "builders"—friends who drop everything and help put out the fire of the immediate crisis, and steady, calm people to build you back up over time.

- Grieving is social; so is healing.

- Don't offer platitudes or comparisons like, "At least it's not as bad as...."

- Allow those suffering to tell their own stories.

- Appreciate love, however unexpected its expression.

**They cried to the Lord in their trouble, and He saved them from their distress. (Psalm 107:13)**

*Jesus, give us strength in times of trauma.*

# A Fall Before the Finish Line

It all happened a few years ago, but what Holland Christian did that day will remain with her forever. She was a high-school junior then, a star runner for her school's cross-country team, taking part in a key state meet. Her coach, Jim Tracy, was there too, but not all was well. The inroads of Lou Gehrig's disease were debilitating him, and the cheer she led for him had an extra-special quality. "I think that made the team really want to win it for Jim," she said later.

Christian was in third place near the end of the 3.1-mile course, ready to make her move, when her legs just gave out. She slowed down as other runners passed her, and right at the end she collapsed. The finish line was only two or three yards away.

She gathered all her strength and crawled her way to the finish, with the encouragement— but not the help—of a race official. Without that crawl she would have been disqualified; with it, even though she finished 37th, her team won the championship. And her coach, ailing but happy, would have nothing but sweet memories of the day.

**I have finished the race. (2 Timothy 4:7)**

*When all seems lost, Lord, give me the strength to endure.*

## The Marriage Couldn't Possibly Last

The bride's father wanted his daughter to marry someone else, but the young woman had made up her mind. And so the couple eloped. Friends of the family told the father not to worry, because the marriage couldn't possibly last. How wrong they were!

John Betar, 102, and his wife Ann, 98, chuckled as they recalled it all—on their 81st wedding anniversary! At the time, Worldwide Marriage Encounter listed the Betars as "the longest-married living couple in the United States" and *Our Sunday Visitor,* which ran their story, said the answer to their long-lasting love wasn't chocolate, roses, jewelry or romantic dinners. Instead it was old-fashioned compromise.

"Marriage isn't just a lovey-dovey thing," said Mrs. Betar. "You learn to accept another's way of life. Agreements. Disagreements."

In short, you have to accept your spouse, warts and all. If anyone wants to argue, they have a right to do so. But they'll have to take it up with the Betars.

**Let marriage be held in honor by all. (Hebrews 13:4)**

*Bless spouses with the willingness to compromise, Jesus.*

## An Unexpected Daddy

Shanell Mouland felt nervous about who would wind up sitting next to her three-year-old daughter Kate during their flight from Orlando, Florida, back home to Canada. The reason? Kate has autism and could be prone to meltdowns.

When a businessman carrying papers sat down and Kate started rubbing his arm, Shanell feared he would give her the look that says, "Manage your child please." Instead, Eric Kunkel engaged Kate in conversation and asked her about her toy turtles. Kate felt such a connection that she started calling him "daddy," not because she thought he was her actual father, but because he gave her a sense of security.

Towards the end of the flight, Kate did have a meltdown, but even then, Kunkel tried to help. Shanell felt grateful. As she wrote in an open letter on her blog, "Thank you for not making me repeat those awful apologetic sentences that I so often say in public. Thank you for entertaining Kate so much that she had her most successful plane ride, yet. And, thank you for putting your papers away and playing turtles with our girl."

**Blessed are you because you had compassion. (Tobit 8:17)**

*Help me show kindness to those with special needs, Father.*

## The Future of Time

As someone whose life has been focused on time, Terry Irby developed a vision for the future that would benefit the next generation. For more than 40 years, Irby has worked as a watchmaker, and now serves as technical director of watch repair for Tourneau. But he and his fellow "artisans" are aging, reports Harry Smith for *NBC News,* and their highly skilled profession isn't drawing a lot of young people in this digital age.

The solution? Irby created a watchmaking program for at-risk high school students in Queens, New York. He teaches them how to take apart the hundreds of tiny pieces that make up a watch, diagnose the problem, fix it, then reassemble it.

The teens have found the work rewarding. Ayushi Pant, age 18, says watch repair has taught her patience and given her insights on how to "solve life's problems." Nineteen-year-old Edwin Larregui goes even further, saying the class helped save his life: "It kept me away from a lot of things. I'm here and learning, I feel good."

**There is...a time for every matter under heaven. (Ecclesiastes 3:1)**

*I pray that I use my time on this earth wisely, Jesus.*

## The Irish Cornerstones

Music and parades mark St. Patrick's Day, but it's also a time to reflect on the role faith played in Irish history. Father Matthew Malone, S.J., commented on that history in his 2014 St. Patrick's Day homily at New York's St. Patrick's Cathedral.

"The Irish experience," he said, "began in a crucible of hardship, starvation and war. For centuries...Ireland placed her desperate faith in the crucified one, the stone that the builders rejected, who had become the cornerstone. Thus with their eyes firmly fixed on the hope of heaven, a long suffering people came to believe in the promise of a new Earth.

"They then set sail for this city, which they would transform into a daring center of unprecedented apostolic activity. From here, the Church would advance across the continent; and everywhere that the Church advanced, the Irish followed, founding parishes and schools, hospitals and orphanages, colleges and sodalities. Here in the land of the free, the stones that the earthly builders had rejected, became the cornerstones of a new church."

**We have hope in God. (2 Maccabees 2:18)**

*Thank You for the gift of faith, Holy Spirit.*

# From Wall Street to the ER

In 2003, Wall Street analyst and consultant Debbie Yi was enjoying a vacation in Mexico when she got the phone call that changed her life. Her sister Christine had her leg ripped off by a New York City subway car after falling into the gap between the train and platform. Yi told the *New York Post* that she slept in a reclining chair by Christine's bed in Bellevue Hospital for a month, giving her ample time to observe the doctors, nurses, and interns at work.

She said, "I saw how much compassion they had—my sister wasn't just a patient, they truly cared about her. Seeing the difference the staff at Bellevue made in my sister's life—my whole family's lives—made me realize I couldn't go back to my consulting job...I wanted to be hands-on, saving people's lives. I would never feel complete until I was a doctor."

Yi soon began her studies at the Albert Einstein College of Medicine in the Bronx. Her work in New York Presbyterian Hospital's ER went on to be profiled in the Christopher Award-winning documentary series *NY Med,* on which she displayed a compassion for patients that was grounded in her own past.

**Honor physicians for their services. (Sirach 38:1)**

*Give doctors and nurses compassionate hearts, Lord.*

## The Homeless Man at the Bistro

Cara Callbeck was relaxing in a Paris bistro during her vacation when a homeless man started wandering between the tables and talking to himself while drinking from a flask. The restaurant staff called the police to complain that his antics were disrupting their business. When the police arrived, they responded that the man wasn't actually doing anything wrong. The restaurant staff protested, but the officers departed.

"It was then that I found God in the police," wrote Callbeck on IgnatianSpirituality.com, "as they approached the fellow and began chatting with him. They didn't yell at him or speak down to him; they just engaged him in normal, idle chit chat. After some time, they left the area together, all the while joking and talking with the man as though they were old friends.

"The police officers treated the homeless man with respect and dignity just as our Lord would want. In this little scene on vacation in Paris, God reminded me of just how important it is to look beyond my own comforts to see the dignity and value of every person around me. There is no taking vacation from that."

**All of you are one in Christ Jesus. (Galatians 3:28)**

*Help me to see Your presence in everyone, Holy Creator.*

## Love What You Do

"Do what you love" is a popular mantra, but *Verily* magazine Lifestyle Editor Krizia Liquido believes the idea falls short because many people have to work jobs that may not be emotionally rewarding in order to pay bills and support their families. As another option, she proposes the mantra, "Love what you do"—and offers suggestions on adopting that mindset.

- "No job is perfect, even if it seems that way on the surface. By carrying out your work well and being conscious of your attitudes toward the tasks that occupy you at each moment, you take control of transforming your actions—big and small—into acts of love. Start by identifying necessary tasks you dislike, then aim to do them a little bit better each time. It's an exercise in humility, determination, and perseverance, more fulfilling to the spirit than any temporary pleasures can allow."

- "Respect even the most mundane tasks—it's mainly in accomplishing them well that we contribute toward a greater good over our lifetimes."

**Commit your work to the Lord, and your plans will be established. (Proverbs 16:3)**

*May I always find purpose in the work I do, Creator.*

## Gotta Have Sole!

Five-year-old Nicholas Lowinger was going to visit a homeless shelter in Cranston, Rhode Island, with his mother. He felt excited for the chance to display his brand-new light-up sneakers, but his mother gently warned him against doing so, since many of the children there were lucky to have shoes at all, let alone the light-up kind.

Something about seeing the kids that day touched Nicholas's young heart. When he went home, he gathered up all his old shoes to donate to homeless shelters in and around Cranston. Yet his generosity didn't end there.

Seven years later, with the help of his parents, Nicholas co-founded the Gotta Have Sole Foundation. Since 2010, it has raised enough funds to provide shoes for more than 10,000 children in 21 states. It also boasts over 1,000 volunteers, including Nicholas himself, who puts 15 hours each week into his organization. "New shoes can make a child feel good about him or herself," Nicholas, now 15, explained to *CNN*. "They gain confidence...Something that seems so simple, a pair of shoes, made the difference."

**You shall love your neighbor as yourself. (Mark 12:31)**

*God, may we always work to make a difference.*

## Generosity from Beyond the Grave

Someone taught Edwin "Bud" Skalla how to keep a secret. The 92-year-old Iowa farmer, a bachelor, hinted at it in a deathbed conversation with the executor of his will, a long-time friend. But he didn't give it away until he died. And then? Boy, did he give it away!

With no descendants to provide for, Skalla left his assets and property to 13 Iowa churches to the tune of $10 million, which means their total receipts will add up to about $700,000 each. And on top of that, he willed his own $3 million farm to his home parish, St. Mary's of Portsmouth. Years of hard work and wise investments in farm properties accounted for the size of the estate, which left its beneficiaries nearly speechless.

Father John Dorton, who presided at Skalla's funeral Mass, said the gift came from a man with a very generous heart.

"His heart never really wandered very far from here," he said. "I think he wanted to make an impact that would benefit the churches and the community."

**For where your treasure is, there your heart will be also. (Matthew 6:21)**

*Father, keep our minds and hearts open to those in need.*

## A 'Hero of the 500'

Arnold Harvey—an Army vet, father of five, and truck driver for a waste management company—was shocked when he saw people sleeping on the streets near the garbage cans on his waste pick-up route in Washington, D.C. He told *People* magazine that he was heartbroken that so much need existed.

Harvey and his wife, Theresa, decided to help out by starting an organization called God's Connection Transition. It provides donated food to thousands of families each month. One young mother was especially appreciative of the help. "Our income is barely enough to get by," she said. "This is a godsend."

As a result of his philanthropy, Harvey is one of more than 50 employees of Fortune 500 companies being honored as part of Fortune's "Heroes of the 500."

So many people not only need someone to care, but they truly appreciate the help they receive. Remember, you don't need a fortune to be a hero.

**We must support the weak, remembering the words of the Lord Jesus, for He Himself said, "It is more blessed to give than to receive." (Acts 20:35)**

*Encourage me, Lord, to help when I see a need.*

## The Patron Saint of Beer?

"From man's sweat and God's love, beer came into the world." Legend has it these words were written by St. Arnulf of Metz, who is considered a patron saint of beer brewers.

As related by Sam Guzman at The Catholic Gentleman blog, Arnulf was a seventh-century bishop and advisor to King Theudebert II of Austrasia (which combined parts of modern-day France, Germany, Belgium, and the Netherlands). Following Arnulf's death, his former parishioners from the diocese of Metz, who already considered him a saint, set out to recover his body.

"The journey was during a particularly hot part of the year," Guzman notes about the legend, "and the travelers were ready to faint of thirst. One of the parishioners, by the name of Duc Notto, cried out, 'By his powerful intercession the Blessed Arnulf will bring us what we lack!' Miraculously, their supply of beer was replenished and lasted until they returned home."

The next time you enjoy a glass of beer, remember to toast St. Arnulf—and say a little prayer while you're at it!

**The Son of Man has come eating and drinking. (Luke 7:34)**

*Help me to enjoy food and drink in moderation, Lord.*

## Tragedy and Prayers

This year marks the 25th anniversary of one of the worst fires in New York City history, but a vigil and Mass at a nearby church will ensure that the 87 victims of the Happy Land Social Club blaze will never be forgotten.

On March 25, 1990, flames engulfed the Bronx social club in a fire set by a young man after a fight with his girlfriend. No fire exits or sprinkler system were provided, and an evening filled with laughter and dancing turned to tragedy. The victims have been remembered each year at a Mass and candlelight vigil at St. Thomas Aquinas R.C. Church.

The fire led to a crackdown on social clubs and fire code violations, and last year's observance included this remembrance by Ivine Galarza, district manager of the local Community Board: "Happy Land reminds us of the importance of ensuring that our neighborhood nightspots are in strict compliance with all relevant licensing and safety requirements."

It also reminds us that life is fragile and precious.

**May my life be precious in the sight of the Lord. (1 Samuel 26:24)**

*Help us to create safe communities, Heavenly Father.*

## Above Earth's Lamentation

While working on her album *Above Earth's Lamentation*, which was inspired by a period of intense grief in her life, singer-songwriter Sarah Hart actually became comfortable with the idea of death—even her own, which she addresses in the song *One Beautiful Day*. Though the topic sounds depressing, the song is one of joy.

During an interview on *Christopher Closeup*, Hart revealed that she wrote those lyrics while thinking of the day her cancer-stricken grandmother died. She said:

"I was with her, my mother and two aunts, and we sat around my grandma, prayed the rosary, told stories, and laughed. When it was over, I remember thinking, 'Please, Lord, let me go like that.' It was sad and there were a lot of tears, but it was also a celebration. That's what I was clinging to in that song. I was thinking, 'When I go, you'll be sad, but I want you to celebrate, too, because we will see each other again and this is not a scary thing. This is a beautiful thing that we as Christians have been hoping for and longing for.'"

**Today you will be with Me in Paradise. (Luke 23:43)**

*Embrace my deceased loved ones in Your care, Messiah.*

## The Weight of a Nation

"The last thought that I had was, I made peace with God." Marine Cpl. William Kyle Carpenter recalled that moment in Afghanistan in 2010 when he believed he was going to die.

During a firefight with the Taliban, Carpenter and Lance Cpl. Nicholas Eufrazio were on a rooftop when an enemy grenade landed near them. Carpenter threw himself between the grenade and Eufrazio, absorbing most of the blast. His right eye and most of his face were destroyed, and his right arm shattered. Other Marines quickly jumped in to tend to Carpenter's wounds.

After many surgeries and two-and-a-half years in the hospital, Carpenter was finally released in 2013. In 2014, he was awarded the Medal of Honor, the nation's highest military honor.

He said, "As the president put the Medal of Honor around my neck, I felt the history and the weight of a nation. I will wear it for those who have been wounded on distant lands who still continue to fight in battle, and through long and difficult days of recovery here at home. And for those who have given it all, I can never express in words what you mean for this nation."

**I will confer great honor on you.
(1 Maccabees 11:42)**

*Inspire us to large and small acts of bravery, Holy Spirit.*

## We Need to Teach Our Daughters

Someone recently shared the following observation about parenting on Facebook:

"We need to teach our daughters to know the difference between:

"A man who flatters her and a man who compliments her;

"A man who spends money on her and a man who invests in her;

"A man who views her as property and a man who views her properly;

"A man who lusts after her and a man who loves her;

"A man who believes he's a gift to women, and a man who believes she's a gift to him.

"And then we need to teach our sons to be that kind of man."

**Train children in the right way, and when old, they will not stray. (Proverbs 22:6)**

*Heavenly Father, guide parents in teaching their children, through words and actions, how to live holy and loving lives.*

## Driving Past the Church

Each day Brett Ramport drove to his workplace and each evening he drove home. Nothing unusual there. But on the way, coming and going, he passed St. Thomas Becket Church in Eagan, Minnesota, and even though he started off with not much in the way of faith, he found the church beckoning to him.

"I would drive by this church every day," he told Dave Hrbacek of *The Catholic Spirit*, newspaper of the St. Paul-Minneapolis Archdiocese. "I kept on thinking, 'Gosh, I have to go there.'" Ramport, 44, married and the father of three, was also listening to *Relevant Radio* as he drove, and even learned a few Catholic prayers, the Hail Mary among them.

And in time, of course, he actually did stop in the church—and eventually became a Catholic there at an Easter Vigil ceremony. Not only that, he still stops in to visit the church's adoration chapel, not to mention the sanctuary for Mass.

It all began with a drive to work—and it's Ramport's faith that still drives him today.

**You did not choose Me but I chose you.
(John 15:16)**

*Holy Spirit, help me to be responsive to Your call and Your wisdom in my life.*

## For Easter and Beyond

Still not sure of how you might celebrate Easter? Here are some suggestions from Father William Byrne of the *Catholic Standard*, newspaper of the Washington (D.C.) Archdiocese:

- **Don't lose ground.** Lent might be over, but be sure you get to Mass.

- **Get out of the house.** "Spring is a clear reminder of the Resurrection, so go out and enjoy some fresh air."

- **Get out of church.** Once you've gone to Mass, take part in the church's evangelizing mission. Bring God's message, by word and example, to those who aren't there.

- **Learn about a new saint.** "The saints are the ones who know most about heaven, so do a little research and see how they got there."

- **Write or call someone you miss.** Easter restores our relationship with God. To build on that, reach out to someone you haven't talked to in a while. "God gave us eternal life. Why? Because He wants to be with us forever—so pass it on."

> **My child, do not forget My teaching. (Proverbs 3:1)**

*May the disciplines I've practiced through Lent, Jesus, lead me closer to You throughout the year.*

# Choosing Fatherhood Over Baseball

At the start of the 2014 baseball season, New York Met second baseman Daniel Murphy found himself in the middle of an unexpected controversy because he took a few days off to be with his wife when she gave birth to their first child, Noah. Some commentators berated him for missing Opening Day, and not prioritizing the game over his personal life.

Ever a class act, Murphy didn't get angry or defensive in response. He simply explained that his wife was physically drained by the birthing experience and he wanted to be there for her— especially since his travel schedule during the season would sometimes keep them apart. He also told the *Daily News*, "Long after they tell me I am not good enough to play baseball anymore, I'll be a husband, and I'll be a father."

Murphy's faith played a role in his decision as well. At a White House forum on fatherhood, he said, "We try to take Jesus Christ and put Him in the center of everything. So instead of thinking, 'I'm a father; I'm a husband; I'm a baseball player,' I just try to take Jesus, put Him right in the middle."

**With all your heart honor your father. (Sirach 7:27)**

*Help me to love my family as selflessly as You love us, Father.*

## 'He Was Not a Faceless Monster'

On June 5, 2014, a mentally-disturbed gunman killed one teen and injured two others on the grounds of Seattle Pacific University in Washington. The death toll would have been higher if student security guard Jon Meis hadn't tackled and pepper-sprayed the shooter while he was reloading.

Meis was hailed as a hero, but felt uncomfortable with the attention. He said, "What I find most difficult about this situation is the devastating reality that a hero cannot come without tragedy. We cannot ignore that a life was taken from us. Others were badly injured... Nonetheless, I would encourage that hate be met with love. When I came face to face with the attacker, God gave me the eyes to see that he was not a faceless monster, but a very sad and troubled young man. While I cannot at this time find it within me to forgive his crime, I desire that he find the grace of God and the forgiveness of our community."

Weis concluded, "We serve a truly awesome God and I firmly believe that it is through Him alone that we will find the strength to heal from this tragedy."

**I am the Lord who heals you. (Exodus 15:26)**

*Grant healing to victims of violence, Prince of Peace.*

## A Lesson in Friendship

On the night of His betrayal, Jesus ate the ritual meal of the Passover with His 12 closest friends. Later, He asked them to keep Him company as He prayed to the Father to strengthen Him for the ordeal He would face the following day.

Jesus was realistic about His friends and their capabilities. He told them that one of them would betray Him, that they would all abandon Him, and that Peter—the man He had named as leader of the apostles—would even deny knowing Him three times before the cock crowed.

But St. John tells us that in spite of their weaknesses, Jesus loved His friends to the end.

When friends disappoint us or fall short of our expectations, our first inclination may be to turn our backs and have nothing more to do with them. In such moments, consider the example of Jesus who forgave His friends even though they bitterly disappointed Him.

**If you forgive others their trespasses, your heavenly Father will also forgive you. (Matthew 6:14)**

*Jesus, help us to pattern our lives on Your example of unlimited forgiveness.*

## 'I'm Supposed to Show You How to Die'

Devastated when his father John was diagnosed with pancreatic cancer, Christopher Award-winning author Jim Ziolkowski started interviewing him on videotape as a way to keep his memory alive after his death.

Jim once asked his dad if he was afraid of dying. As recounted in Jim's book *Walk In Their Shoes,* John, a lifelong Catholic, responded, "Sometimes I am sad, but never afraid. It makes me sad because I would like to live longer. I would like to be a part of your life. I don't look at this as hardship or adversity, though. I look at it as God's will. It has drawn our family together and helped us to understand our own mortality. I think this is all God's will, and with my remaining time I am supposed to show you how to die. Every living creature eventually dies. This is part of life."

Reflecting on his father's subsequent passing, Jim wrote, "I came to see that [Dad's] faith, far from being unapproachable, was a model for us all...I pray for him each day."

**The last enemy to be destroyed is death.**
**(1 Corinthians 15:26)**

*Comfort those grieving the deaths of loved ones, Savior.*

## A Reunion for the Ages

He was saved by a miracle—and it took another miracle to meet his savior. That's the story of Leon Gersten, a Holocaust survivor and now a psychologist in Long Island, New York—and Czeslaw Polziec of Poland, a member of the Catholic family that saved Gersten's life. As reported by the *New York Post*, they were reunited for the first time in nearly 70 years at JFK Airport.

"We never forget the fact that you and your parents are the ones who saved our lives," said Gersten, 79. "The only reason we are alive is because of you and your family."

Polziec, 81, said through an interpreter that he could hardly believe the meeting was taking place. "We lived in terrible circumstances," he said. "Poland was occupied by the Nazis, and they were killing the Jews."

Gersten spent two years of his childhood, with his Jewish family, living in hiding with the Polziecs. "This is why our gratitude is so great, because of them," Gersten said. "The Germans did not succeed, and this was our triumph."

**When the righteous triumph, there is great glory. (Proverbs 28:12)**

*Instill me with the courage to defend the defenseless, Lord.*

## A Christopher Prayer for Easter

Lord, instill us with the hope we celebrate this Easter, the hope that's difficult to believe in when we live in a world with much pain and suffering. Good people suffer hardship and we wonder why a loving God would allow these things to happen. But then we remember that Jesus, too, experienced intense suffering: Betrayal, persecution, crucifixion.

He didn't exempt Himself from human hardships. Instead, He humbled Himself in order to identify with those of us who live in this broken, yet beautiful world, thereby allowing us to identify with Him, and reminding us that God does not cause suffering, but rather that He walks through it with us.

By believing in Jesus as "the way, the truth and the life," our defeats can be turned into victories just like His death led to the greatest victory of all. Through His resurrection, Jesus brought light to the world in a new way that offers us all the opportunity to receive mercy and redemption.

This Easter, we choose hope in You, O Lord. Amen.

**He sent redemption to His people. (Psalm 111:9)**

*Thank You, Jesus, for the gift of eternal life with You!*

## Between a Laugh and a Tear

Tom Leopold has been making people laugh for decades as a writer on TV series like *Cheers* and *Seinfeld*. But he and his wife Barbara experienced an intense period of darkness when their 12-year-old daughter began struggling with a life-threatening eating disorder. He wrote, "It's a whole lot easier to hold your heart together when it's you who does the suffering, but when it's your child and nobody can fix her...Well, it would take more than a comedy writer to say how it feels."

Two years later, with progress still hard to come by, Leopold prayed to God for help, saying, "I just can't make it alone." That simple prayer set him on a spiritual journey that eventually led him to convert to Catholicism.

The Christophers honored Tom Leopold with our 2014 Christopher Spirit Award for bringing laughter into people's lives and for being a candle in the darkness to families struggling with eating disorders. As he says, "Does my daughter still suffer? She does, we all still do, but now I feel the Lord's grace. We are not alone."

**The Lord alone guided him.
(Deuteronomy 32:12)**

*Walk with me through my sufferings, Lord.*

## Tips for a Better World

Father Joseph Breighner of the Baltimore Archdiocese once had a popular radio program called *Ask Father Joe*. He still dispenses advice through his highly readable column in the *Catholic Review*—including this favorite, headed "Five tips for a better world."

- **Smile.** "The smile you give may be the only smile someone else receives that day. It's impossible to smile and not feel better yourself."

- **Be happy.** "There's an old saying: 'Two men looked out through prison bars. One saw mud. The other stars.' What we focus on we get to keep."

- **Listen to others.** "Just listen, and you give one of life's greatest gifts."

- **Speak kindness.** "Don't say the mean or hurtful thing. Praise others. Tell them how good they look or how helpful they were. Kindness costs nothing and can mean everything."

- **Be happy with what you have.** "Don't go chasing after all the stuff that others do, Jesus reminded us, but 'seek first the kingdom of God.'"

**Happy is the person who meditates on wisdom. (Sirach 14:20)**

*Help me become a better, more selfless person, Father.*

## Homeless is My Address, Not My Name

What exactly do we see when we look at a homeless person on the street? The traveling Minnesota exhibit entitled "Homeless is My Address, Not My Name" shows we should look beyond their current living situation to the people inside.

Sponsored by St. Stephen's Human Services in conjunction with Family Housing Fund, this display features black-and-white portraits of the homeless. A telephone number printed underneath each picture connects to a personalized recording by the photographed man or woman relating their story.

"We don't ever want to think about being homeless," Carol Gregg, director of Care and Share Shelter in Crookston, tells *Our Northland Diocese*. "But the fact is these pictures could be of you or me, our neighbors, anyone.... Many of us are just one paycheck from homelessness."

Jesus saw the goodness in everyone, no matter how dire their present predicament. May we be inspired to show similar compassion towards those in need of a helping hand.

**Whoever is kind to the poor lends to the Lord, and will be repaid. (Proverbs 19:17)**

*Jesus, open our hearts to the possibility of giving.*

# A Triathlon to Remember

Air Force Major John Berger endured a broken pelvis and other injuries when he became the victim of a hit-and-run accident in St. Louis. On the bright side, he soon became fast friends with his ER doctor, Scott Farber.

One day, Berger suggested to Dr. Farber the possibility of them racing in the Ironman Triathlon, held every June in France, to raise money for The Wounded Warrior Project. After some deliberation, Dr. Farber agreed, and he and Berger began training in January, 2012. They worked out up to 20 hours a week in preparation for the event, which includes a 2.4-mile swim, a 112-mile bike ride and a 26.2-mile run.

Although Major Berger finished the triathlon in less than 13 hours, Dr. Farber was unable to complete it. However, they raised $10,000 for wounded warriors, and Farber and Berger both look forward to participating again next year.

"One of the big reasons I did this was to say thank you to all the people who helped me along the way," Berger told the *Catholic Globe.* "Everybody had a big role in helping me."

**Two are better than one...if they fall, one will lift up the other. (Ecclesiastes 4:9-10)**

*Messiah, bless our friends, and all who encourage us.*

## Coping With Tragedies

As adults we've heard about and experienced far too many tragedies; some of us might have become inured to them. Not so for innocent children who may be faced with new and bewildering situations.

Parents and other responsible adults can do a lot to help youngsters cope with and learn from difficult experiences.

Writing in the *Manhattan Times*, Carolina Pichardo says she's constantly looking for the right balance between shielding her daughter, and sharing age-appropriate information with her, whether the destructive event is a violent gun attack or a violent act of nature.

Pichardo advises adults to assess their own reactions and then devise a plan of how and when to introduce the tragic news to their children. Be prepared to answer questions and to help them face any strong emotions. But remind children that "there is also a lot of kindness and happiness in the world."

**In the world you face persecution. But take courage; I have conquered the world! (John 16:33)**

*Merciful Father, protect our children and help us guide them as they face life's adversities.*

## The Mourners Were Surprised

People who attend funerals are seldom asked for their names and addresses, but that's what happened at the funeral of James Wilkie on the Isle of Man. The hundred or so people who supplied the information had their curiosity satisfied a few days later.

Wilkie, a lifelong bachelor who sometimes found himself lonely, had set aside 30 percent of his estate to be divided among the people who showed up for his funeral. It was his small way of thanking them for taking the time to pay their respects.

Those who respond with kindness and love to the lonely can seldom expect financial reward for their thoughtfulness. They should be content with having relieved the isolation of another human being. Remember: in the beginning, when God decreed that it was not good for man to be alone, each of us received a commission to reach out to others in love.

**The Lord God said, "It is not good that the man should be alone." (Genesis 2:18)**

*Help me, Jesus, to find a way to make at least one life a little bit less lonely.*

## Yankees Celebrate HOPE

Every year, the New York Yankees celebrate HOPE week—but it's got nothing to do with where they want to be in the baseball standings. Instead, HOPE stands for "Helping Others Persevere and Excel," and it celebrates individuals who model giving and selflessness.

One of the 2014 honorees was Quai Jefferson, a senior at St. Joseph's Regional High School in Montvale, New Jersey. As reported by *WCBS,* Jefferson has served as the primary caregiver for his mom Vaida, who suffers from multiple sclerosis. He also kept up his grades, became a "two-sport star athlete" at St. Joe's, and earned a scholarship to the University of Delaware.

When Jefferson arrived at the picnic at which the Yankees honored him, he walked in literally carrying his mother, thinking he was getting an award for athletic achievements. He was happily surprised to find Bronx Bombers like CC Sabathia and Mark Teixeira praising his goodness and spirit. Even then, the humble Jefferson deflected attention from himself by telling his mom, "I love you. You're my shining light."

**Your care has preserved my spirit. (Job 10:12)**

*Help me balance all my responsibilities, Loving Father.*

## Standards of Beauty

Women's magazine covers are known for featuring "perfect looking" models, whose physical flaws or imperfections are airbrushed out of the picture. That's why Turia Pitt's appearance on the cover of *Australian Women's Weekly* was a groundbreaking moment.

In September 2011, Pitt was an ultra-marathoner running a race in Kimberley, Australia, when she got caught in a brush fire that burned over 65 percent of her body. She spent 864 days in the hospital and endured 100 surgeries. But the 29-year-old wouldn't let her injuries keep her down.

Following her lengthy recovery, she raised funds for the reconstructive surgery charity Interplast by biking over 1,300 miles in Australia and walking part of the Great Wall of China. She's also earning her master's degree in engineering.

Writer Kate Leaver noted the importance of using Pitt as a cover model: "It will give parents a chance to talk to their kids about bravery, strength and courage and about beauty being so much more than what you see on the outside."

**Let your adornment be the inner self.**
**(1 Peter 3:4)**

*Lord, keep me from judging people based on superficial qualities.*

## Is God Giving Me the Cold Shoulder?

Sometimes prayer can be frustrating because it seems like God doesn't hear us. So should we keep praying anyway? An answer can be found in the Christopher Award-winning film *Gravity,* which stars Sandra Bullock and George Clooney as two astronauts stranded in outer space after their ship is destroyed.

Their communication lines to earth appear to be severed, so they can't hear mission control in Houston. Clooney, however, keeps talking to mission control, and Bullock doesn't understand why. He tells her that the two of them may not be able to hear what's happening on earth, but it's possible that Houston can hear them. No response doesn't mean you're not being heard, so it's always best to keep communicating just in case.

In a movie with several spiritual overtones, that's a relevant point. There are times when we feel as if God doesn't hear our prayers. But a silent response doesn't mean He doesn't hear us. We have to continue with the belief that we are being heard—and ask for the patience and humility to wait for God to respond in His own way and time.

**Pray without ceasing. (1 Thessalonians 5:17)**

*Hear and answer my prayers, Lord. I need Your help.*

## Amy Adams' First-Class Heart

Spotting a celebrity at the airport can be an unexpected treat. But seeing that same celebrity perform a good deed makes it a truly memorable moment.

In June 2014, *ESPN* host Jemele Hill observed actress Amy Adams sitting in first class after boarding a flight from Detroit to Los Angeles. Later, she saw a soldier in uniform being escorted to Adams' seat—but Adams was no longer there. The actress, whose father was a member of the U.S. military, had quietly arranged to give the soldier her seat, while she took his reservation in coach.

Hill shared what she saw on her Twitter account, making the story national news even though Adams had deliberately avoided attracting attention for her charitable act. Still, Adams' first-class heart can serve as an example for all of us to model kindness and humility when the opportunity arises.

**When you give alms, do not let your left hand know what your right hand is doing, so that your alms may be done in secret; and your Father who sees in secret will reward you. (Matthew 6:3-4)**

*Encourage me, Lord, to perform random acts of kindness.*

## Making Peace at the End of the Day

Heaven knows there's no shortage of advice for a man and woman who decide to get married, but this time they might listen a bit more closely. It comes right from the top, from Pope Francis himself, who had the answer for the troubles that couples often encounter in their journey through life.

"There are problems in marriage: different points of view, jealousies, arguments, but tell young couples to never let the day end without making peace," the pope said. "The sacrament of matrimony is renewed in this act of peace."

Not surprisingly, the pope spoke in his usual straight-from-the-shoulder style to the Pontifical Council for the Family, as Cindy Wooden of *Catholic News Service* reported. He departed from his text to say that he always asks young married people how many children they have, and then is likely to challenge them: "Do you play with your children? The free gift of a parent's time is so important."

The Catholic Church realizes that marriage isn't always easy. But as Pope Francis said, "It is so beautiful!"

**Peace be to you. (Judges 6:23)**

*Strengthen the bonds of love between couples, Lord.*

## Touched by Words of Encouragement

The Christopher Award-winning TV series *Touched by an Angel* ran on CBS for nine seasons (1994 to 2003), after which the show's writer and executive producer Martha Williamson felt exhausted. She decided to take a break from TV and focus on her husband and two daughters.

A few years into her sabbatical, she started to wonder if the work she had done really mattered. Around the same time, she was going through a storage room and discovered fan letters she had never seen.

Not only did these letters—many of them handwritten—praise *Touched by an Angel,* they revealed stories about ways in which the show had changed viewers' lives. For instance, said Williamson on *Christopher Closeup,* "We got a letter from a man who was in prison and said that he and his fellow inmates would watch the show every Sunday night because it was the only time all week they heard the words, 'You are loved.'"

Those letters became a source of encouragement for Williamson. She felt grateful that they arrived in her life just when she needed them most.

**How sweet are Your words to my taste. (Psalm 119:103)**

*May my words convey encouragement, Holy Spirit.*

## The Need to Be Right

An Iowa man was so right that he was wrong.

His wife returned home complaining that a traffic radar unit had erred in ticketing her for doing 38 miles per hour in a 25-mile zone. It was impossible, she claimed, to accelerate that fast in that area. Her husband disagreed and said he would prove it.

With him at the wheel, they returned to the scene of the infraction. He succeeded in reaching 38 miles per hour at the point where his wife had been stopped by the police. However, he couldn't enjoy his "I told you so" moment very long because the radar was still operating. The police gave him a speeding ticket as well. (Unfortunately, there was no family discount.)

Most of us have to resist the tendency to prove that we are right at another's expense. Instead of using someone's shortcomings to build up our ego, we ought to be more concerned about ways to assist that person. That's closer to God's way of dealing with us, so we should model that behavior ourselves.

**Agree with one another, live in peace; and the God of love and peace will be with you. (2 Corinthians 13:11)**

*Jesus, make me quick to be understanding toward others.*

## The Promise of Retirement

One man put it well when he said, "Retirement is a time for rebirth." It's important for people to retire *to* something, not just *from* a job. Retirement can be:

- a time to do some well-deserved relaxing;
- an opportunity to seek emotional tranquility and engage in constructive leisure;
- a release from the burdens of responsibility before they become too hard to deal with;
- a chance to reintegrate one's life and even to embark on a second career.

Age, like youth, has problems—and promise—of its own. We can too easily overlook the promise. The deep-seated yearning by people of every age to be purposeful is rooted in the creative activity of God Himself.

Anything you can do to stir up your own willingness to serve, and encourage such desire in others, is a step toward bringing out the best in humanity.

**Teach us to count our days that we may gain a wise heart. (Psalm 90:12)**

*Whatever our age, Jesus, enable us to use our full potential.*

## Bronze is as Good as Gold

When an ice skater falls down three times during an Olympic performance, it can feel impossible to move forward. That was the case for Italy's Carolina Kostner after the 2010 Vancouver Olympics, where she was expected to win a medal. Her failure to do so led her to retire from the sport, deciding she needed time away from the constant pressure of competition. That time gave her new perspective on her ice-skating career.

With a newfound maturity, the 27-year-old entered the 2014 Olympics in Sochi, Russia, focused on her love of skating, not thoughts of winning a medal. Ironically, that's when she finally won a medal.

After the beautiful artistry she exhibited during her skates to "Ave Maria" and "Bolero," Kostner earned a bronze medal, making her the first Italian to ever win an Olympic figure skating singles medal. She told *ESPN*, "This medal is absolutely worth gold. I will cherish it in my heart. It feels so great that patience and sacrifice and hard work and faith are paid at the end."

**Endurance produces character, and character produces hope. (Romans 5:4)**

*Grant me a new perspective after difficult times, Lord.*

## A Washington Monument

Our Lady of Mercy Church in Potomac, Maryland, was filled for the funeral of Maurice "Mac" McGarry, a beloved Washington-area broadcaster who had died at the age of 87.

Before his retirement in 2011, he was host for 50 years of the popular televised *It's Academic,* which quizzed thousands of high schoolers on general knowledge questions. "Mac" had a huge following, and worked in dozens of charity events in addition to his quiz-show duties.

"He was indeed a Washington monument," said Msgr. Joseph Ranieri, the celebrant of the funeral Mass.

Msgr. Ranieri brought a touch of humor to his homily when he recalled McGarry's favorite moment among all his programs.

The host had asked who defeated Napoleon at the Battle of Waterloo, and a student calmly replied, "Duke Ellington." (Never mind that the correct answer was the Duke of Wellington; let's hope that the creative-minded student received an "A" for coming pretty darn close.)

**Give me now wisdom and knowledge.
(2 Chronicles 1:10)**

*Send us good and humble teachers, Divine King.*

## The Learning Tea

Seven years ago, Katrell Christie opened a tea-and-coffee shop called Dr. Bombay's Underwater Tea Party in Atlanta. In 2009, she took a trip to India with some college students. On a private trip to the town of Darjeeling, Katrell met three orphan girls she learned would be evicted from their orphanage within a year, as they could only be kept there until age 16.

Christie, moved by the plight of these young women, promised to return in six months to help them. Selling donated books from her shop, she soon raised a few thousand dollars, which covered her return trip to India, a rented apartment, and high-school tuition for all three of these girls.

Five years later, Christie now carries a special line of Darjeeling tea in her store, most appropriately dubbed "The Learning Tea." All proceeds from these purchases go directly to paying for the education of orphaned young women in India.

Christie told *Christian Science Monitor* contributor Stell Simonton, "It [education] is the only way I see that you can stop the vicious cycle of poverty in India."

**Wisdom is a fountain of life. (Proverbs 16:22)**

*God, bless all teachers, educators of our future leaders*

## Trusting Your Future to God

As a college student at the University of Southern California, DeVon Franklin chose to interview Tracey Edmonds, the CEO and President of her own entertainment company, for a school project. Several years later, she gave Franklin his first junior executive job because he had made such a good impression when they met.

Franklin, now a successful film executive himself, is grateful to both Edmonds and God for his big break. Why God?

He writes, "When I met with Tracey as a student, I knew that was part of God's process. I had no notion of how it would play out, but because I trust the Lord I made sure I conducted myself appropriately. If I hadn't made an impression as someone of passion, desire, and principles, I doubt Tracey would have remembered me four years later."

Franklin concludes, "What matters is not where you are today, but what kind of person God is shaping you to become in preparation for the time when He brings His vision for your life to fruition."

**I trusted in Your steadfast love. (Psalm 13:5)**

*May prayer, preparation, and trust guide me to success, Lord.*

## Building a Budget

"If the prospect of your credit-card bill arriving puts you in a cold sweat, you, my friend, need a budget." So writes Kara Eschbach in *Verily* magazine, noting that you need to analyze your spending and break it into five categories.

First, there are Fixed Expenses, like "rent/mortgage, student-loan payments, car payments, insurance, and utilities." Next come Living Expenses, including groceries, eating out, movies or gas. Third is your Rainy-Day Fund, "in the case of an unforeseen event, like getting into a car accident or being laid off." Fourth comes your Retirement Fund, in which you should invest, even if the prospect of retiring seems far off. Finally, there's Fun Savings, like a down payment on a house.

Eschbach advises you to be completely honest about every penny you spend so you can "visualize how your current lifestyle will need to change so you can shift money into different categories. Remember, a budget isn't so much a constraint as an empowering tool to help you take control of your financial life."

**The borrower is the slave of the lender. (Proverbs 22:7)**

*Guide me in spending money responsibly, Lord, and may I always contribute to those in need.*

# Year Up

Millionaire Gerald Chertavian built a successful career on Wall Street, but it was his friendship with 10-year-old David Heredia that became his most life-defining experience. During the 1980s, Chertavian spent every Saturday with David as part of a Big Brother program. Though the youngster lived in one of New York City's most crime-infested housing projects, he still dreamed of a better future.

In 2000, Chertavian thought of a way to help kids like David and founded Year Up. As he told the website Nation Swell, "Year Up works with low-income 18-to-24 year olds, and in one year moves them from poverty to a professional career [through] intensive training and development for six months, and then an internship with a Fortune 1000 company."

The program has helped thousands, but over six million young adults are still without jobs in the U.S. Chertavian remains optimistic, though: "What fuels me the most is seeing a young person that has taken control of their life…[That's] one of the most inspirational and spiritual experiences one could have."

**Prosper for us the work of our hands.**
**(Psalm 90:17)**

*Direct young people to good jobs, Heavenly Father.*

## Why I Care

Whether by talent, luck or hard work, people who "make it" can help create a better world by caring about others who are less fortunate. Some successful and caring people lend their names and efforts to important causes.

For instance, Nick Lachey—a noted writer, singer, and producer—contributes by working with the Autism Speaks campaign. He helps raise awareness about the challenges faced by people with Asperger's, a syndrome that his younger brother Zac was diagnosed with at age seven. "It's a great way to contribute," he says, "to raise money and improve the quality of life for those on the autism spectrum and their families."

Lachey adds that his brother is a high-functioning young man talented in math and technology. But Zac "thinks in a way we don't" and struggles socially.

Special-needs people need to be loved and respected just like anyone else. Learn more about their condition so you can help them live the best lives they possibly can.

**Love one another with mutual affection; outdo one another in showing honor. (Romans 12:10)**

*Encourage us, Jesus, to share our abundance with others.*

## Critics Are People Too

Nancy Banks-Smith writes TV reviews in the British newspaper *The Guardian*, but not everyone agrees with her opinions. One reader once wrote her a stinging letter complaining, "For months I've had to read the tripe you write."

Unruffled by the attack, Banks-Smith responded: "I don't know what you have to complain about. You've only had to read it for months. I've had to write it for years."

That story provides an important lesson about feedback. It's usually valued by those engaged in any form of public work, such as writers, producers, broadcasters, and elected officials. But to be effective, such criticism should refrain from merely negative carping.

When airing a grievance, point out specific flaws gently but firmly—and try to include specific suggestions for improvement. God is the cause of our integrity and dignity. We must strive to recognize these qualities in others.

**Let no evil talk come out of your mouths, but only what is useful for building up.**
**(Ephesians 4:29)**

*Holy Spirit, never let me lose sight of the power of gentle persuasion.*

## A Wing and a Prayer

It was 1968 when Canadian bush pilot Brian Steed severed his right arm at the elbow, but still managed to fly his plane 15 miles for help. "God definitely had a part in this," the 28-year-old said of his rescue after a propeller sliced off his arm. He had slipped from a pontoon into the whirling blades after landing on a wilderness lake.

"I said a simple prayer," he related. Dragging himself from the water into his cockpit, he looped a rough rope-tourniquet around his arm, then managed a shaky take-off with one hand. "Blood was squirting all over," he recounted. "I was having a conversation with God all the time."

At the forest station, an employee completed the dramatic rescue by flying the craft on to Port Arthur, Ontario, where the pilot was hospitalized.

Divine help is available to all who call upon it. But God ordinarily assists those who use common sense and uncommon courage in carrying out their duties to self and others.

**I have filled him with divine spirit, with ability, intelligence. (Exodus 31:3)**

*I pray for Your aid in difficult situations, Savior.*

## The Optimist and the Pessimist

Our happiness is often determined by how we look at things. Consider this amusing story which was featured in Father Brian Cavanaugh's book *The Sower's Seeds:*

"There were two identical twins. One was an eternal optimist. The other twin was a sad and hopeless pessimist. The worried parents of the boys brought them to a local psychologist. He suggested to the parents a plan to balance their personalities, saying, 'On their next birthday, put them in separate rooms to open their gifts. Give the pessimist the best toys you can afford and give the optimist a box of manure.'

"The parents did as instructed and observed the results. When they peeked in on the pessimist, they heard him complaining, 'I don't like the color of this computer. I don't like this game. I know someone who's got a bigger toy car.'

"Tiptoeing across the corridor, the parents peeked in and saw their little optimist gleefully throwing the manure up in the air. He exclaimed, 'You can't fool me! Where there's this much manure, there's gotta be a pony!!!'"

**A cheerful heart is a good medicine.**
**(Proverbs 17:22)**

*Help me to find the silver lining in dark clouds, Redeemer.*

## Amputation Brings Opportunity

Franciscan Sister Pat Taube, age 75, couldn't believe it when the doctors told her they would have to amputate her hands and feet following a life-threatening bout with septic shock. After all, she had spent her life ministering to people enduring illness or disease. She was supposed to be the caretaker, not the care recipient. Yet, Sister Taube is approaching her problem with an impressive level of hope and faith.

The Sylvania, Ohio nun believes that her suffering will make her more relatable to the sick when she resumes her ministry in the future. She told the *Catholic Chronicle*, "When this happened, I thought, 'Well, this is a new opportunity.' I feel that God has something in store for me to do and I need to follow through on that."

Currently at the Rosary Care Center on her motherhouse's grounds, Sister Taube received prostheses for her arms and legs and is undergoing rehabilitation. She said, "I don't have hands or feet—but there's so much more to life. And it's still me. I'm still the person that I always was."

**No purpose of Yours can be thwarted. (Job 42:2)**

*Use me to achieve Your will, Heavenly Father.*

## A Parent's Prayer

Many years ago, Father James Meana wrote a special prayer for parents. Here is an excerpt:

"O Heavenly Father, make me a better parent. Teach me to understand my children, to listen patiently to what they have to say, and to answer all their questions kindly...Let me not tempt my children to lie or steal. And guide me hour by hour that I may demonstrate by all that I say and do that honesty produces happiness.

"When I'm out of sorts, help me, O Lord, to hold my tongue. May I ever be mindful that my children are children and I should not expect of them the judgment of adults. Let me not rob them of the opportunity to wait on themselves and to make decisions.

"Bless me with the bigness to grant them all their reasonable requests and the courage to deny them privileges I know will do them harm. Make me fair and just and kind—and fit me, O Lord, to be loved and respected and imitated by my children. Amen."

**The glory of children is their parents.**
**(Proverbs 17:6)**

*Give parents wisdom, patience, and compassion, Father.*

## Happy Flower Day!

Trisha Gallagher turned her desire to brighten the days of nursing home residents into a ministry that's touching thousands.

In May 2013, the 62-year-old Philadelphia resident discovered that her local Trader Joe's supermarket was willing to donate day-old flower bouquets to charity. As someone who already worked with the elderly, she asked the store manager if she could distribute some of them.

Gallagher told *Woman Alive* magazine that she received 60 colorful bouquets her first day and took them to a nearby nursing home, where she handed them out with the greeting, "Happy Flower Day!" Residents were overjoyed by the unexpected gift.

Since then, Gallagher has distributed over 17,000 bouquets to lonely seniors, people on the street, hospital patients, recovery houses and more. And she's done it 355 days out of the last 365 because she loves the thrill of making people happy. How does Gallagher know to whom she should give flowers on any particular day? She says, "Every day, I ask for the knowledge of God's will and the ability to carry it out."

**Let no flower of spring pass us by.
(Wisdom 2:7)**

*May a spirit of giving bloom in my heart, Holy Spirit.*

## A Prom Mitzvah

James Maslow has attracted a lot of fans as a singer with the band Big Time Rush. One of those fans, 23-year-old Hannah Wackernagle of Grove City, Ohio, who was born with Down syndrome, likes him so much that she made a video asking him to go to her high school prom with her.

After Hannah posted it online, the video went viral and came to Maslow's attention. Since he was a contestant on *Dancing with the Stars* at the time her prom was taking place, he couldn't oblige Hannah's request, but he did the next best thing.

Maslow flew her and her family from Ohio out to Los Angeles, spent a day with them in Disneyland, had his dance partner Peta Murgatroyd teach Hannah some dance moves, then gave her a special mini-prom with him in the *Dancing with the Stars* ballroom.

Considering that Maslow was raised Jewish and "believes in religion wholeheartedly," despite not being able to practice it as much as he used to, this act of goodness and charity can definitely be considered a "mitzvah" (a blessing).

**May Your blessing be on Your people. (Psalm 3:8)**

*May I always take time to bestow kindnesses, Father.*

## The Relief of Forgiveness

When Kerry Weber, the managing editor of *America* magazine, traveled to Rwanda in 2013 as part of Catholic Relief Services' Egan Journalism Fellowship, she witnessed an unfathomable level of mercy. The trip's purpose was to report on the state of society 20 years after the government-sanctioned genocide, during which nearly a million people were killed—many by their own neighbors—over a period of 100 days.

Weber spoke with the genocide's survivors and perpetrators, along with government and church officials who had worked to rebuild their country from the ashes. During one meeting, she learned that people whose family members had been murdered were living in the same village as their killers.

"Not only lived with them," she said, "but in our group, sat next to each other and hugged each other. All the people who spoke to us about forgiveness said that it was a relief for them. They could not go through life with this anger. One woman even, while the man that killed her family was in prison, helped support *his* family. It was more mercy than I can imagine."

**Love your enemies. (Matthew 5:44)**

*Move me past anger toward forgiveness, Divine Savior.*

## The Berzins Bunch

Every day must feel like Mother's Day to Eileen Berzins of Annapolis, Maryland, whose family is really large. You can't accuse her of being superstitious, either. In 2014, she gave birth to her 13th child, Francis, and through it all, at 39 years of age, still manages to look just like a model.

The subject of a profile by Maria Wiering in the *Catholic Review*, newspaper of the Baltimore Archdiocese, Berzins had a ready answer on how to run a household with six girls, seven boys, and her husband, Tim.

"I do the same as everybody else does," Eileen says. "Just a little bit of it. It's not like God gave us 13 at once."

Her husband, a U.S. Naval Academy graduate now involved in defense contracting, summed up the family outlook: "When people say, 'Does your wife work?' I kind of laugh because there's no tougher job."

However, Mrs. Berzins doesn't look at what she does as a "job." A Georgetown graduate and a former teacher, she says of motherhood: "It's all I ever wanted to be."

**Sons are indeed a heritage...a reward. (Psalm 127:3)**

*Abba, guide all families, keeping them grounded in love and faith.*

## Only God Can Make a Tree

One of nature's thirstiest forms of life is the tree. A large oak can drink 300 gallons of water in a day, yet it uses less than a quart for making wood.

Far from being wasteful, this enormous absorption is necessary to operate an air conditioning system of sorts to maintain the cool temperature needed for photosynthesis—the basic food-making process in plant life. Also, vast quantities of water are required to supply the minerals for the tree's growth.

To fill these needs, the entire root system is designed to probe the soil with millions of microscopic root hairs, which slip between individual grains of earth to absorb moisture.

The intricate and purposeful workings of nature often bring us to a renewed appreciation for God's marvelous design. Occasionally stop and look around. Find reasons to be thankful for the natural wonder in trees, plants, animals, and humanity itself.

**Lift up your eyes on high and see: Who created these? He who brings out their host and numbers them, calling them all by name. (Isaiah 40:26)**

*Help me better appreciate nature's wonders, Lord.*

## When God Cheers

Five-year-old Jimmy stood nervously at home plate, waiting for his first-ever at bat in a baseball game. Diagnosed with cerebral palsy at age 15 months, Jimmy needed leg braces to walk, but he could take comfort in the fact that all the kids on the field were living with some physical disability. They were simply here today for love of the game.

As recounted by John Shaughnessy in his book *When God Cheers,* Jimmy got a hit and started running to first base, then second base. The crowd chanted, "Go Jimmy! Go Jimmy!" But running with leg braces had taken a toll by the time he neared third base, and he struggled to move forward.

That's when the opposing team's shortstop, who was playing his position from a motorized wheelchair, drove up to Jimmy and said, "Hop on back, I'll take you home." That's exactly what he did. Jimmy and his new friend crossed home plate to cheers from the crowd, delivering the lesson that some things in life are more important than winning.

**Two are better than one...For if they fall, one will lift up the other. (Ecclesiastes 4:9-10)**

*Holy Spirit, inspire me to perform more acts of kindness.*

## Balancing It All

Busy moms may find it difficult to make time for God in the course of their daily responsibilities. Candace Cameron Bure can relate. However, the actress and author of *Balancing It All* noted that experience has taught her that Scripture reading and prayer are crucial to maintaining a sense of balance in her life.

She said on *Christopher Closeup,* "I just read the Bible this morning with the kids. Before going to school, at 6:45, we all sit on the couch and read a chapter. We talk about it for 15 minutes, but it sets your day. That's the only way that I'm able to balance the things that God has given me to balance."

Though she wants to do everything that's asked of her, Bure realizes that sometimes achieving balance requires saying "no." It was a difficult lesson, but the 38-year-old laughingly admits that she's finally getting there "in my old age."

"You can get overwhelmed and then priorities that really need to be done are being put aside," said Bure. "Just because things are good doesn't mean that they need to be done by *you*—[or that] God wants *you* to do them."

**Do not busy yourself with many matters. (Sirach 11:10)**

*Lord, help me find the balance that eludes me.*

## Most Valuable Mom

It wasn't Mother's Day last year when the star of basketball's Oklahoma City Thunder, Kevin Durant, accepted his league's Most Valuable Player award. But no one could have paid a finer tribute to his mother than Durant did that day, with an acceptance speech that deserves to be ranked at the very top.

Durant started and finished by thanking God. Then, he voiced his gratitude to teammates, coaches and other staff members and the fans of Oklahoma City. Finally, tears flowing down his face, Durant turned to address his Mom:

"I don't know how you did what you did. You were a single parent with two boys by the time you were 21. We moved from one apartment to another by ourselves. One of my best memories is when we moved into our first apartment...We hugged each other, and we thought we had made it.

"When you didn't eat, you made sure we ate. You went to sleep hungry. You sacrificed for us. You're the real MVP."

**Strength and dignity are her clothing...Her children rise up and call her blessed. (Proverbs 31:25,28)**

*Mother of God, bless and protect all the mothers of this world, strengthening them in wisdom and faith.*

## Because You Gave Me Life

With Rita Respass-Brown's kidney function at only six percent, she would need either dialysis or a transplant in order to stay alive. When her 24-year-old son Tony heard the news, he secretly went to get tested to see if his kidney would be a match for his mom. It turned out to be a perfect match, so he told her that he would be her donor.

Rita felt reluctant at first because she didn't want Tony to make such a big sacrifice for her. But as she recalled on the TV series *NY Med,* he asked her, "Mom, what does it mean to you for someone to give you a kidney?"

Rita responded, "Life!"

Tony answered, "That's why I'm going to give you my kidney. You gave me life—and you don't have the right to deny me the ability to do for you what you did for me."

Thankfully, the transplant went well, giving both mother and son a new appreciation for the precious gift of life—and each other.

**There is no fear in love, but perfect love casts out fear. (1 John 4:18)**

*Father, help me to serve my family fearlessly and selflessly. Also, bring healing to all those facing severe health issues.*

## Canceled Wedding, Homeless Feast

When Willie and Carol Fowler's daughter canceled her wedding 40 days before the event, they were left facing not only great emotional pain but steep financial loss as well. The Fowlers had already booked a wedding reception at the prestigious Villa Christina in Atlanta. They wisely turned to prayer for guidance on what to do next, and instantly found their answer.

"I was in the process of canceling out the venue," Carol Fowler told *ABC News's* Christina Ng, "and he [Willie] said, 'No, what we'll do is donate it to Hosea Feed the Hungry.'…It was a vision. He said he had prayed on it during the night and that's what we were going to do."

Talk about every cloud having a silver lining! Hosea Feed the Hungry, a nonprofit that supplies the homeless with necessary goods and services every year, was overwhelmed by the Fowlers' generous donation. The intended wedding feast was transformed into a sumptuous banquet for 200 grateful individuals, 50 of them children.

"It was a wonderful event," said Quisa Foster of Hosea. "It brought tears to my eyes."

**And all ate and were filled. (Matthew 14:20)**

*Abba, may we seek to turn every negative into a positive.*

# A Homecoming Queen's Kind Gesture

Mary Urtuzuastegui was a bright 11-year-old at Most Holy Redeemer School in Montgomery, Minnesota. She loved playing volleyball, and she dreamed of competing for—and winning—the title of Homecoming Queen at Tri-City United High School.

That dream was crushed in 2013 when a car accident took Mary's life. But the crown would be hers nonetheless. The actual winner, Kayla Treka, who had known Mary as coach of her volleyball team, presented the tiara to her family in a gesture of sympathy. "Mary was always her Dad's little princess," said Mary's mother. "He'll really appreciate this."

Kayla, a member of her parish's youth group, decided to give up the crown as a symbol of her faith after talking over the matter with her parents. The gift moved many people, including Mindy Reeder, principal of Most Holy Redeemer School. "We call Mary our angel now," she said. "She's crowned in heaven with Jesus, and we have that crown here to be symbolic of that."

**Rejoice with those who rejoice, weep with those who weep. (Romans 12:15)**

*Teach young people to reflect compassion, Jesus.*

## Doing God's Work

It's great to be remembered, especially when you're known for what you did in life. That's the case with Kenneth Jernigan, whose career was recalled a couple of years ago in a regular *Catholic Review* feature called "Our Back Pages"—and who was celebrated as "The Martin Luther King Jr. of the Blind."

Jernigan died in his Baltimore home in 1998, sure in the knowledge that as longtime president of the National Federation of the Blind, he had worked hard to eliminate discrimination against those who, like himself, were unable to see. He was also concerned with providing training of the blind so they could compete in the business world.

Not long before he died, Jernigan and his wife, Mary, were received into the Catholic Church. His widow, interviewed for the "Our Back Pages" feature, said: "After we converted, we realized that all that he had been doing for the blind was really God's work."

**Through such works You have taught Your people that the righteous must be kind, and You have filled Your children with good hope. (Wisdom 12:19)**

*May all my works please You, Gracious Father.*

## How Will the World be Converted?

As recorded in the gospel of Matthew, Jesus tells His disciples, "Go therefore and make disciples of all nations" prior to His ascension into heaven. When He did ascend, the book of Acts notes that the apostles stood staring intently into the sky.

Reflecting on these passages for Ascension Thursday, Patheos.com blogger Deacon Greg Kandra offered this interpretation of the story's meaning:

"It is tempting on this feast of the Ascension to experience it the way the apostles did, to gaze into the heavens and to ponder the clouds and to pray over the miracle of this great moment. But Christ's words to His apostles are words to us all. Go. The world will not be converted on a mountaintop. The message will not be spread in the clouds. It will happen in the streets and the synagogues, in public squares and private homes, in books and newspapers and media of all kinds. It needs to be lived in the world."

**And remember, I am with you always, until the end of the age. (Matthew 28:20)**

*Jesus, instill me with the courage and wisdom to share Your life and message with the people around me.*

## Guardians of Rescue

Like many other veterans who fought in Iraq and Afghanistan, former Marine Jarrett Gimbl was unsure of where to turn for help when he returned home. Honorably discharged in 2009, he suffers periodically from irritability, aggravation and headaches, all classic symptoms of post-traumatic stress syndrome.

Then help arrived—in the form of Gunny, a yellow Labrador-hound mix provided by Guardians of Rescue, a Long Island (New York) organization that supplies service dogs to veterans in need. Gimbl depends on Gunny for just about everything. "If I'm losing my balance," he said, "he leans on that leg. He knows everything."

The founder of Guardians of Rescue, Robert Misseri, had an easy explanation of the organization's mission. "This is my opportunity to serve those who have served," he told the *Daily News.* And the dogs "give the veterans a trust level that they don't have with people anymore."

As for Gimbl, he knows what his dog has done for him. "If it wasn't for Gunny," he said, "I wouldn't be here."

**May He rescue me from all tribulation. (1 Samuel 26:24)**

*Give veterans the healing they need, Prince of Peace.*

# Letter Carrier's Vigilance Saves a Life

Michael "Mickey" Wheeley has worked as a letter carrier in Graham, North Carolina for more than 20 years, and knows all his patrons like family. So when Wheeley noticed one of his client's mailboxes overflowing with at least a few days' worth of medicine packages, he knew that something must be wrong. He knocked on the door and heard a voice tell him to come in.

As it turns out, Wheeley's patron, both a veteran and recent stroke victim, had been put on bed rest. His caretaker had quit earlier that week, and the man had had nothing to eat or drink for three days. Immediately, Wheeley called his postal supervisor, Carole Eckstrom, who phoned 911. The mailman waited with his patron until an ambulance arrived to take the latter to the Durham VA Hospital.

"Mickey very well could have saved that man's life," Eckstrom told *WFMY News 2*. "I told our carriers, 'This is what we do, we are the contact for most people we serve.'"

"He needed some help," Wheeley concluded, humbly deflecting any praise. "We all need some help."

**Love one another as I have loved you. (John 15:12)**

*Master, open our eyes and hearts to those in need.*

## Adopting a War Orphan

A Dutch couple found a dramatic way to be instruments of God's peace shortly after World War II. At a time when anti-German feelings ran high in the Netherlands, Dr. and Mrs. Jan Tinbergen opened their home to a seven-year-old German war orphan.

This incident was reported in the world's press the day after Dr. Tinbergen was nominated to share the first Nobel Prize in Economic Science. An American friend explained his motives:

"Adopting that little girl instead of just sitting around hating the Germans was typical of the way Tinbergen thinks. It sounds corny, but he really seems to be one of those people who live their Christianity."

What is accomplished by those who just sit around and hate or complain? If more of us risked seeming a little "corny" by living the Gospel Christ preached, we'd make a significant step toward bringing about the reign of the Prince of Peace.

**Live your life in a manner worthy of the gospel of Christ. (Philippians 1:27)**

*Holy Spirit, show me where in my life I can become a peacemaker.*

## Leisure Time

Can you relax without feeling guilty? Although not everyone can, there are good reasons to try.

In their book, *Spiritual Literacy: Reading the Sacred in Everyday Life,* editors Frederic and Mary Ann Brussat devote a section to leisure.

They note that leisure activities run the gamut and can include cooking, sharing meals, exercise and sports. Hobbies might "offer us opportunities to express ourselves and to nurture our growth through silence, attention, imagination, and wonder."

Leisure activities can also help us find meaning and discover spiritual truths—good reasons to take a break.

As William Penn (quoted by the Brussats) once said, "In the rush and noise of life, as you have intervals, step within yourselves and be still. Wait upon God and feel His good presence; this will carry you through your day's business."

**He said to them, "Come away to a deserted place...and rest a while." For many were coming and going, and they had no leisure even to eat. (Mark 6:31)**

*Increase our ability to relax and appreciate Your goodness, Father.*

## A Motivated Runner

In the late 1960s, while her fellow students at Brooklyn's Erasmus High School studied international problems in textbooks, Cheryl Toussaint got a first-hand glimpse of Russia and West Germany.

Toussaint, who would go on to become a silver medalist in the 1972 Olympics, was the youngest member of a group of 30 U.S. track and field athletes who flew overseas for an international competition. How did she earn this distinction?

She said, "To be good, you have to sacrifice. I can't remember the last time I went to a party."

Her coach added, "Cheryl has worked hard for this trip. She deserves it. But there are hundreds of other youngsters who could have the same chance if they only put their minds on running toward a goal instead of away from it."

There is no substitute for hard work in achieving anything worthwhile. In God's world, as in athletic competition, those who work the hardest often achieve the most.

**Let us run with perseverance the race that is set before us. (Hebrews 12:1)**

*Lord, help me persevere when giving up would be easier.*

## Come On Up to the House

"The world is not my home. I'm just a' passin' through."

Those lyrics from the Tom Waits song "Come on Up to the House" hold special meaning for author and catechist Jonathan F. Sullivan. Due to a long battle with alcoholism and depression, Sullivan's father could never find peace in this world despite being a man with a strong sense of faith.

After he died, Jonathan found comfort in this song that was both "mournful" and "hopeful" —in the idea that God had invited his father to "come on up to" His house.

As Jonathan wrote in a blog post, "That suffering can be transformed for the salvation of the world is the mystery of the cross. God calls us all to pass through this world to His home—a lavish home of grace and abundance where we can surrender our hardships. 'Come On Up to the House' will always remind me of my father's pain and how it has been transformed, and I hope one day we will meet in that house and sing together in praise of God's wondrous love."

**I have seen the suffering of My people. (1 Samuel 9:16)**

*Holy Spirit, bring peace to those struggling with addiction and depression.*

## Retirement — Not a Door Marked Exit

The good news: American life spans are extending. As a result, we need to rethink our attitudes about retirement.

Jane Pauley, broadcaster and writer, is a baby boomer who isn't ready to retire in any traditional sense of the word. She has a lot of company.

Many people with the health, resources, desire, physical and/or emotional ability to work beyond typical retirement years stay on the job; others tackle new challenges.

Pauley, author of *Your Life Calling: Reimagining the Rest of Your Life,* says the meaning of retirement is changing. She writes, "Retirement is not a door marked Exit. Think instead of a door leading us to something new...Unlike previous generations, who retired *from* something, we can imagine retiring *to* something."

As you prepare for the future, nurture your health and wellbeing and maintain social support.

**I have been young, and now am old, yet I have not seen the righteous forsaken or their children begging bread. (Psalm 37:25)**

*May Jesus be our guide through unfamiliar territory.*

# Why Jim Caviezel Jumped Off Stage

During a panel discussion at San Diego Comic-Con featuring the cast of the action-adventure TV series *Person of Interest,* a nervous young girl from the audience asked star Jim Caviezel, "Which was more fun to work on? *Person of Interest* or *The Passion of the Christ?*" (in which Caviezel played Jesus).

The room erupted in laughter. Considering that Caviezel endured a lightning strike and other injuries on *The Passion,* he jokingly answered, "*Person of Interest* is a little more funner."

With a sense of parental curiosity, Caviezel, a father of three, then asked the girl, "How old are you, sweetheart?" She responded, "I'm 11 years old." Caviezel smiled, "You're the same age as my daughter and you're beautiful."

The girl approached the stage in the hopes of shaking Caviezel's hand. Co-star Sarah Shahi said, "Give her a hug"—so Caviezel followed his TV partner's advice. Using some action-hero moves, he climbed over the table, jumped off the stage, and embraced the obviously-thrilled girl. It was a simple gesture of kindness, but it meant the world to one young fan.

**The fruit of the Spirit is...kindness.**
**(Galatians 5:22)**

*Remind me that no act of kindness is too small, Father.*

## A Fearless and Holy Leader

By the time his battalion was captured during the Korean War, U.S. Army chaplain Father Emil Kapaun already had a reputation as a fearless and holy leader because of the way he braved enemy fire to rescue the wounded during battle. As he and his fellow soldiers were being marched to their prisoner of war camp by their Chinese and North Korean captors, the priest engaged in another remarkable act of courage.

Roy Wenzl—co-author of the Christopher Award-winning book *The Miracle of Father Kapaun*—explained that Father Kapaun saw a Chinese soldier with his rifle pointed at the head of Sgt. Herb Miller, who was lying in a ditch with a broken ankle. It was routine for the Chinese to execute wounded enemy soldiers.

Wenzl said, "Father Kapaun breaks away from his captors, strides over, brushes the Chinese soldier's rifle up in the air, then leans down right in front of him, picks the sergeant up and carries him away. And the sergeant's still alive today."

Father Kapaun continued to be a lifesaver in the POW camp as well. More of his story tomorrow.

**His heart was courageous. (2 Chronicles 17:6)**

*Grant me courage in the face of strife, Prince of Peace.*

## No Act of Service Was Beneath Him

Life in the North Korean POW camp was brutal for Father Kapaun and the Allied soldiers, but once again, the chaplain provided material relief and moral leadership. For instance, the Chinese and North Koreans only gave their captives a handful of birdseed to eat daily. Despite feeling starved himself, Father Kapaun often gave his seeds away to set an example of sharing.

The Allies also didn't receive any water to drink, so they scraped snow and ice off the ground to hydrate themselves. As a result of ingesting unclean water, they often got dysentery.

Because of his youth working on a farm, Father Kapaun took roofing tin from bombed-out buildings and formed them into bowls that they could use as little cooking pots. That saved lives because it allowed them to boil water before drinking it. And for the soldiers who did suffer from dysentery, Father Kapaun would hand-wash their underwear, demonstrating that absolutely no act of service was beneath him.

The spiritual guidance Father Kapaun gave his fellow POWs was also invaluable. That part of his story tomorrow.

**Those who are generous are blessed. (Proverbs 22:9)**

*Help me endure sacrifice to help others in need, Lord.*

## Prayer and Defiance

The practice of Catholic prayers and rituals became another way for Father Kapaun to defy the enemy in the POW camp. Roy Wenzl, co-author of the book *The Miracle of Father Kapaun,* said during an interview on *Christopher Closeup,* "The guards banned any sort of religious services, so Father would sneak around at night, go into the huts and say the rosary. The Protestants and the Jews and the agnostics would pray the rosary because it was a way to support him. He was also trying to keep them alive by creating a spirit of defiance and purpose."

The camp's communist commanders saw Father Kapaun as a threat, so they put him in a place dubbed "the Death House" when he grew weak and sick. Wenzl said, "The Allied soldiers volunteered to carry him, as sort of an honor guard, to his own death. And on the way into the Death House, Father's hand came up off of the stretcher and he blessed the Chinese guards who were participating in his murder and he asked their forgiveness, and then said, 'Father, forgive them.'" He died soon after.

The conclusion of Father Kapaun's story tomorrow.

**I will pray to the Lord for you. (1 Samuel 7:5)**

*Replace hatred with forgiveness in my heart, Redeemer.*

## Christ Was His Model

The levels of selflessness and sacrifice displayed by Father Emil Kapaun throughout the Korean War were heroic and saintly, to say the least. Where did he get the strength and character to act that way? To his biographer Roy Wenzl, the answer is obvious: "Christ was his model."

The surviving POWs who had been with Father Kapaun during his final months immediately tried to get him recognized posthumously with the Medal of Honor. For bureaucratic reasons, it took 50 years before their efforts finally came to fruition in 2013.

In addition, the chaplain is also on the road to sainthood after several seemingly-incurable patients were recently healed following prayers for his intercession. Wenzl notes that many of the people supporting Father Kapaun's cause for sainthood are Protestants who are "baffled about why this guy hasn't been named a saint." It seems that even in death, Father Kapaun is crossing denominational lines just as he did in life.

**The hour is coming when all who are in their graves will hear His voice and will come out — those who have done good, to the resurrection of life. (John 5:28-29)**

*May we all aspire to be saints in Your heavenly kingdom, Lord.*

## Bring on the Laughs

Never underestimate the power of laughter. That was the gist of actor and comedian Bob Newhart's commencement address at the Catholic University of America in 1997.

Humor isn't frivolous, Newhart reminded the graduates; it's necessary. He said, "It allows us to step back from an event over which we have no control and deal with it and then move on with our lives...We had an earthquake a couple of years ago in Los Angeles, and it wasn't more than three or four days later that I heard the first earthquake joke. Someone said, 'The traffic is stopped, but the freeways are moving.'"

Newhart concluded, "People with a sense of humor tend to be less egocentric and more realistic in their view of the world, more humble in moments of success, and less defeated in times of travail. I certainly don't delude myself that there aren't more important things to do in life than make people laugh, but I can't imagine anything that would bring me more joy."

**He will yet fill your mouth with laughter, and your lips with shouts of joy. (Job 8:21)**

*Keep my eyes, heart, and spirit open to the humor in everyday situations, Divine Creator.*

## Love and Grand Gestures

Calah Alexander, a wife and mother of five in Florida, admits that she used to "buy into the cultural lie that love is measured in Grand Gestures," like champagne and diamonds. And since her husband, a teacher, wasn't good at grand gestures, she would often lapse into a "woe is me" attitude.

Then she started paying more attention to her husband's actions on a day-to-day basis and discovered just how special their relationship was.

On her Patheos blog, Alexander wrote, "During the school year he works from 9 to 6, comes home for an hour for dinner, and then goes straight back to the writing center until 10:30 or 11. And in that hour, he never comes home and relaxes. He comes home and helps me feed the kids dinner, get them in bed, then cleans and sweeps the kitchen before going back to work."

Alexander now realizes that she's got a spouse who appreciates everything she does as a wife and mom, and does his best to selflessly support her. And that kind of love serves a much bigger purpose than champagne and diamonds.

**He who loves his wife loves himself. (Ephesians 5:28)**

*Help spouses love each other like You love us, Lord.*

## Attention, Control Freaks!

The need to be in control. Many of us struggle with it, and Catholic writer Mary DeTurris Poust is no exception.

As she recalled on her blog Not Strictly Spiritual, she was meeting with her spiritual director, a Sister of Saint Joseph of Carondolet, a few years ago and told her, "I want to be in the spiritual groove. Sometimes I've got it going on in my spiritual life, and then I hit dark and dry patches and everything falls apart. I feel like I'll never get back to where I was."

The nun suggested that DeTurris Poust's focus on "I" may be contributing to the problem—and that she needed to give up her "illusion of control" and instead tell God, "I know I can't do this without You."

DeTurris Poust acknowledged that she still struggles with this same issue and plans to reflect on the idea "that I cannot do anything without God, but with God all things are possible."

Reflect on your life and see if your desire for control is impacting you in a negative way. Then pray for the grace to trust God—and be humble enough to let Him lead the way.

**Trust in Him, and He will act. (Psalm 37:5)**

*Lord, increase my faith and my trust in You.*

## Living with Attila the Teen

If you're a parent living with "Attila the Teen"—a teen who constantly acts disgruntled—Marybeth Hicks has some advice for you. It doesn't have to be that way.

Writing in *Catholic Digest,* she bemoans the fact that parents and other authority figures today often act as if it's impossible for young people to exhibit manners and self-control. On the other hand, if you set high expectations for teens, like Hicks does with her kids, they may rise to the occasion.

She writes, "At our house, we all pitch in. Chores aren't fun, but you don't have to apologize because you can't make emptying the dishwasher more fun. It's fun when kids have a positive attitude, chat with family members, and work together. If you're being manipulated into excusing your disgruntled teen without her doing her fair share of the work, the only thing you should be sorry about is allowing her to intimidate you."

Hicks concludes, "Worry less about managing your daughter's behavior, and more about building her character. If you focus on her good character, her good behavior will follow."

**Discipline your children while there is hope. (Psalm 19:18)**

*Help me raise kind and compassionate children, Lord.*

## Helping a Loved One Grieve

We all have friends and family who must cope with the deaths of loved ones. Here are some tips from *Catholic Digest* on how to help someone who is grieving.

- **Don't fall back on clichés, such as "It all happens for a reason."** Just say, "I'm sorry for your loss," and mean it.
- **Offer specific help like writing thank-you notes, cooking meals, or providing childcare.** Vague offers of "call me if you need anything" will likely not be taken up.
- **Remember to pray for them, and let them know it.** Have a Mass said, send a spiritual bouquet.
- **Don't forget that grief remains after the funeral is over.** Patience and compassion will be needed for a long time.
- **Talk about the person who is gone.** Even if it brings on tears, it feels good to know a loved one is remembered.
- **Don't be offended if phone calls or texts go unanswered.** They can seem overwhelming to a bereaved person, so just keep in touch and know your concern is appreciated.

> **Blessed be he by the Lord, whose kindness has not forsaken the living or the dead! (Ruth 2:20)**

*Holy Spirit, bolster the spirits of the grieving.*

## Father's Instinct Saves Newborn

Three weeks from her due date, *CNN* reporter Josh Levs' pregnant wife started having contractions at their home, then fell to her knees in pain. Levs called 911 for an ambulance, but the baby's birth had already begun.

Following the 911 operator's instructions, the anxious father managed to ease his newborn son out, but saw to his horror that the umbilical cord was wrapped five times around his baby's neck—and the child didn't seem to be breathing. Levs unraveled the cord as calmly as possible, then laid his son down on the floor.

"When I stroked him gently a couple of times, the baby opened his eyes, began to move, began to breathe," he recalled. "I can still see and feel everything about that moment."

Levs concludes that he's glad nothing went wrong with the birth, and feels grateful he was able to be there for his son in such a unique way: "It reinforces, in a powerful way, what just about all dads want our kids to have—the feeling, the knowledge that we will take care of them, protect them."

**Love one another with mutual affection. (Romans 12:10)**

*Father, guide our earthly fathers in Your ways.*

## Be in the Business of Loving People

Brian Bird has worked in Hollywood for 25 years, most notably as an executive producer on the TV series *Touched by an Angel* and *When Calls the Heart*. While serving as the keynote speaker at a brunch for a Christian group in Hollywood, he shared several "commandments" for Christians who work in media. One of them—Thou Shalt be in the Business of Loving People—can apply to anyone in any walk of life.

Bird said, "I'm talking about the people we have to work alongside to get the message out — the people in Hollywood whose lifestyles and values may offend us, but whom God has not given up on. Because Hollywood is a town of great insecurity and betrayal, loyal friends rarely exist. I've learned that the people I work with don't care how much I know until they know how I much I care."

Bird concluded, "We also don't need to feel the burden of cleaning up the lives of those we work with. If we love unconditionally in the name of Christ, the Holy Spirit will do the cleaning up."

**Let all you do be done in love.**
**(1 Corinthians 16:14)**

*Holy Spirit, may the unconditional love of Christ guide all that I do and say.*

## Fear Brings on Failure

In his book *Enjoy Your Precious Life,* Father John Catoir shares insights about living a joyful life versus a fearful life:

"A successful athlete has a winning attitude. He or she gets in the flow of the game confidently playing to win. The fearful opponent plays defensively, and tries to keep from losing. The fear of losing inhibits the athlete's skills."

"A happy pianist delights in the sounds he creates for his audience; whereas a tense pianist pounds away at the piano worrying about what the critics might say if he makes a mistake. He worries about failure, and brings on failure."

"A happy physician exudes confidence in his skills. In the process he or she gives much needed assurance and comfort to all. A greedy physician sees dollar signs in his service. The patients are seen more as units of income than suffering human beings. This attitude translates into a spirit of arrogance."

"Love is the motivation that makes the difference. With love comes joy and freedom."

**Truly the eye of the Lord is on those who fear Him, on those who hope in His steadfast love. (Psalm 33:18)**

*Help me rest in Your love, Lord, and find joy in my work.*

## The Legacy of a Playground

Her family found a unique and wonderful way to celebrate the life of Mary Sherlach, 56, a counselor killed in the shooting massacre at Newtown, Connecticut. They dedicated a playground in her memory for the children in another disaster area: Breezy Point in Queens, New York, hit hard by the ravages of Hurricane Sandy.

Bill Sherlach, Mary's husband, and their two daughters, Maura Schwartz and Katy Sherlach, visited the playground—which they helped design—for the dedication. "You can run under the covers and stay there," Bill told Simone Weichselbaum of the *Daily News.* "Or you can carry on whatever your loved one was all about. Mary was all about the kids."

Sean Fitzgerald of Breezy Point considered the gift as his son tried out the new equipment. "It's amazing that this is here," he said. "That the people of Newtown thought of us after what they went through."

**May His name endure forever, His fame continue as long as the sun. (Psalm 72:17)**

*Holy Redeemer, inspire us to bring hope out of tragedy through compassion and action.*

# Surviving Disasters with a Little Help

A roof over your head? That's just the beginning for Catholic Relief Services, which supplies tarpaulins not only to tornado and typhoon victims, but to catastrophic disaster areas all over the world. Consider these advantages, provided by Jim Stipe in *The Wooden Bell*, CRS's newsmagazine:

- **Shelter keeps you and your food dry.** CRS uses tarps designed to offer long-term protection for homes and food.

- **Shelter allows you to sleep.** When it rains at night, without a roof you can't sleep. A long list of health problems are related to lack of sleep.

- **Shelter protects you from the sun.** CRS uses tarps with built-in UV protection.

- **Shelter keeps families together.** The simple act of eating together, as a family, can be emotionally healing.

- **Shelter offers a sense of normalcy.** In a disaster, families experience an incredible loss of control, as possessions and homes are ripped from them. Having a tarp for a roof allows families to stay where they are, in the community they know.

**You have been a...shelter from the rainstorm. (Isaiah 25:4)**

*Bring relief and hope to those suffering in natural disasters, Lord.*

## Something Special for the Marines

It only took one phone call to the right person, and miracles started to happen. That's how a heroic group of Marines, heading home from Afghanistan, found a dream trip for the last leg of their journey.

The 13 Marines, led by Capt. Pravan Rajan, had had a tough itinerary thus far—four flights, with close connections, en route to their California base. That's when Capt. Rajan's fiancée had an idea: she called O'Hare Airport in Chicago to ask if "something special" could be done for their final flight.

She happened to get John Colas, 74, a former Marine now a USO volunteer, and he swung into action. He had little trouble persuading 15 Chicago police officers and a like number of firefighters to serve as an honor guard when the Marines got off their flight; then they escorted them—to the cheers of dozens of passengers— through the terminal.

The best was yet to come. They flew first class to California, courtesy of American Airlines and seven anonymous first-class fliers who gave up their seats. Said Colas: "We want these kids to realize that they haven't been forgotten."

**You will increase my honor. (Psalm 71:21)**

*May we find ways to honor those who serve us, Lord.*

## Attention, Newlyweds!

"No newly married couple knows what they are doing when it comes to marriage."

So say marriage counselors Dr. Greg and Lisa Popcak in their book *Just Married*—and they admit that held true for them as well when they tied the knot 24 years ago.

During an interview on *Christopher Closeup,* Lisa said, "There's a culture shock to being married: joining your traditions, working out the everyday ins and outs of life, having to live with somebody during all their moods. The Church knows what it's talking about when it says the vows are 'for better or for worse, for richer, for poorer, in sickness and in health.' Most people don't realize how quickly you'll go through all those stages, even in the first year of marriage!"

Greg added, "Couples...shouldn't be surprised when they wake up and think, 'What did I do?' That's perfectly normal. But you can get through that so long as you're committed [to each other] and going back to God and asking Him to teach you to love each other with His love."

**Love is patient; love is kind. (1 Corinthians 13:4)**

*Help me to appreciate my spouse, Holy Spirit.*

## More Important Than Gold

Coach Holly Metcalf wanted to lead the United States' eight-women rowing team to victory in the world championships. To do so, she knew they'd need to beat the favored Romanians. But at the competition, the Romanians had a strike against them because all their boats had been destroyed during a violent rebellion in their country. They had no boat in which to compete.

In his book *When God Cheers,* John Shaughnessy writes that Metcalf faced a dilemma: "Her U.S. team had an extra boat. If she didn't offer it to the Romanians, the Americans would dramatically increase their chances of winning the title."

Metcalf didn't believe that would be a victory her team could be proud of, so she lent the Romanians the boat, leading to a heart-pounding race in which each team gave their very best.

In the end, the Romanians squeaked out a victory. When asked afterwards why she gave away her team's chance at a gold medal, Metcalf said, "The demands of a sport bring out your character and inner strength. Character in sports is everything."

**Character produces hope. (Romans 5:4)**

*May all of our victories be justly earned, Messiah.*

## A Lesson from the Past

The 1960s were a time when policemen didn't seem to get along with so-called "hippies." But sometimes, appearances can be deceiving. For instance, consider this story that took place in Seneca Falls, New York, during this tempestuous time.

The local police department received a letter containing six dollars. It read, "Enclosed is $6 for the cop who lent me $5 for gas on Saturday. I lost the paper with his name. Thanks very much. I guess some cops aren't so bad after all." It was signed, "Young Hippie Peace Freak."

A patrolman explained that the young man had come to the station house after midnight and asked where he could obtain gas money to get to Buffalo, 100 miles away. The policeman handed him five dollars out of his own pocket, asking for no receipt and never expecting to see the money again.

Most people aren't so bad if we look beyond stereotypes to see the real person inside. Remember, a reflection of God is often revealed to us in the goodness of diverse people.

**He judges the peoples with equity. (Psalm 9:8)**

*Father, make me willing to go beyond superficial impressions when dealing with others.*

## The Meaning of Life

Some people dread old age, but 90-year-old former philosophy professor Alice von Hildebrand still finds a joy in living that's grounded firmly in her faith. The New Yorker told *Rich in Years* author Johann Christoph Arnold:

"When I was still teaching, I rode on the subway and looked at the faces: boredom, despair, sadness. This, in the richest country in the world! But the moment that you relate to God—and thank Him for your existence, for loving you, for being your savior—you can establish a most beautiful relationship with other people. You love and help one another.

"You realize the meaning of your life is not luxury and fun, but it is helping. Once you radiate joy, people are going to say, 'What's her secret?' And then gently, without preaching, without saying 'I'm superior to you,' you just share. After all, the meaning of the word 'gospel' is 'the happy message.' Obviously there are moments of darkness and discouragement. But...we are made for joy. Don't expect Paradise on this earth. But there is meaning, and this meaning is the love of God."

**The joy of the Lord is your strength.
(Nehemiah 8:10)**

*Help me to remember, Lord, that we are made for spreading joy, not sadness.*

## What Are You Doing With Your Face?

"As you are reading this right now, what are you doing with your face?" asked singer-songwriter Brooke White on her blog. White was reflecting on the fact that people's faces often look serious because of stresses they're enduring. But she also shared that the simple act of smiling can make us happier.

White wrote, "I'm not suggesting putting on a facade, or being inauthentic. What I am [suggesting] is finding it in ourselves to say, 'Despite these blues, despite the struggle, I believe happiness can be found. I can smile, and I will smile!' Sometimes, a smile is an act of faith. We will find, however, it is also a joy magnet. It attracts people, it opens the door to good things, new possibilities."

White concluded, "Try it right now! Go ahead and smile! Do you feel what I feel? Like a boost up into your brain, like energy in your cheeks! Also, notice the state of your heart and the track of your thoughts. Might it bring a recollection of your blessings? Spark even a little feeling of gratitude? I have tried it, tested it, lived it [and I know]—smiling works."

**Happy are all who take refuge in Him. (Psalm 2:12)**

*Lord, when I'm distressed, help me to take refuge in the richness of my blessings.*

## Disabilities Are Not Contagious

When Dan LaHood and his wife Cubby first started St. Joseph's House, a home-based daycare center in Silver Spring, Maryland, they took in kids with spina bifida, muscular dystrophy, and other special needs. Their own three children were still young, so they got involved with their parents' work, too. Some people thought this might lead to problems.

During an interview on *Christopher Closeup,* Dan explained, "When we first started, people said, 'But what's it going to do to your children?' As if the disability was catching! We said, 'We're going to live with any eventuality because we're committed to doing this.' Now our children are as natural with these kids as you could imagine. They're more like brothers and sisters than acquaintances or friends."

Dan concluded with a thought about the effect this kind of work has on his kids and everyone: "It expanded their hearts like it expands everybody's hearts, in a milieu of love. Feel that love, sense that love, and communicate that love to others."

**Everyone who loves is born of God. (1 John 4:7)**

*Increase my capacity to love those with special needs, Jesus, and bless all those who care for them.*

## In the Limelight

The renowned priest and author Henri Nouwen once wrote the following about our culture's worship of celebrity:

"There is much emphasis on notoriety and fame in our society. Our newspapers and television keep giving us the message: What counts is to be known, praised, and admired, whether you are a writer, an actor, a musician, or a politician.

"Still, real greatness is often hidden, humble, simple, and unobtrusive. It is not easy to trust ourselves and our actions without public affirmation. We must have strong self-confidence combined with deep humility. Some of the greatest works of art and the most important works of peace were created by people who had no need for the limelight. They knew that what they were doing was their call, and they did it with great patience, perseverance, and love."

Don't worry if the world doesn't notice your good deeds. God sees all—and He admires the humility and dedication you bring to building His Kingdom.

**Perform your tasks with humility; then you will be loved by those whom God accepts. (Sirach 3:17)**

*Let me seek Your will above all else, Beloved Teacher.*

## The Last of the Original Code Talkers

With the U.S. fighting in the Pacific during World War II, the military needed to develop a code to transmit classified information—a code that couldn't be deciphered by the Japanese. An Army engineer suggested they try using the Navajo language. As reported by *CNN*, Navajo was "almost impossible for a non-Navajo to learn, and it had no written form."

In 1942, recruiters visited a Navajo school in New Mexico, looking for volunteers to create the code. Chester Nez signed up, becoming a member of the all-Navajo 382nd Marine Platoon—aka, the Navajo Code Talkers. He also became part of the messenger team in war-zones like Guadalcanal and Guam. Nez and his fellow Code Talkers wound up completely stumping the Japanese, thereby helping the U.S. win the war.

Nez once said, "The feeling that I could make it in both the white world and the Navajo world began there, and it has stayed with me all of my life. For that I am grateful."

Chester Nez was the last of the original Code Talkers when he passed away at age 93 in June 2014. May he rest in peace.

**He replied in the language of his ancestors.**
**(2 Maccabees 7:8)**

*Teach Your children to learn the language of peace, Father.*

## Adjusting to Retirement

The late Anna Olsson of Omaha, Nebraska, didn't let age, arthritis, or retirement hinder her from living a full and active life. She had worked as a teacher, secretary, and successful businesswoman. After retirement, she delivered speeches to naturalized citizens at the local Federal District Court, on behalf of the Chamber of Commerce.

Olsson also circled the globe twice. At Point Barrow, Alaska, she dined with local villagers on whale blubber. A few years earlier, in Jordan, she rode horseback through a narrow mountain pass to view the ruins of the ancient city of Petra.

People like Anna Olsson, who refuse to let grass grow under their feet, manage to accomplish a great deal. They achieve even more when their desire to "do something" is joined with a sincere intention to help others.

If God had wanted us to be rooted in one spot, He would have made us trees. Since He gave us the power to love and to move, He obviously expects something more. What does He expect of you?

**What does the Lord require of you but to do justice, and to love kindness? (Micah 6:8)**

*Remind me, Holy Spirit, to live each day fully.*

## Angels on the Rails

His wife knows who pushed her husband from a subway platform to the tracks below, but she doesn't know the identity of the two "angels" who risked their lives to jump down and save him. She wishes that she did, but they simply vanished into the crowd once they had performed their life-saving deed.

Yumen Li is the wife of Shou Kuan Lin, 72, the retired factory worker who was seriously injured in the fall. "God sent angels to come help, and I'm very grateful," she said of the rescuers. "They just brought my husband back up to me without thinking about their own lives. They came and helped save my husband. I was shocked but also very moved." Elizabeth Hagen and Daniel Prendergast told their story in the *New York Post*.

Police think that Lin's attacker, who is homeless, was intoxicated and did not deliberately push him onto the tracks. Nonetheless, they charged the man with attempted murder and felony assault. Meanwhile, Lin's wife concentrated on her husband's rescuers. She doesn't know their names, but they have her eternal thanks.

### Come and rescue us. (1 Maccabees 5:12)

*Use me as an angel to help someone in trouble, Lord.*

## Miracles On and Off the Field

After seven seasons with a losing record, the 1969 New York Mets pulled off a "miracle" win in the World Series. Some of their accomplishments off the field were pretty admirable too.

They often visited children in hospitals to share the message, "You can't count anybody out. Look at us." First baseman Ed Kranepool said their testimony had a remarkable effect on the young patients.

He recalled, "There was this one kid in a hospital I went to. The doctor said he was dying. They told us he was a ball fan. I saw him, talked to him, and the kid looked like he wouldn't make it. During the season, the doctor calls me for tickets. The kid got better. The doctor said it was a miracle."

Ability on the diamond is no guarantee of achievement in other fields of endeavor. But an all-out effort to win, combined with teamwork, can help anyone be effective in encouraging others to do their best. These qualities will strengthen us if we, like the Miracle Mets, refuse to be counted out. And God will strengthen us too.

**Keep the way of the Lord by doing righteousness and justice. (Genesis 18:19)**

*Grant us the strength of mind and soul to take a "never say die" attitude towards our problems, Lord.*

## Grace versus Despair

Terrible tragedies occur in many people's lives, pushing them to the edge of despair and hopelessness. It's a problem Tod Worner wrestled with on his Patheos blog—and he found some answers in the life of Jesus.

Worner wrote, "We cannot give in to despair. Despair is endless blackness. It is ruthless isolation from God and man, but also from love, faith and hope. It sees no way out. And yet there is a way out. There is light. There is an unbreakable thread that forever connects us to God and man. The suffering Christ hoped. Because He saw the key, the redemption, the paradise that we in our deepest despair cannot see. And He bids us to believe."

Worner concludes, "We will be consoled. Be it in days or years, grace will win out. Even if it is in the long-awaited reunited embrace in heaven."

**God, who is rich in mercy, out of the great love with which He loved us even when we were dead through our trespasses, made us alive together with Christ—by grace you have been saved. (Ephesians 2:4-5)**

*Be near me in times of tragedy, Jesus. Help me to believe that my loved ones and I will be united with You some day.*

## Golden Rules for Supervisors

Personnel specialist Edward E. Marcus shared the following suggestions for becoming an effective supervisor:

- **Don't select employees on the basis of snap judgments.** Screen them thoroughly.
- **Give clear instructions.** Be sure they're understood.
- **Lead people; don't boss them.** Foster a spirit of "can do" and inspire others by your own example.
- **Don't play things "close to the chest."** Be willing to communicate "downward, upward, and sideways."
- **Follow the one rule that takes care of all the others.** Treat employees as you would like to be treated as an employer.

Like most time-tested maxims, the Golden Rule contains a rich store of truth. But it's only a principle—of little value unless activated. God leaves it to each of us to take it off the shelf and apply it in our relationships.

**Do to others as you would have them do to you. (Luke 6:31)**

*May all leaders emulate Your fair and loving example, Heavenly King.*

## Lessons from a Tank

As a child, columnist Rich Lowry learned a valuable life lesson while building a scale model of a U.S. M-3 Lee tank with his father, who was fascinated by military history.

His dad bought the model so the two of them could work on it together after dinner every night. The picture of the completed tank on the box looked "gloriously realized," wrote Lowry, but the road to getting there—through complex instructions and a multitude of tiny parts, decals, paints, and glue—proved to be an exercise in patience that added "up to hours and hours of concentration."

In retrospect, Lowry realized, "[Models] are an implicit education in following directions, in getting details right and in delayed gratification—in short, in all the qualities that are important to success later on in almost any walk of life."

When the tank was finished, Lowry notes that he and his dad felt "the deep satisfaction of an intricate project done right." It remains one of his fondest memories of time well spent between a father and a son.

**If you pay attention, you will become wise. (Sirach 6:33)**

*Help me approach life's tasks with patience, Creator.*

## Choosing Fatherhood Over Fame

Talk-show host Arsenio Hall never had the desire to be a father until he started babysitting the son of his friend, basketball star Magic Johnson. On *Access Hollywood,* Hall recalled bringing the boy to a game that Johnson was coaching and witnessing a kind of love between the two that he'd never seen before. He realized, "I don't think I want to leave this earth without being a father."

In 1999, Hall had a son he named Arsenio Jr. Choosing family over fame, he decided to become a stay-at-home dad. It's a decision he never regretted.

Hall said, "Being a father changes a man. It explains life in a very interesting way, and it explains your purpose on this earth. I think it makes you a smarter, less selfish person. And what I needed a lot is to step outside of this body and be less concerned about me...You've heard parents say, 'Take me. Don't take my baby.' I didn't understand that. When you have that kind of love for someone on this planet, it changes who you are."

**Sons are indeed a heritage from the Lord. (Psalm 127:3)**

*Lord, bless fathers with a selfless love for their children, and sustain them when burdens arise.*

## Ace Pit Bull's Lick Saves Owner's Life

It was a hot, July day when 13-year-old Nick Lamb of Indianapolis was literally licked awake by his two-year-old pit bull, Ace. Lamb is deaf, and had his "cochlear implants" out while he was napping, so he didn't hear the fire alarm's ominous warning. But luckily, Ace did, and it was because of the dog's persistent licking that his young owner's life was saved.

After he and Ace evacuated their burning home, Nick immediately called his mother, Lindsay Bernard, and then 911. Although naturally distressed over the significant damage done to their house, Bernard was thankful that her son, as well as Ace and their pet cat, Pixie, all escaped unharmed.

"[Lamb] told firefighters that this was the first summer he was old enough to stay home alone and was excited to have reached that milestone," Indianapolis Fire Department Capt. Rita Reith reported to Justin L. Mack of *The Indianapolis Star.*

Thankfully, Bernard could not have asked for a more faithful companion for her son than their "Ace" of a pit bull.

**Who teaches us more than the animals of the earth? (Job 35:11)**

*God, bless our pets, loving caretakers of all children.*

# 'Miss Amazing' Pageant Crowns Winners

In 2007, 13-year-old Nebraskan Jordan Somer founded the Miss Amazing pageant, designed specifically for girls with physical and mental disabilities. It's a contest composed of traditional categories such as evening wear and talent.

The only real difference between the Miss Amazing pageant and other beauty competitions is that even though there are official first-, second-, and third-place prizes, every participant goes home a winner. "Every girl at the Miss Amazing pageant receives a crown because every girl in her own way is Miss Amazing, just by participating in the event and pushing her limits," Somer, now 20, told *Today* reporter Jillian Eugenois.

For the Miss Amazing contestants, it truly is the journey and not the destination that matters most to them, and to their parents as well. Somer, whose contest is now held nationwide, says that taking part in this pageant allows young girls to see firsthand what it means to be accepted and appreciated for their talents. This, Somer maintains, is how it should always be for these special needs young women, every day.

**I am...wonderfully made. (Psalm 139:14)**

*God, bless all those who have the courage to be different.*

## The Candy Bomber

During the 1948 Berlin Airlift, at least one American pilot gave special thought to the needs of children. Air Force Col. Gail Halvorsen won the title of the "Candy Bomber" by dropping bags of candy to thousands of little Berliners.

Out of special consideration for the children, Col. Halvorsen and his crew used string and handkerchiefs to parachute candy to the youngsters.

He later recalled, "You have to remember the conditions that existed in Berlin at the time. The war had been a particular hardship on children. When the airlift began, most of them were living under extremely difficult conditions. To those kids, a candy bar or a stick of gum was a real luxury."

One of the most powerful motives for laboring tirelessly for peace today is to save tomorrow's youth from the horrors of war. In other words, pray for peace, but don't neglect to work for it, too.

**Pursue peace with everyone, and the holiness without which no one will see the Lord. (Hebrews 12:14)**

*Divine Redeemer, make me "an instrument of Your peace," a tireless worker for harmony among all people.*

## Prayers and Baby Bottles

When Dan Almeter was a young husband and father, his job as a social worker and his family obligations took up most of his time. Despite his busy schedule—or maybe because of it—he yearned for a more active prayer life.

In an interview with Rachel Balducci for *Catholic Digest*, Almeter recalled that his wife gave birth to their sixth child around this time. Since he would get up for the baby's 2 a.m. bottle feedings, he started to multitask: "I'd warm up the bottle, light a candle, and sit in the rocking chair. The whole time I'd say, 'Jesus, I love You.'"

Almeter notes that those moments opened him up to a whole new experience of God's presence, which led him to spend more time in quiet, contemplative prayer.

Now retired, he's glad he made the effort to grow spiritually when he did: "We were created for union with God, but people are very distracted today. Breaking through that distraction and making time is the biggest challenge, but deep prayer is meant for everybody. It helps us grow in love and charity and holiness. It's a gift."

**To You, O Lord, I lift up my soul. (Psalm 25:1)**

*Savior, lead me towards a deeper, more fulfilling prayer life.*

## A Life of Service

When Dick Ridgway died at 76 in August of 2013, nearly 1,000 mourners filled Holy Redeemer Church in Kensington, Maryland, for his funeral. An attorney, Ridgway lived a life of service to others, which he attributed to the altruistic actions of his former pastor, the late Msgr. James Caulfield.

He never forgot how Msgr. Caulfield helped him out after Ridgway's father passed away, and paid for his first year of college to help him get started. Ridgway followed Msgr. Caulfield's example throughout his life. Among other things, he co-founded the Shepherd Foundation, which has provided $7 million in tuition assistance to more than 9,000 students, enabling them to attend Catholic schools in the Washington Archdiocese.

Msgr. John Enzler, one of the foundation's co-founders and now CEO of archdiocesan Catholic Charities, said Ridgway "inspired me by his care for others," citing the many organizations that his long-time friend had helped with his presence, purse and personality. Msgr. Enzler added: "He loved to share in the work of the church through my priesthood."

**Render service with enthusiasm. (Ephesians 6:7)**

*May I reflect a spirit of selflessness, Bountiful Savior.*

## Pet Ownership and Health

Can having a pet be a health hazard? In some cases, yes.

A cat litter box, for instance, might expose you to *toxoplasmosis*, a disease with potential risk for pregnant women and people with weakened immune systems. Cat scratches or bites can cause flu-like illnesses. Pet allergies send some people to the hospital with an exacerbation of asthma symptoms.

But despite potential downsides, an article in the *AM/New York* newspaper states the obvious: pet lovers believe their cats and dogs are good for their health. And they are.

"Studies have shown lower blood pressure in people with pets," said Dr. Susan Hirsch, an internal medicine physician. And "recent studies have linked pet ownership to healthier bodies, longer life and less depression after heart attacks."

This is encouraging news for all those who find the animal/human bond that God created so special.

**The righteous know the needs of their animals, but the mercy of the wicked is cruel. (Proverbs 12:10)**

*Thank you, God, for Your gift of creation, including our beloved cats, dogs and other animals.*

## On These Courts

Injuries prevented retired NBA All Star Anfernee "Penny" Hardaway from ever winning a championship during his career. But the values and selflessness he learned from his grandmother growing up in a rough part of Memphis brought him victory of a different kind.

After his friend, youth basketball coach Desmond Merriweather, was stricken with cancer, Hardaway returned to his hometown and took over as head coach of Lester Middle School's basketball team. In addition to teaching the students how to play the game, he became a role model who helped guide them through struggles with crime, gang pressures and failing grades. In the end, his efforts bolstered the entire community—and earned Hardaway his first-ever championship season.

CNN.com writer/producer Wayne B. Drash told that story in his 2013 book *On These Courts: A Miracle Season that Changed a City, a Once-Future Star, and a Team Forever.* We were happy to honor it with a Christopher Award.

**From my youth, You have taught me. (Psalm 71:17)**

*Bless young people with positive role models, Holy Spirit.*

## Big Man Has Big Aim in Life

The late Max Palmer, a wrestler-turned-preacher, credited a renewed faith in God with freeing him from a long period of alcoholism.

The Oklahoma City native attributed his drinking to a desire to deaden the embarrassment he felt due to his towering height. You see, Palmer was seven-foot eight.

He said, "I started drinking then, and just didn't stop until I converted more than five years ago. For the first time, I am not ashamed of my size. In fact, I have accepted myself as I am, and with a task Christ has for me. I'm happy."

Acceptance of self and recognition that God has a task for each of us can add new dimension to any life. Ask for His help in discovering the divine purpose He had in mind when placing you on this earth. And remember that He loves you just the way He created you.

**Do not look on his appearance or on the height of his stature...for the Lord does not see as mortals see; they look on the outward appearance, but the Lord looks on the heart. (1 Samuel 16:7)**

*Jesus, give me the vision to carry out my mission in life.*

## Homeless Doesn't Mean Criminal

James Brady, a homeless man from Hackensack, New Jersey, made news when he found $850 and turned it in to police rather than keep it. He made further news when a welfare official denied him benefits because he didn't report what he found as income.

He drew contributions of nearly $10,000 from readers of his story for his medical needs. But he really made news, reported by Hannon Adely in *The Record*, when he used his new-found fame to plead for better treatment for the homeless.

"'Homeless' and 'criminal' are not synonymous," said Brady, a former data technician who has been treated for depression. "I have no problem with cracking down on homeless people when they're doing something wrong. When they're not doing something wrong, they should be treated with the same respect as anyone else.

"We're not criminals," he added. "We're just down on our luck."

**Let us therefore no longer pass judgment on one another. (Romans 14:13)**

*Open my eyes to see others as You see them, Lord.*

## A Sign of the Times

How can a waiter or waitress take your order if they can't hear you? Signs Restaurant in Toronto has the answer.

When owner Anjan Manikumar worked as a server years ago, he had a deaf customer who needed to point to the menu to order his food. Manikumar wondered how the hearing impaired could be provided a more interactive and personal dining experience, so he came up with Signs.

It's a first-of-its-kind business in Canada in which all the servers are deaf—and customers order food and drinks via sign language which is incorporated into the menu. As reported by *CBC News*, "The restaurant wants to become the meeting place for the deaf community and any hearing customers interested in learning and practicing sign language in a casual atmosphere."

Signs' manager Rachel Shemuel says, "We want to create awareness for the hearing community that the deaf community has the ability to do anything and everything."

Manikumar adds, "I hope this encourages people in other sectors to hire deaf people as well."

**You shall not revile the deaf. (Leviticus 19:14)**

*Guide us all in reaching our potential, Holy Spirit.*

## People Power

The power of people working together saved the leg of a commuter in Perth, Australia.

In August 2014, an unidentified man was rushing to get on his morning train to work. He slipped and his leg became wedged into the two inch space between the train car and platform. Another commuter saw what happened and called for help immediately.

Soon after, passengers were asked to get off the train. About 50 of them then lined up in a row, pushed on the train car simultaneously, and tilted it just enough for the man to remove his leg. He was treated by paramedics and deemed well enough to go to work

Claire Krol—a spokeswoman for Transperth, Australia's public transportation system—said, "It is the first time we've seen something like this happen. This is a real case of passengers working together, and 'people power' are the perfect words to describe it."

**Woe to one who is alone and falls and does not have another to help. (Ecclesiastes 4:10)**

*When troubles arise, Lord, help us to work as one.*

## Joy and the Grit of Service

At age 24, Brandon Vogt—the author of *Saints and Social Justice*—was looking for a saint that seemed relatable to him as a young Catholic man interested in living his faith. He found one in Pier Giorgio Frassati, who died at age 24 in 1925.

What was it about St. Pier Giorgio that appealed to Vogt? He told interviewer Elizabeth Scalia, "He was an adventurous young man who scaled mountains throughout Italy. He was also politically active, championing social causes…Yet he was also an extremely devout Catholic. He attended Mass every day and wouldn't go on a mountain climb unless there was a church nearby. He prayed the Rosary daily, sometimes five times per day, and often had deep, mystical experiences in prayer."

In addition, St. Pier Giorgio served the poor daily, giving them "food, money, and even the clothes off his own back."

Vogt sees him as a model for anyone who seeks to reflect Catholic social teaching: "He fuses all its elements: faith with charity, contemplation with activism, personal care with institutional reform, and boundless joy with the grit of service."

**He loves righteousness and justice. (Psalm 33:5)**

*Help me look to the saints as role models for life, Savior.*

# Regenerating Our National Character

Anyone disturbed about signs of moral breakdown in our country and world might reflect on these words of historian James Truslow Adams (1878–1949):

"If there is to be a regeneration of the national character, it can come about only by the regeneration of each of us as individuals. It is not a matter of committees, machinery, and organization. It can only come about from subtle change in the heart of the individual man and woman."

The structures of our civilization are in constant need of renewal and reform. Denunciation and name-calling won't do the job. Neither will a flight from reality or a complacent "business as usual" attitude.

Only people—intelligent, dedicated, compassionate people—with God's help, can bring about the improvements our world so sorely needs. Will you do your part?

**We are what He has made us, created in Christ Jesus for good works. (Ephesians 2:10)**

*Instead of complaining about what's wrong with the world, Father, give me the grace to work to improve it.*

## Gimme Shelter

One day, someone asked filmmaker Ronald Krauss, "Have you heard about this shelter that's helping young women get off the streets?" The facility in question was Several Sources Shelters in New Jersey, founded by Kathy DiFiore. Her ministry has supported homeless, pregnant young women for over 30 years, and saved the lives of thousands of babies.

Though Krauss hadn't heard of DiFiore, he visited the shelter while staying at his brother's house for the holidays. As he explained during a *Christopher Closeup* interview, "One of the girls that I met had walked 25 miles to get there, and I helped her into the shelter. That was transformative! It reached into my heart that I had helped somebody…I approached Kathy one day and said, 'I think more people need to find out about this place because this [story] could spread kindness and compassion.'"

And that was the origin of the Christopher Award-winning film *Gimme Shelter.* More about DiFiore's work tomorrow.

**He will hide me in His shelter in the day of trouble. (Psalm 27:5)**

*Help us provide safe havens to those in need, Messiah.*

## Out of the Darkness

As the movie *Gimme Shelter* reflects, some of the young women who come to Kathy DiFiore's shelter have endured some horrific experiences. She explained on *Christopher Closeup*, "If a young lady seems like she has a dark side, it's because she was physically abused or mentally tormented. We have professional staff that work with them so, over time, through God's love and an understanding of the Holy Scriptures, they heal."

Filmmaker Ronald Krauss added that he came to see the shelter as "holy ground" because of DiFiore's successful approach to lifting these young women out of darkness.

He said, "She shows them that not everybody is bad. The number one word I'd say that she develops with them is 'trust.' Because that's the thing that was broken the most; that somebody would actually be willing to help them is something that they can't believe when they've been kicked down so many times in their lives and told that they're no good and worthless...When they trust, they give you their heart."

The conclusion of DiFiore's efforts tomorrow.

**I trusted in Your steadfast love. (Psalm 13:5)**

*Strengthen all victims of abuse, Jesus, and help them to regain trust in You, in others, and in themselves.*

## God Will Be There for You

Though *Gimme Shelter* is a dramatized version of Ronald Krauss's experiences at Kathy DiFiore's shelter, the film—which stars Vanessa Hudgens, Rosario Dawson and James Earl Jones—is grounded in truth. Not only does DiFiore hope it encourages young women in crisis pregnancies to seek help, she wants individuals around the country to create shelters of their own. To give those interested a foundation, she provides a free "How to Open a Shelter Kit" on her website, SeveralSourcesFD.org.

DiFiore wants the film to touch viewers in a different way as well: "I want people to get closer to God. And through the power of prayer, I want people to be inspired to do something, whether it's for one individual that they personally know— or for something greater than that, like opening a shelter. God will direct them."

Krauss added, "My hopes as the filmmaker is that this film will give people hope. If you think God's not there for you, He is. If you just reach out. He'll be there for you."

**When you search for Me, you will find Me. (Jeremiah 29:13)**

*Guide the lost and the lonely to Your healing heart, Lord.*

## Hit Like a Girl

If the Toms River, New Jersey, Little League team reaches the 2014 Little League World Series, "girl power" will be partially responsible. That's because their best pitcher and hitter is 12-year-old Kayla Roncin.

Kayla grew up watching Yankee games with her dad, and soon developed a love for baseball. More importantly, she demonstrated a talent for the game that surpassed many of the local boys.

When Toms River manager Pete Avallone first brought her onto the team, the boys were skeptical. Kayla's power at the plate and on the mound, however, made their skepticism short-lived. And when an opposing team laughed at her after seeing she would be pitching to them, Kayla simply struck out the side and quieted everyone down.

Kayla hopes that her team will bring home a championship. Regardless, she's already a champion to many.

**In passing judgment on another you condemn yourself, because you, the judge, are doing the very same things. (Romans 2:1)**

*Holy Spirit, help me resist the urge to be judgmental.*

## Thanks for the Ticket, Trooper!

Tana Baumler was in a hurry. Way too much of a hurry. In fact, she was driving 95 miles per hour in a 75-mile-per-hour zone in Boise, Idaho, when Trooper Mike Nelson pulled her over. Not only was she nervous for herself, but she feared her two granddaughters, who were with her in the car, might get scared.

In that respect, Baumler had nothing to worry about. She told *KBOI TV,* "[Trooper Nelson] was giving the kids stickers and little sheriff badges. He was just really nice to them."

Trooper Nelson explained his approach: "I usually just talk to the kids. Kids are always really inquisitive when the guy with the big hat walks up to their car on the side of the highway so sometimes they are a little nervous."

The trooper left such a good impression on Baumler that she sent a thank-you note to the Idaho State Police praising his "great attitude." And whereas the kids got stickers and badges, Baumler also received a gift: a $150 ticket. She admitted she deserved it and felt grateful that the whole experience taught her an important lesson about kindness—and slowing down.

**Only acknowledge your guilt. (Jeremiah 3:13)**

*Holy Spirit, help me to acknowledge and confess my sins.*

## 'The Voice' of Italy

Contestants who win the televised singing competition *The Voice* would ordinarily say their priority moving forward is building a music career. Sister Cristina Scuccia, who won Italy's version of the show, gave a different answer. She named her priorities as "Jesus and prayer."

The 25-year-old Ursuline Sister of the Holy Family gained worldwide attention for her performances on the show. In June 2014, she earned 62 percent of the final vote by the public, thereby winning. She went on to lead the crowd in reciting the Lord's Prayer, explaining, "I want Jesus to enter here."

In an interview with the website TGcom24, Sister Cristina revealed why she auditioned for *The Voice* in the first place: "The Lord has given me a gift and, honestly, it would have been easy for me to stay hidden in a corner at home. I wanted to also show that God has not taken anything away from my life, but rather He has given me so much more."

**No one after lighting a lamp puts it under the bushel basket, but on the lampstand, and it gives light to all in the house. (Matthew 5:15)**

*Help me to use my talents, not hide them, Creator.*

## Doris Day Still Feels Young at 90

"I'm positive," Doris Day recently told *People* magazine. "I just am. And I still feel like the best is yet to come."

Day, a noted actress and singer, gave the interview during a rare public appearance to benefit her foundation on behalf of animals. "I don't feel like I'm aging or anything like that," the 90-year-old said. "I feel young!"

Doris Day was a big box-office star known for such romantic comedies as *Pillow Talk* and *That Touch of Mink*—as well as for songs such as *Que Sera, Sera*. She reminisced, "I couldn't wait to get to work. I was just thrilled to be there."

Day left the movie business when she felt it was time to pursue other interests—but she never gave up her sense of purpose. She also continues to maintain a sunny, upbeat attitude. While it won't stop the changes and challenges of extreme hardship or aging, it does help her appreciate the blessings she's been given.

**May the God of hope fill you with all joy and peace in believing. (Romans 15:13)**

*Infuse us, Holy Spirit, with the ability to find and value "the sunny side of the street."*

## 'Erling, Got Any 'Matoes?'

Three-year-old Emmett Rychner loves spending time with his best friend, Erling Kindem. What makes their relationship unusual is that Kindem is 89 years old.

Bryan and Anika, Emmett's parents, didn't really know their Farmington, Minnesota neighbor well until their tomato-loving toddler noticed the tomatoes Kindem was growing in his garden. The youngster started visiting regularly and asking, "Erling, got any 'matoes?"

Charmed by Emmett's personality, the World War II veteran started looking for ways the two of them could have fun together. As reported by *KARE-TV,* "Soon Erling and Emmett were racing lawn mowers, Erling on his John Deere garden tractor and Emmett on his battery-operated toy riding tractor."

Erling and Emmett's relationship will be facing a challenge soon. The Rychners are moving to a larger house, while Kindem and his ailing wife are relocating to a senior apartment. But in light of the strong bond the two have formed, this might be a friendship that can survive a few extra miles.

**Come over, friend; sit down here. (Ruth 4:1)**

*Lord, let children look to seniors for friendship.*

## One Church, One Child

Chicago's Father George Clements gained national attention in 1981 when he became the first Catholic priest to adopt a child. After realizing that black children had a difficult time getting adopted by black parents, the African-American cleric decided to set an example himself. He earned the support of Pope John Paul II and wound up adopting a total of four sons.

That decision led him to start the One Church, One Child program, which facilitates adoptions for church members, and has resulted in more than 100,000 adoptions nationwide.

In addition, Father Clements went on to minister to troubled people through two other projects: 1) One Church, One Addict, which supports churches that reach out to drug addicts through counseling and treatment, and 2) One Church, One Inmate, which assists those making the transition from inmate to law-abiding citizen.

How did he accomplish all that? One admirer told the Archdiocese of Milwaukee's *Catholic Herald*, "It's based on the Gospel and it's based on faith."

**The Lord preserves the faithful. (Psalm 31:23)**

*Guide me in being a problem solver, Holy Spirit.*

## The Unnoticed Flower

In his book *The Sower's Seeds,* Father Brian Cavanaugh, T.O.R. shares this story by an anonymous author.

Once a wise old botany teacher was speaking to a group of young and eager students. He told them to go out by the side of some lonely road and find a small, unnoticed flower.

"Get a magnifying glass and study the delicate veins in the leaves, and notice the nuances and shades of color," the teacher said. "Turn the leaf slowly and observe its symmetry. And remember: this flower might have gone unnoticed and unappreciated if you had not found and admired it."

When the class returned after carrying out the assignment, the teacher observed: "People are just like that unnoticed flower, too. Each one is different, carefully crafted, uniquely endowed. But you have to spend time with a person to realize this. So many people go unnoticed and unappreciated because no one has ever taken time with them and admired their uniqueness."

**So God created humankind in His image. (Genesis 1:27)**

*Instead of overlooking those who don't conform to modern standards of beauty, Lord, open my eyes to their uniqueness and worth as Your children.*

## Gratitude is a Free Hot Dog

It was 1968 when 200 children threw a farewell party for their favorite hot dog vendor who was retiring.

Isodoros "Pop" Pantelaros had sold hot dogs in New York's East Harlem for years. He often gave away franks to hungry youngsters without much money.

His generosity reached overseas as well. In 1965, he bought and shipped a bus to his native village of Pyrgy, Greece, so that 72 children could more easily get to their school six miles away.

Recalling two narrow escapes from death in his early life, Pantelaros said, "God has given me back my life twice, so I always have a debt to Him and I try to say 'thank You' every way I can."

"Pops" Pantelaros knew the power of offering cheerful, efficient, and selfless service to his customers and community. His willingness to respond generously to people's needs were an expression of the joy that God had put in his heart.

**The one who sows bountifully will also reap bountifully. (2 Corinthians 9:6)**

*Father, instill me with the love to give generously to others.*

## God's Obituary?

One theologian's statement of faith was a response to the idea that "God is dead." Dr. Norman Pittenger of Cambridge University explained his concept of God in *Christian Century* magazine. The god who is dead, he claimed, never existed anyway—the moral dictator, the deity who reinforces our prejudices. This is what is dead.

The real God, Dr. Pittenger believes, is "the active and loving God...the dynamic, personal Love Who is ever at work to establish in the world more love and goodness." He can be discerned in history through "an increasing purpose forcing us to live together in justice and charity."

"I for one," he summarized, "am prepared to risk everything I am and everything I have on that faith."

When we question God's existence, we are more likely examining our concept of Him, which is often limited and incomplete. Seek knowledge of God in the Scriptures, as well as in books by writers like C.S. Lewis, who have explored these questions themselves.

**My thoughts are not your thoughts. (Isaiah 55:8)**

*Guide us to expand our knowledge of You, Creator.*

## A Growth Opportunity

Veteran farmer Michael O'Gorman, 65, started a nonprofit organization to help war veterans become farmers. Why?

Several years ago O'Gorman noticed that the average age of American farmers was rising—and the unemployment rate of returning military personnel was unacceptably high.

O'Gorman, an organic farmer from California, started the Farmer Veteran Coalition. "You go back to the Bible and you see the verse about turning swords into plowshares," he said. "There's a power in the transition between those two things."

The Farmer Veteran Coalition matches seasoned farmers with returning military vets and helps them transition from warrior to farmer. The nonprofit includes a job-placement feature and a fellowship fund which offers financial grants.

One 31-year-old Army reservist and Iraq veteran, who now grows vegetables, points out that both the military and farming are tough but meaningful pursuits.

There will always be growth opportunities waiting for someone who sees needs and determines to meet them.

**Our land will yield its increase. (Psalm 85:12)**

*Encourage us, Jesus, to work for meaningful causes.*

## Get in the Middle of This

Brayden Banner, age eight, met Josh Jones, age 12, when they were both being treated at M.D. Anderson Cancer Center in Houston, Texas. Though Banner's cancer was found to be benign, Jones was fighting a six-year battle with the disease.

Things weren't much better for Josh at home 600 miles away in Canyon. His grandmother Peggy was raising him because his mom was killed in a car crash. And as reported by *Amarillo Globe-News,* "Medical bills had them way behind on mortgage payments and in danger of losing their car."

That's when Brayden stepped in. Despite the fact that he and Josh lived hundreds of miles apart, he organized a benefit pancake breakfast to raise funds for his new friend. Locals who wanted to support Brayden's initiative turned out in larger numbers than expected, collecting $6,500. In addition, a local used-car dealer donated a vehicle to the Jones family.

Brayden said, "I learned that it's important to help people when you see [a need], and not say, 'I don't want to get in the middle of this.'"

**A little child shall lead them. (Isaiah 11:6)**

*Holy Spirit, instill me with the initiative to help others.*

## A Janitor's Education

Gabe Sonnier's parents had taught him the value of getting an education. Unfortunately, his parents split up when he was a college freshman, and he was forced to leave school and go to work. Subsequently, his jobs included working at construction sites and at a supermarket. He eventually became a school janitor, just like his father.

"It was my intention to stay five, maybe 10 years," says Sonnier of his work at Port Barre Elementary in Louisiana. But 33 years later he was still at the school: this time, as its principal.

Sonnier saw his own children through college before attending night school himself, earning Bachelor's and Master's degrees. As his education increased, he was promoted through the ranks until he advanced to become principal. Along the way, he also became a role model to others. He now reminds students, "Don't let the situation you're in define you."

If you don't get all the breaks you hoped for in life, try not to limit yourself. Your goals may take longer to reach, but you can still achieve them—or find new ones that are even better.

**The plans of the diligent lead surely to abundance. (Proverbs 21:5)**

*Lord, may we remember that we are never too old to stop learning*

## Guardian Dog Changes a Life

On Shoreditch High Street in East London, a Staffordshire terrier named George sits while his owner, John Dolan, draws a picture. This pair has been a familiar sight to East Londoners for the past three years.

Dolan, a 43-year-old former heroin addict who did 30 stints in prison by the year 2009, was given an unexpected second chance at life with a "guardian dog." Given to him by a homeless couple that were about to move into their own flat, George was just the inspiration Dolan needed to clean up his act.

"It was only because I had the animal and he's a responsibility," John told London's *The Guardian*. "He's like my child in a sense." After a couple of years selling his portraits off the street, Dolan was discovered by a gallery director named Richard Howard-Griffin, who offered the artist an opportunity to display his pictures publicly.

Today, John Dolan's art is well-known in East London. He has also written a memoir about "the dog who changed my life."

**The righteous know the needs of their animals. (Proverbs 12:10)**

*God, may we never underestimate the power of love and responsibility.*

## The Only Way to Heal

In 2003, while driving in Tallahassee, Florida, with his blood alcohol content twice the legal limit, Eric Smallridge hit a car carrying Meagan Napier and Lisa Dickson, both age 20. The young women were killed on impact.

At the time of Smallridge's sentencing, Meagan's mother, Renee, stated that she forgave her daughter's killer—though she later admitted that her expression of mercy was not sincere. Three years later, her attitude changed.

"I could hate him [Smallridge] forever and the world would tell me I have a right to do that," Renee told *CBS News* reporter Steve Hartman. "It's not going to do me any good...In my opinion, forgiveness is the only way to heal."

Renee's compassion did not stop there. She also asked the judge to cut Smallridge's 22-year prison sentence in half—a plea which was granted. The penitent Smallridge, moved by Renee's actions, gave her his first genuine apology. He also agreed to travel with her to local high schools, preaching the consequences of drunk driving. "I'm going to go wherever we need to go to spread this message," he concluded.

**For freedom Christ has set us free. (Galatians 5:1)**

*Messiah, release us from self-made prisons of resentment.*

## Five Tips for a Great Wedding

Father William Byrne is at it again. The popular pastor of St. Peter's in Washington, D.C., is known for his listings of five ways to do this or that (and having them printed in the *Catholic Standard*, the archdiocesan paper). Here he is with "Five Tips for a Great Wedding," good at this or any other time of year:

- **Expect something to go wrong.** Perfection only happens in heaven. If Jesus is invited, you can always work things out.

- **Invite Mary.** Ever since "that wedding," Mary has been interceding for couples who turn to her.

- **Fill the jars.** Budget for a gift to the poor when you plan your wedding. In addition to a fun party, why not spend part of the day in the soup kitchen?

- **Fill the jars again.** Letting Jesus Christ into our empty jars or yearning hearts results in a superabundance of joy.

- **Best wine for last.** "Good things are worth waiting for, especially honeymoons. 'Nuff said."

> **With merriment they celebrated Tobias's wedding feast for seven days, and many gifts were given to him. (Tobit 11:18)**

> *Guide couples toward happy, holy marriages, Father.*

## Moving Beyond the Superficial

A lot of young girls aren't sure about the way they look, and Elisha Maldonado of the *New York Post* thinks she knows what's to blame. It's "a culture obsessed with the superficial," she writes, one that's only grown worse with the Internet and the rise of social media. Citing the increase in girls from 9 to 14 who send videos to YouTube to get opinions as to whether or not they're pretty, Maldonado writes:

"What's particularly disconcerting about these inquiries by young girls, who barely know who they are as individuals, is that the focus on looks at such a young age comes from insecurity."

Further, she has some advice to give.

"What these girls should be asking is not how they look to the rest of the world, but how they can give, out of their own unique abilities, to the world. Physical beauty," she concludes, "changes none of that."

**Let your adornment be the inner self with the lasting beauty of a gentle and quiet spirit, which is very precious in God's sight. (1 Peter 3:4)**

*Guide me in developing my inner beauty, Heavenly Father.*

## The Day You Became a Missionary Disciple

Do you know the date on which you were baptized? Few of us do, and according to syndicated columnist George Weigel that's not a good thing. In fact, it can be a great tool when it comes to evangelizing, and that comes from none other than Pope Francis himself.

In one of his homilies at daily Mass, the Holy Father suggested that his listeners not only learn when they were baptized, but celebrate the day as a reminder of their becoming commissioned as missionary disciples.

Weigel himself concedes that the idea came to him while he was working with evangelical Protestants on a number of issues. They invariably introduced themselves by name and then added, "I was born again on such-and-such a date." For Weigel and most "cradle Catholics," it's a relatively easy assignment—a few days or weeks, usually, after their actual birth.

Weigel doesn't expect an onrush of seekers looking to determine the date of their baptism right away, but, he says, the idea might just catch on. After all, now it has the encouragement of the pope himself!

**Repent, and be baptized. (Acts 2:38)**

*May I always stay true to my baptismal vows, Jesus.*

## Dignity in Death

His job is to ensure that no one from Staten Island dies without a proper burial, and to date, he's batting 1,000 percent. No one told Gary Gotlin he had to do that, but as his borough's public administrator, he decided to take this task upon himself.

"Everybody deserves the dignity of a proper burial," he said. "So my policy is, I won't let anyone under my jurisdiction go to potter's field."

As administrator for Staten Island, one of the five boroughs that comprise New York City, he's responsible for handling the estates of Staten Islanders who die without a will or people listed as next of kin. Without Gotlin, these people would be buried in a mass grave on Hart Island, a bleak piece of land off the Bronx.

The subject of a profile by Corey Kilgannon in *The New York Times,* Gotlin, 66, relies on cemeteries, funeral directors, religious leaders and others to help with burials. "Staten Island is like a small town," Gotlin concludes. "It's got a lot of heart."

**Precious in the sight of the Lord is the death of His faithful ones. (Psalm 116:15)**

*Messiah, may we give the deceased the respect they deserve.*

## Elderly Doesn't Mean Worthless

"Old age should not be a withdrawal from the mainstream of society," but rather a time to pursue a more relaxed but still meaningful life. So says retired doctor Ken Johnson in Johann Christoph Arnold's book *Rich in Years*.

Dr. Johnson notes that every community includes disabled, lonely seniors who don't have a lot of "family, social, or financial support." As a result, he "envisioned a multitude of the nation's churches, temples, and mosques forming local interfaith coalitions to recruit and train volunteers, many of them elderly themselves, to serve the needs" of this group.

In addition to restoring a sense of dignity to care recipients who had felt abandoned and worthless, this mission added meaning to the lives of volunteers by having them perform simple tasks like changing a light bulb for someone, or driving them to a doctor's office. One volunteer explained that he now feels "special" because "someone really depends on me."

A lack of purpose can be debilitating to someone of any age. See where you're needed—and get to work.

**Walk according to the purpose of God. (Wisdom 6:4)**

*May we treat the elderly with dignity, God of all Ages.*

## Respite Renews Hope

When Lon and Brenda Solomon's daughter Jill was born with a seizure disorder and brain damage, her constant need for care drained the couple physically and even spiritually.

As reported by *Christianity Today,* a friend of theirs "organized a group of caregivers to care for Jill and give her parents a break." Those regular intervals of "respite" renewed the Solomons' sense of hope. That's why the Vienna, Virginia couple opened a facility called Jill's House in 2010. Children with special needs spend a weeknight or weekend there, enjoying good meals, a playground, an art room and more. A specially-trained staff and nursing team provide 24-hour supervision.

Jill's House president Cameron Doolittle notes the difference respite care can make: "Katie, another child we serve, sleeps less than five hours per night. Her parents were exhausted and ready to give up on their marriage. Now, during Katie's weekly visits to Jill's House, her parents have time to rest and reconnect with each other and their other daughter. Katie's mom recently told us, 'Jill's House saved our lives.'"

**I will give you rest. (Exodus 33:14)**

*Guide me in offering rest to the weary, Divine Savior.*

## The Power of Mary Poppins

Phil Rosenthal created the popular TV series *Everybody Loves Raymond,* which often combined humor with moments of truth and poignancy. In his memoir *You're Lucky You're Funny,* he reveals that he learned how to tell entertaining-but-meaningful stories at age four from watching the movie *Mary Poppins.*

He writes, "If you've had the pleasure of watching it with your kids recently, you'll appreciate that this film, unlike almost everything else out there now, is about something. There's a point to the magic and the fun—there's something underneath—and it's something that stays with you when the two hours are over, that you can integrate into your life."

Rosenthal concludes, "You don't get it consciously when you're four, but the reason you have to see it six times is because this deceptively simple entertainment has been sophisticatedly designed to impart its themes: Kindness. Love your family. Feed the birds. Enjoy your life. Find a wife like Mary. It's not a lesson, just a strong point of view that comes through while you're enjoying yourself."

**The teaching of kindness is on her tongue. (Proverbs 31:26)**

*Guide storytellers toward sharing truth, Divine Creator.*

## Is Religion Good or Bad?

Author Melissa Kuch set her debut young adult fantasy novel *The Hypothesis of Giants: Book One—The Assumption* in a fictional version of our country called the United States of the Common Good. In this land, freedom of speech and religion have been outlawed. Why? Because the government believes that religion is destructive to society.

With religious freedom issues in the news, Kuch uses her book to reflect the fact that faith has inspired many more unheralded acts of virtue in our world than acts of evil.

Her views on this topic are inspired by her own experiences: "The main thing about religion, I feel, is hope. It brings hope to people in times of loss, depression and despair—and it [adds a] sense of community, having people be together and look for this higher cause, this higher meaning of life. Growing up Catholic, and also having attended St. John's University, which is a Vincentian university, doing those types of good deeds and being able to give back to the community is a wonderful thing that people all across the world are doing."

**For freedom, Christ has set us free. (Galatians 5:1)**

*Strengthen our commitment to freedom of religion, Savior.*

## When the Baby Stopped Breathing

Pamela Rauseo was driving her baby nephew, Sebastian de la Cruz, to a doctor's appointment when the unthinkable happened. While they were stuck in traffic on Miami's Dolphin Expressway, Sebastian stopped breathing.

Frantic, Rauseo jumped out of the car, screamed for help, and started administering CPR. *Miami Herald* news photographer Al Diaz happened to be in the car behind Rauseo, so he ran to alert a police officer. When he returned to the scene, he captured a picture of Rauseo and Officer Amauris Bastidas performing CPR on Sebastian and resuscitating him.

At Jackson Memorial Hospital, doctors removed three previously-undiscovered cysts in Sebastian's trachea that were making it impossible for him to breathe. The boy's parents were grateful that Rauseo still remembered the CPR techniques she had learned seven years earlier after her own children were born.

One of the hospital's doctors concluded, "The big take-home message is that CPR does save lives."

**Wisdom will come into your heart, and knowledge will be pleasant to your soul. (Proverbs 2:10)**

*Guide us toward knowledge that can help save others, Divine Comforter.*

# The Ghostbuster Miracle

After actor, writer and director Harold Ramis's death in 2014, Laura Keeney revealed in the *Denver Post* that he gave her one of the most joyful experiences of her life.

Keeney's step-brother Bill had autism and though he possessed a creative talent that would allow him to masterfully recreate the paintings of famous artists, he didn't speak as a small child. One day, the family watched the movie *Ghostbusters* together, which Ramis co-wrote and starred in.

Keeney wrote, "[Bill] giggled and laughed and cried from laughing and it was magnificent." In fact, it was the first time she ever heard him laugh. Bill went on to memorize every line of dialogue in the film and recite it along with the actors.

"Each viewing was a new and delightful gift created just for him," Kenney recalled. "Each laugh was like the first—full of mirth and glee, sometimes completely gut-busting, but always genuine...It might seem small, but it was the closest thing to a miracle I've ever witnessed."

**God has brought laughter for me; everyone who hears will laugh with me. (Genesis 21:6)**

*Help me to always retain a sense of humor, Savior.*

## The Rabbi's Advice for His Son

As his son prepared to start college, Rabbi Matt Cutler shared some words of wisdom for him—and all students—on the website of Albany, New York's *Times Union*.

- **Learning is not just about acquiring knowledge; it is about engaging in material and making it a part of you.** The real results of learning cannot be marked on a multiple-choice exam; they are found when you are away from class and you find yourself thinking about the material.

- **Push the limits of what you think you can do.** Take a couple of classes that will truly challenge your intellectual abilities.

- **The key to your education is sharing it with others by leaving your community better than you found it.** Remember, at your Jewish core, you value *Tikun Olam* [repairing the world]. Sharing what you learn by turning it into action is essential. But it is not your job to save the world. In the *Pirke Avot* it is written, "It is not incumbent for you to complete the task, but neither are you at liberty from doing your fair share."

> **Let the wise also hear and gain in learning, and the discerning acquire skill. (Proverbs 1:5)**

*Bless young people with both knowledge and wisdom, Lord.*

## Threads for Teens

Sixteen-year-old Californian Allyson Ahlstrom knows how important new school clothes are to young girls. Teens, ages 13 to 17 in particular, feel prettier and more confident in clothing that is made to fit them. Why should young women who can't afford brand-new outfits every year be deprived of this simple joy? Thus, Allyson's idea for a clothing store for teens in need was born. Her boutique, Threads for Teens, provides two new outfits, free of charge, to every visiting customer.

Allyson is helped by 30 volunteers, and has been awarded almost $20,000 in cash prizes for her altruism. As of 2012, Alyson herself raised $140,000 in cash and clothing for her store. Keeping with her back-to-school theme, she has also collected over 70 backpacks of school supplies for her annual Back-to-School Backpack Event.

Alyson Ahlstrom's Threads for Teens is now an official 501 (c-3) charity, guided by an inspirational quote attributed to St. Francis of Assisi: "For it is in giving that we receive."

That's a good rule for all of us to follow, no matter our age.

**A generous person will be enriched. (Proverbs 11:25)**

*Lord, may we remember it is better to give than to receive.*

## Selflessness Leads Teacher to Rwanda

In August 2013, 30-year-old Heather Quinlan left her California home to embark on the adventure of her lifetime. The former campus minister and evangelization director chose to spend a year as an English teacher and mentor at a Catholic boarding school for girls in Rwanda.

As reported by *Catholic News Agency*, Quinlan is a missionary with the Catholic organization Fidesco, which sends volunteers to developing countries to help them with their needs.

Quinlan made her decision because she had spent the previous four years doing a lot of soul-searching about her life, relationships, and vocation. She said, "My prayers were about my life, my thoughts were about my life. When I was thinking about Fidesco, I thought, 'It would be so good to stop thinking about myself, and go someplace where people need love and are in so much need that my prayers revolve around them.' So I look forward to that: to stop being selfish, and to just live for others."

**Turn my heart to Your decrees, and not to selfish gain. (Psalm 119:36)**

*When I'm too preoccupied with myself, Lord, help me to expand my horizons.*

## Year of the Jungle

Author Suzanne Collins is best-known for writing *The Hunger Games* trilogy, but in 2013 she and illustrator James Proimos published a book for children called *Year of the Jungle*. It was inspired by Collins' childhood, and we were happy to recognize it with a Christopher Award.

The main character is a girl named Suzy, who loves the Ogden Nash poem her dad always reads to her about a dragon who acts bravely despite feeling afraid. This poem becomes more relevant when her father is sent to fight in Viet Nam.

At first, Suzy imagines him in a jungle like her favorite cartoon character. But as time passes and his postcards ask for prayers, her worries grow. When Suzy's dad finally returns home, he seems haunted by his wartime experiences. Ultimately, father and daughter find comfort and healing in their relationship with each other—and in a poem about a scared-but-brave dragon.

This autobiographical story offers a timeless reflection on the anxieties of children when their parents are at war.

**Cast all your anxiety on Him, because He cares for you. (1 Peter 5:7)**

*Give children the strength to deal with anxieties, Father.*

## Stumbling Blocks to Faith

Faith, doubt, and trust in God. For singer-songwriter Audrey Assad, addressing those topics on her album *Fortunate Fall* served as a way to find the good after undergoing struggles such as her parents' divorce and her husband's bout with cancer.

As she explained during an interview on *Christopher Closeup,* "When it comes to faith, I tend to write about the things that are stumbling blocks for me. So because I spend time writing songs to wrestle out those ideas and points of confusion, I sometimes find resolution and peace where I didn't have it."

Assad learned the necessity of dealing with problems head on through experience. She said, "I've never gotten anywhere in life by denying I'm struggling with something. So for me to take a step forward into the path of healing or renewal or joy or gratitude has always come through a darker period. Not everyone may function that way, but I know that I do, so I have become willing to embrace those seasons [of life] because I know that they hold something [good] on the other side."

**We call blessed those who showed endurance. (James 5:11)**

*Lead me out of the darkness into the light, Divine Savior.*

## The Columbo Technique

Want to make a lasting impression on your boss or a potential employer? Try emulating Lieutenant Columbo.

That's blogger Greg Lhamon's advice, but he doesn't mean that you should dress in a rumpled raincoat like the shrewd TV detective played by Peter Falk. Instead, it's about a technique Columbo used as he finished interviewing a suspect.

Lhamon writes, "He'd thank the suspect profusely, step toward the door, and then turn back, and say, 'Oh, just one more thing.' Then he'd ask one last question, a particularly damning question that let the suspect know he was onto him."

How can this apply in business situations? Lhamon says, "Hold back a critical piece of information and reserve it for the end of the meeting; right before you part company, share the information or ask a question...Sincerity is critical. The goal is simply to make a strong, memorable point."

Remember, the right words at the right time can make you stand out from the crowd.

**A word fitly spoken is like apples of gold. (Proverbs 25:11)**

*Just one more thing, Lord. Thank You for my blessings.*

## A Murder Leads to a Mission

Matthew Barnett's ministry as the pastor of Bethel Temple in Los Angeles' Skid Row began 19 years ago with an incident that would have scared most people away. On his first day, a teenage boy was shot and murdered outside the church door.

Though he wasn't sure he could handle this type of environment, Pastor Barnett got to work doing what needed to be done. During a *Christopher Closeup* interview, he said, "What kept me going, I believe, was ministering to the family [of the boy that was killed]. We paid for the funeral, and we walked into their house and said, 'We're gonna make sure that we're there for you.' It was one of the most meaningful experiences in my life. After that day, there was no way I could ever quit."

That commitment eventually led Pastor Barnett to take in someone suffering from drug addiction. Then he took in a homeless family. As the dream of helping others grew, he knew he'd need a bigger facility to accommodate everyone. He found it in an unexpected place. That part of the story tomorrow.

**Let us consider how to provoke one another to love and good deeds. (Hebrews 10:24)**

*Instill me with trust in You, Lord, whenever fear threatens.*

# A Not-So-Impossible Dream

As Pastor Matthew Barnett's dream of helping others grew, he noticed that Queen of Angels Hospital in Echo Park was shut down. Though entertainment companies wanted to buy the property, the Los Angeles Archdiocese sold it to his church at a discount because he promised to make it a place of spiritual healing.

Now named the Dream Center, it serves and houses the homeless and addicted, victims of sex trafficking and domestic violence, troubled youth, and more. Pastor Barnett says that he modeled the Dream Center's inclusive approach of offering material and spiritual support after Jesus's approach:

"Jesus didn't say, 'When you believe, then we'll let you belong.' He allowed people to belong first in order that they might believe. Compassion opens up the door where people begin to understand that we're gonna love them unconditionally, whether they receive the message of Christ and His compelling love for them, or not. But it gets hard not to believe when people have loved you so long and been so consistent in your life."

More of Pastor Barnett's story tomorrow.

**See what love the Father has given us.**
**(1 John 3:1)**

*Teach me to love others as You love us, Jesus.*

## The Broken and the Holy

Many of the people Pastor Matthew Barnett has encountered in Los Angeles have pasts that would shock most of us. There was one 14-year-old, for instance, whose mother got him hooked on the drug crystal meth. Though that teen managed to turn his life around, not all do. Not being able to save everyone took a toll on Pastor Barnett for a while, and left him wondering why a good God allows such horrific things to happen.

Time and experience have given him a new perspective, though. He said, "I began to find that you can't let your heart be destroyed by the ones that fall on the wayside. You have to build upon something, and that's the success of the ones who make it."

Pastor Barnett concluded, "Sixty percent of my staff are graduates of our Drug and Alcohol Rehab program. In our church, we've got ex-pimps, ex-murderers. And that's just the pastoral staff. When I started to see what God can do with these people, then I began to realize that some of the finest people I've ever met are some of the most broken people I've ever met."

**The Lord is near to the brokenhearted, and saves the crushed in spirit. (Psalm 34:18)**

*May my brokenness lead me closer to You, Lord.*

## Roving Preacher Unmasks Thief

Lorenzo Dow roamed Burlington, New Jersey, in the 19th century, preaching the gospel and helping folks solve their problems, sometimes in offbeat ways.

Once, the preacher was asked to determine who had stolen a farmer's wallet. He asked for a rooster and a blackened, dirty pot. Then, he put the rooster in the pot, and covered it. "When I darken the room," he said, "each man is to press his hands firmly on the pot. When the thief touches it, the rooster will crow."

Everyone did as instructed, but the rooster didn't make a sound. Then, Parson Dow examined everyone's hands. All were blackened except one man's. He confessed his guilt and admitted that he hadn't touched the pot because he was afraid the rooster would crow.

Within each of us, there is a conscience. It can be ignored, stifled, or twisted, but never wholly stilled. This faculty of moral judgment is our surest point of contact with the inner workings of God's grace and the call of His word.

**By rejecting conscience, certain persons have suffered shipwreck in the faith. (1 Timothy 1:19)**

*Father, instill me with the courage to be honest.*

## Composing a Life

Beethoven frequently got his outstanding musical ideas while he walked alone through the countryside and listened to nature, according to author Colton Waugh.

Upon returning home, he would immediately go to his piano and struggle to work out in notes what he had heard in his mind.

Composers write their music in different ways, according to their individual temperaments. The brilliant Mozart, for instance, seemed to develop his compositions almost effortlessly. He might write down some of the notes while chatting with a group of friends.

The musical writings of the great composers express a wide range of human feeling—sadness, longing, hope, and joy.

Few people have either the inspiration or the ability to compose a musical masterpiece. But each of us without exception can play a creative role in bringing some of God's love and harmony into the lives of the people around us.

**Clothe yourselves with love, which binds everything together in perfect harmony. (Colossians 3:14)**

*Enable me, Lord, to be an instrument of Your truth and joy.*

## Awesome Dad

"You really couldn't ask for anything better as a young kid. It was awesome," said Chase Elliott, 18. Quoted in *USA Today,* Elliott spoke admiringly about his father Bill, a NASCAR icon who won many races during his nearly 40-year career. "It was the coolest thing ever," said the younger man. "Getting to watch your dad race on weekends was a dream come true."

Although the racetrack was significant for this family, what's most important for kids is quality time with parents. If you can be together that's great, but it's key for children to know their dads care about them. For Chase, now a racer himself, Bill modeled a solid work ethic, shared his accumulated knowledge, and taught his son practical skills.

Dads don't have to win the Daytona 500 to be special. Youngsters thrive when their fathers are emotionally present in their lives and when they feel their love and support.

**As a father has compassion for his children, so the Lord has compassion for those who fear Him. (Psalm 103:13)**

*Father, help dads appreciate their importance in the lives of their children.*

# Blind and Autistic Musical Genius

Tony DeBlois was born blind and weighing a little over one pound. He also had autism, which was not a condition understood by the American medical community in 1974.

DeBlois could not speak until age 17, and still cannot read or write. But long before he found his voice, he was able to speak through his music. Perhaps that's why he not only attended the Perkins School for the Blind, but also graduated with honors from the Berklee College of Music in Boston.

Today, at 40, he plays 23 instruments and can sing in 11 languages. His nationwide concerts are enjoyable and inspiring. "Tony has a real gift and I just love his personality," 12-year-old Cody Dauby, a parishioner of St. Thomas Aquinas Church in West Lafayette, Indiana, told *The Catholic Moment* reporter Caroline B. Mooney.

"We are here to tell you that it is okay to be different," DeBlois told his St. Thomas audience. "Believe in yourself. Don't give up on your dreams—and have high hopes."

**My grace is sufficient for you, for power is made perfect in weakness. (2 Corinthians 12:9)**

*Abba, may we utilize our gifts for Your glorification.*

# Sons to the Rescue

It was the day after Father's Day. Fifty-one-year-old Michael Meigh of Garnerville, New York, reentered his home, complaining of heat exhaustion after doing cement work outside. When Sean, 19, saw his father sweating profusely, he asked his 11-year-old brother Connor to keep an eye on him while he went to take a shower. Soon after, Michael passed out in front of his youngest son. Connor ran to get his brother, and called 911.

While Connor waited outside for the ambulance to arrive, Sean performed CPR on his father, which he later found out had a life-saving effect, as Michael had suffered a heart attack due to a blocked artery.

"I cannot express how proud I am of them," says Marian Meigh of her two sons, as quoted in *Catholic New York*. "They were willing and able to jump into an emergency situation and take action immediately."

For their bravery and courage, Sean and Connor will receive the Heartsaver Hero Award from the American Heart Association of Hudson Valley.

**Sons are indeed a heritage from the Lord. (Psalm 127:3)**

*May we lean upon You, Father, for love and strength.*

## Our Spiritual Mother in Heaven

While celebrating mass at Indiana State Prison on the Feast of the Assumption several years ago, prison chaplain Father David T. Link told the inmates that they've got a spiritual mother in heaven who can relate to their troubles. Mary, he pointed out, came from a poor village. She faced many other hardships in her life, including the crucifixion of her beloved Son. But why do Catholics believe that Mary was assumed into heaven?

As recounted in the biography *Camerado, I Give You My Hand,* Father Link explained, "Maybe God wanted to save Mary from the power of death. It may have been to reward Mary for having endured great sorrow. But most likely God assumed Mary into heaven because He wants us to know for sure that our spiritual mother is in heaven, where she is caring for us. Be assured that right now Mary is looking down on this chapel with pride and love for all who have come to honor her Son."

That message resonated with these men, who may not have received much love during their lives. It gave them an ever-present mother to whom they can always turn for comfort.

**Mary...you have found favor with God. (Luke 1:30)**

*Help me to be as loving as Mary, Lord.*

## The Sower of Love

Pope Francis continues to fascinate the world, and among the reasons he does so are the talks he gives each day. *Catholic News Service* reported on this one, which asked pilgrims gathered for his Angelus blessing to consider what really is their heart's desire.

"All of us have a desire," the pope said to thousands in St. Peter's Square. "Pity the person who doesn't have a desire. Desire moves us forward, toward the horizon, and for us Christians that horizon is an encounter with Jesus."

Pope Francis told his listeners to reflect on what Jesus had taught: "Where your treasure is, there also will your heart be."

Many people would respond that their family is the most important thing, he said, and that's good. But, he added: "What is the force that holds your family together? It's love, and the one who sows love in our hearts is God."

**Sow for yourselves righteousness; reap steadfast love; break up your fallow ground; for it is time to seek the Lord, that He may come and rain righteousness upon you. (Hosea 10:12)**

*Guide me in sowing seeds of Your love, Father.*

## Lessons from a Homeless Man

Among the features in *The New York Times* is "Metropolitan Diary," a weekly potpourri of items sent in by readers that illustrate, for better or worse, life in New York. One issue included a submission by Barbara Nahmias about a homeless man named Joe that she sees as she exits her subway car.

"He gives me a big smile as he sees me approach," she wrote. "I give him his breakfast, as I have every day for five months."

Joe is known for helping people, and for finding temporary work wherever he can. Barbara worried when she didn't see him for a few days, then discovered he'd heroically saved a woman who nearly fell off the subway platform. She wrote:

"Joe says he feels so lucky that so many kind people like me help him. What he doesn't know is that he is my teacher, my inspiration—and that when my sweetheart asks me every evening, 'How was your day?' I tell him that the best part of it was my time with Joe."

**The rich and the poor have this in common: the Lord is the maker of them all. (Proverbs 22:2)**

*God, may we learn from people from all walks of life.*

# A Father's Hope

In 2005, when she was only five days old, Sarah Jane Donohue was shaken so violently by her baby nurse that she ended up with broken bones and permanent brain damage. Doctors said the girl would never walk, talk or function normally. Sarah Jane's father Patrick refused to accept that diagnosis, however, so he has devoted his life to helping her and other children like her.

As reported by Andrea Peyser in the *New York Post*, Patrick created the Sarah Jane Brain Project in 2007, to develop better treatments for kids with Pediatric Acquired Brain Injuries (PABI). In 2013, he founded the International Academy of Hope in Harlem, New York, to provide an educational environment for PABI-afflicted kids who can't function in public schools. Currently there are 19 students, including Sarah Jane.

Patrick notes that one girl is now walking around the school and telling her mother, "I love you," after doctors said she would never progress. He also remains optimistic about Sarah Jane's future. "She can't walk or talk, yet," he said, "but she will!"

**See what love the Father has given us.
(1 John 3:1)**

*Enable us, Lord, to bring healing to those with disabilities.*

## Traveling 4,200 Miles for Puppy Love

When Christine Davies was deployed in Kuwait as a member of the U.S. National Guard, her young daughter Lylia understandably missed her absent mom. One thing that lessened the loneliness was an abandoned dog named Nigel that they found online through Greg Mahle's Rescue Road Trips website. Christine promised Lylia they would adopt Nigel when she returned home.

As profiled by Christopher Award-winning author Bob Dotson on his *American Story* segment for the *Today Show,* Mahle rescues thousands of dogs every year who are abandoned by their breeders, tries to find them loving homes, then delivers them to their adoptive families.

Every other week, Mahle travels 4,200 miles for just that purpose. He leaves his Zanesville, Ohio home in his tractor trailer to pick up dogs that have been abandoned in Texas, Louisiana, Alabama, and Pennsylvania. Then he heads north to New England, where an abundance of people are willing to adopt rescued dogs. Why does he do it? Because his work brings others a lot of joy. The sight of Lylia exclaiming, "He loves me!" while Nigel licks her face is proof enough of that.

**The Lord of heaven grant you joy. (Tobit 7:16)**

*Create in me, O Lord, a heart of compassion.*

## Sandra Bullock's Life Lessons

After Hurricane Katrina severely damaged New Orleans' Warren Easton Charter High School in 2005, Academy Award-winning actress Sandra Bullock financially supported its restoration. In 2014, she personally attended the school's graduation ceremony to share some life lessons with the students.

One of those lessons was, "Stop being scared of the unknown, because anything I worried about didn't happen. Other stuff happened, but not what I worried about. The unknown we can't do anything about, and I don't remember any of the moments in my life where I worried. So that's a lot of time I couldn't get back."

Along those lines, Bullock also advised, "Go find your joy. Are you going to have a good day or are you going to have a great day, because it's completely up to you. It's what you're going to remember in the end. You're not going to remember how you worried. You're not going to remember the 'what ifs' or the whys or who wronged you. It's the joy that stays with you."

**I have said these things to you so that My joy may be in you, and that your joy may be complete. (John 15:11)**

*When worries plague me, Lord, send me Your peace.*

## Holding Civilization Together

In a scene from author Dean Koontz's novel *The City*, which takes place in the 1960s, 10-year-old Jonah Kirk is watching the news on television. The images he sees consist of nothing but riots, looting, and violence, leading him to wonder if the world is falling apart.

Jonah's mother Sylvia then offers him a different perspective, one that's just as valid for those of us surrounded by bad news today. She says, "There's something you need to understand, Jonah. For every person who's stealing and setting fires and turning over police cars, there are three or four others in the same neighborhood who want no part of it."

"The news isn't *all* the news, Jonah," she concludes. "Not by a long shot. It's just what reporters want to tell you about. Riots come and go, wars come and go, but under the tumult, day after day, century after century, millions of people are doing nice things for one another, making sacrifices, mostly small things, but it's all those little kindnesses that hold civilization together, all those people who live quiet lives and never make the news."

**Kindness is like a garden of blessings. (Sirach 40:17)**

*May small acts of kindness build up the world, Father.*

## When is the Right Time?

When Kara Eschbach worked on Wall Street, a mentor cautioned her about the inclination to always wait for "the right time" to do something.

Eschbach recalled, "So often we're told to hold off marriage until that next promotion; postpone kids until you find a larger house; wait until you have the perfect set of credentials before striking out on your own. You can certainly do this, but who's to say those times will be any better? Life will always bring struggles and joy in unpredictable ways, so why wait to do the things you want most?"

As a result of that advice, Eschbach chose to start her own women's magazine and website called *Verily* in 2012. Though the effort has been full of challenges, she's happy she embarked on this new adventure when she did, saying, "I had a growing realization that today would be just as scary as tomorrow."

Sometimes moving forward in life requires us to take a leap of faith. Pray for God to guide you down the right path.

**Only fear the Lord, and serve Him faithfully with all your heart. (1 Samuel 12:24)**

*Move me beyond fear to faith and hope, Father.*

## Lessons from a Root Canal

When leadership expert Michael Hyatt was told that he needed an emergency root canal, he imagined "unspeakable pain." Yet his experience with endodontist Dr. Daniel Price left him feeling great and admiring the doctor's leadership skills.

- Dr. Price demonstrated empathy by listening to Hyatt's concerns and making him feel safe.
- He clarified expectations by explaining that technology had made the procedure less intrusive than in the past.
- He under-promised by saying his goal was a "pain free experience," but that Hyatt would occasionally feel some pressure or a pinch.
- He provided updates, explaining what he was doing so Hyatt wouldn't feel "out of the loop."
- He over-delivered, by finishing in less time than expected—and with "zero pain" on top of that.

Hyatt concluded that empathy, clear expectations, providing updates, under-promising and over-delivering are the marks of a good leader. Pretty insightful lessons to learn from a root canal.

**All who humble themselves will be exalted. (Matthew 23:12)**

*Open my eyes to see life lessons in unusual places, Lord.*

## Begin Again and Again

Who was the guest speaker at the graduation of the Catholic University of America's Class of 2014? Why, none other than Phil Rivers, the quarterback for the San Diego Chargers of the National Football League. What's more, the 32-year-old, a Catholic husband and father of seven, did a great job challenging the new graduates to begin again—and again.

"Whether I have a bad play or a good play, whether I throw a touchdown or an interception, I must begin again," Rivers said. "It certainly applies to you graduates who now are beginning the next chapter in your lives."

Along with these challenges, he also offered some personal insights. "I knew as long as I stayed focused on my priorities, I would be ready for life's ups and downs," he concluded. "What are your priorities? What is the foundation on which you will build your future? Mine are very simple: faith, family and football, in that order."

**If anyone is in Christ, there is a new creation. (2 Corinthians 5:17)**

*Lord, may I never fear the future, for You are always present.*

## The Banana Solution

Many years ago, an enterprising factory foreman discovered a new use for bananas—and solved a problem that had everyone else stymied.

When an aluminum plant in Sheffield, Alabama, had to move a 100-ton piece of delicate machinery 25 feet, no one could figure out how to do it. Then, foreman Robert McDonald got his brainstorm.

He spread 100 pounds of bananas and their peels on the floor around the machine. Workmen then slid the equipment to its new position without trouble. For his efforts, the foreman was promptly dubbed "Slippery McDonald."

Pleasant surprises can occur when we move beyond our usual ways of thinking. Pray for the guidance and wisdom to find creative solutions to difficult problems.

**Trust in the Lord with all your heart, and do not rely on your own insight. (Proverbs 3:5)**

*Father, make us willing to break new ground in bringing help to a troubled world.*

# Bikers Against Child Abuse

It's not surprising to hear that bikers decked out in leather and chains can be intimidating to some people, but there's a particular group that is intimidating for a good cause.

They're called Bikers Against Child Abuse International, and the motto they wear on their leather vests and t-shirts reads, "No child deserves to live in fear."

The Arizona chapter recently visited a young girl, who was abused by a relative, to introduce themselves and let them know they're watching out for her. When the case against the abuser proceeds, the bikers will accompany the girl to the trial, walk her to the witness stand, then walk her out when she's done.

All the bikers are volunteers who receive training from a licensed mental health professional. They also undergo criminal background checks. At heart, they're just good souls who want to help. As reported by the website ViralNova, "These bikers aren't looking for trouble. The only thing they want is to make sure innocent children don't feel alone or powerless."

**Take care that you do not despise one of these little ones. (Matthew 18:10)**

*Bring healing to the victims of child abuse, Divine Savior.*

## 'That Woman Would Have Been Dead'

Many years ago, a four-year-old boy saved his mother's life by trudging miles through the snow to get help.

After their car skidded out of control on a remote Colorado road, mother and son set out on foot. When the woman slipped and hit her head against a rock, the youngster went on alone. After a four-mile hike, he reached a Denver policeman's cabin and announced, "My mother is sick and in the snow."

The officer and boy returned to the still-unconscious mother. She was taken to Denver's Lutheran Hospital and treated for frostbite and a head injury.

"If it hadn't been for that little boy walking out," remarked one sheriff's deputy, "that woman would have been dead this morning."

Achievement knows no size limit or age. Young or old, big or small, we are all capable of efforts that may surprise even ourselves. When capability is joined to good will, God can accomplish much good through us.

**Let Your work be manifest to Your servants, and Your glorious power to their children. (Psalm 90:16)**

*Jesus, guide us in accomplishing Your saving work.*

## When You Thought I Wasn't Looking

Mary Rita Schilke Korzan wrote a poem of appreciation to her mother 30 years ago. Its words about the influence of adults on children still ring true today. Here's an excerpt:

"When you thought I wasn't looking, you hung my first painting on the refrigerator and I wanted to paint another...When you thought I wasn't looking, you baked a birthday cake just for me and I knew that little things were special things.

"When you thought I wasn't looking, you said a prayer and I believed there was a God that I could always talk to. When you thought I wasn't looking, you kissed me good-night and I felt loved. When you thought I wasn't looking, I saw tears come from your eyes and I learned that sometimes things hurt—but that it's alright to cry.

"When you thought I wasn't looking, you smiled and it made me want to look that pretty too...When you thought I wasn't looking—I looked...and wanted to say thanks for all those things you did when you thought I wasn't looking."

**The righteous walk in integrity—happy are the children who follow them! (Proverbs 20:7)**

*Lord, bless our parents and teachers, and all mentors who strive to set a good example.*

## Something Other Than God

During her early 20s, Jennifer Fulwiler was living a comfortable life in material terms. She had a good job, just got married to a successful man, drove a Jaguar, and enjoyed the finer things in life in her 21st floor condo in Austin, Texas. But having been raised an atheist, she'd been plagued by a spiritual emptiness for years—a fear that life was ultimately meaningless.

After investigating Christianity—and Catholicism in particular—Fulwiler found the fulfillment she'd always been seeking. This led to her and her husband Joe seeking a simpler, more self-sacrificial life, which now includes six children.

During a *Christopher Closeup* interview about her book *Something Other Than God*, she explained, "When we first left the fancy lifestyle, we suddenly had all of these problems and crosses that we didn't have before…To this day, we struggle so much more than we did when we were living our worldly, secular lives. And yet, our lives are bursting with life and with love and with joy. God is very real in our lives and we are trying to follow Him the best we can."

**Rejoice in hope, be patient in suffering. (Romans 12:12)**

*Help me to find Your peace and joy amidst hardship, Jesus.*

## Never Forget to Remember

Profound truths can often be expressed in simple ways. This Irish poem by an anonymous writer, reprinted in the newsletter *Apple Seeds*, offers a perfect example:

"Always remember to forget
The things that made you sad.
But never forget to remember
The things that made you glad.
Always remember to forget
The friends that proved untrue.
But never forget to remember
Those that have stuck by you.
Always remember to forget
The troubles that passed away.
But never forget to remember
The blessings that come each day."

**Seek the Lord and His strength; seek His presence continually. Remember the wonderful works He has done, His miracles, and the judgments He has uttered. (Psalm 105:4-5)**

*Help me focus on my blessings, Heavenly Redeemer.*

## Turning Down a Raise?

Blogger Matthew Warner thinks you should tell your boss that you "don't want a raise." Before you call him crazy, hear out his argument.

Warner points out that despite advancements in technology and efficiency that are supposed to make our lives easier, "we work more so we can consume more, which requires us to work more." He suggests that if your boss offers you a higher salary, you should say, "No, thank you. But I would like a shorter work week instead. I'd like to keep my salary the same, actually, but I'd like to work fewer hours."

Why? Warner concludes, "We have the chance here to be spending more time and energy with loved ones, nurturing our souls, pursuing God and truth and helping others more than ever before...At the end of your life, are you going to wish you had twice the salary? Or twice the time spent with loved ones helping each other become the people we were made to be? That seems like an easy answer to me."

**Riches do not profit in the day of wrath, but righteousness delivers from death. (Proverbs 11:4)**

*May I always value people over possessions, Lord.*

# A Link in the Chain of Rebuilding Lives

"Maybe this is how we recover," said Bill Lavin, a firefighter still grieving the loss of buddies who died in the World Trade Center on 9/11. During that time, Lavin received a bundle of letters from compassionate grammar-school children in Bay St. Louis, Mississippi. Those notes gave him hope.

Amazingly, four years later, Hurricane Katrina destroyed the same kids' school. This time Lavin helped them by mobilizing assistance from firefighter colleagues, who constructed new playgrounds. But that wasn't the end of Lavin's "paying it forward."

As noted in *People* magazine, twin tragedies struck the East in 2012: Superstorm Sandy, and the horrific shootings at Sandy Hook Elementary School. "I was as depressed as I've ever been," the father of three said. He became determined to rebuild 26 playgrounds ruined during the hurricane and to dedicate each to a Sandy Hook victim. Donations are pouring in and the project is underway.

Helping others is helping Lavin—and he reminds us that the same approach towards life can help us as well.

**Give, and it will be given to you. (Luke 6:38)**

*May we remember the ripple effect of good deeds, Lord.*

## A Broken Leg Changes a Life

A broken leg changed Dan Moran's life. So writes Dave Hrbacek in the *Catholic Spirit* of St. Paul-Minneapolis. It happened in March 1981, and it seemed at the time to be utter tragedy. Moran had made his high-school hockey team, which had qualified him for the all-important state tourney. Then came the break—on the ice, in his hockey uniform—and despair set in.

Moran was fitted with a cast, and in keeping with tradition, all his friends signed it. One of them wrote "Romans 8:28" on the cast, and Moran looked it up in the Bible. "All things work together for good for those who love God," he read, "and have been called according to His purpose." Moran decided to live by that maxim, and simply put, it changed his life.

Now an investment counselor with a family, he devotes himself to faith and prayer. "Prayer has significantly helped me in my life," he says. "It's helped me grow in my relationship with God and with Jesus, helped me to be a better husband, helped me to be a better father."

And to think it all started with a broken leg!

**To set the mind on the spirit is life and peace. (Romans 8:6)**

*Christ, may I trust You to work out all things in my life for good purposes.*

## God Helps Those Who Help Themselves

Harry Houdini died in 1926, but his fame as one of the greatest escape artists and magicians of all time lives on.

Houdini came from a family that struggled constantly with poverty. His father, a rabbi of great faith, reassured his wife and children that "God would provide."

One day, the cupboards were bare, so ten-year-old Harry took his tricks to the sidewalks of his Appleton, Wisconsin hometown. People stopped, applauded—and filled his hat with coins. Then he ran home and gave money to his astonished parents, saying, "It's true. God does provide. But it's also true that God helps those who help themselves."

There's a huge difference between trusting God and just waiting for Him to do our work for us. We can't escape the fact that God depends on us to do our share for ourselves and our world.

**Whatever your task, put yourselves into it, as done for the Lord. (Colossians 3:23)**

*There's work to be done, Holy Spirit. Grant me the stamina and understanding to do it well.*

## Are You Really Listening?

Most people spend more time and effort trying to become effective speakers and writers than they do in learning how to listen, according to communications expert Edwin Johnson.

Listening is not a passive function, he points out. It is an active process involving thought and the expenditure of energy. Neither is listening simply a way to absorb information about things, processes, and technical data. It is the key to effective human relations, the key to understanding other people.

A good listener seeks first to understand, then to judge, Johnson emphasized. Many people judge first, then feel there is no need to listen. To get the other person's point of view, you have to listen creatively, uncritically, sympathetically, and attentively.

God sends some of His knowledge and wisdom to each of us through other people. The more we realize this, the more inclined we'll be to listen to others—and really hear Him.

**If you love to listen you will gain knowledge, and if you pay attention you will become wise. (Sirach 6:33)**

*Teach me, Holy Spirit, to be an attentive listener.*

## Securing Heaven

Blessed Mother Teresa of Calcutta, who dedicated her life to serving Christ by ministering to the poorest of the poor, shared the following advice in her book *No Greater Love:*

"One thing will always secure heaven for us: the acts of charity and kindness with which we have filled our lives. We will never know how much good just a simple smile can do. We tell people how kind, forgiving, and understanding God is, but are we the living proof? Can they really see this kindness, this forgiveness, this understanding alive in us?

"Let us be very sincere in our dealings with each other and have the courage to accept each other as we are. Do not be surprised or become preoccupied at each other's failure; rather see and find the good in each other, for each one of us is created in the image of God. Keep in mind that our community is not composed of those who are already saints, but of those trying to become saints. Therefore, let us be extremely patient with each other's faults and failures."

**Why do you see the speck in your neighbor's eye, but do not notice the log in your own eye? (Matthew 7:3)**

*May I always remain humble enough to be forgiving, Jesus.*

## You Can't Take It with You

On the Greek island of Crete 3,500 years ago, some people lived in lavish luxury. Archaeologists dug up a 250-room palace built 16 centuries before Christ. Partially destroyed by a volcanic earthquake, the palace still held artifacts of an advanced culture.

Kitchens and pantries held cooking pots and hundreds of terra-cotta wine cups. The ruler's private apartments included a gymnasium and a 17-foot spring-fed swimming pool. Other rooms included elaborate reception and banquet halls, waiting rooms, archives, and a treasury.

In every age of history, human beings have desired the comforts and refinements of gracious living for themselves. Yet we must remember that all these vestiges of power and wealth may eventually be lost and forgotten—or even buried in the ground. Like the old saying goes, "You can't take it with you."

What you can take into the next life is the love you showed for God and others. Now that's an eternal treasure.

**Do not store up for yourselves treasures on earth, where moth and rust consume...but store up for yourselves treasures in heaven. (Matthew 6:19-20)**

*May I never be consumed by greed, Divine Giver.*

## Looking for the Perfect Career?

Mike Rowe, former host of the TV show *Dirty Jobs* and advocate for careers in the skilled trades, shared a letter on his Facebook page from a fan named Parker.

Parker wanted advice on finding a career that would provide him with excitement, adventure, and good money while always leaving him happy. Rowe responded honestly and bluntly:

"Stop looking for the 'right' career, and start looking for a job. Any job. Forget about what you like. Focus on what's available. Get yourself hired. Show up early. Stay late. Volunteer for the scut work. Become indispensable. You can always quit later, and be no worse off than you are today. But don't waste another year looking for a career that doesn't exist. And most of all, stop worrying about your happiness. Happiness does not come from a job. It comes from knowing what you truly value, and behaving in a way that's consistent with those beliefs."

**You have an abundance of workers: stonecutters, masons, carpenters...Now begin the work, and the Lord be with you. (1 Chronicles 22:15-16)**

*Holy Spirit, lead all the unemployed toward good jobs.*

## Prayer for My Children

The following prayer was posted on the website Catholic-Christian.Tumblr.com:

"Dear Lord, I ask a special blessing upon my children. Fill them with Your grace and bless them with every gift they need to live their lives in faithful obedience to You. Touch their hearts and minds and fill them with wisdom, knowledge, hope, and understanding. Help them to be loving, kind, and compassionate. Be their protector and send holy angels to lead them and guide them as they go through their day.

"Bless their lives with peace, joy, and true happiness. Send loving friends into their lives who will be blessings to them. Keep them healthy and whole spiritually, relationally, emotionally, and physically. Let Your light shine brightly in them...Bless them with healthy self-images and may they always know how precious they are to You and me. May they grow to be responsible, generous, humble people of integrity and good sense. Lord, I place them in Your loving care and trust that You will always guide them and love them. Amen."

**Train children in the right way. (Proverbs 22:6)**

*Guide children down the right paths, Loving Father.*

## Breaking Out of an Insulated World

A mother from Youngstown, Ohio, described her years of raising a child with Down syndrome as "something very different than what we ever imagined or hoped it could be. My standards, my values, my sense of what is beautiful, my acceptance of reality today, now have meaning."

She continued, "These years have been fruitful. Our child took us out of our insulated world and opened many closed doors in our hearts. We broke out of those walls and saw the need of other human beings. As a result, we became actively involved in social justice in the world around us."

When we meet challenges in life, we can often take refuge in self-pity. But this mother reminds us that facing our struggles creatively can open us up to a whole new world, one that is far richer and more fulfilling than we ever dreamed.

**I consider that the sufferings of this present time are not worth comparing with the glory about to be revealed to us. (Romans 8:18)**

*Father, in a world full of suffering, give me the wisdom and grace to be an instrument of Your compassion.*

## The Things We Often Take for Granted

On *Good Morning America*, Lisa Beamer—the widow of 9/11 hero Todd Beamer, who helped stop a hijacked plane from reaching Washington, D.C.—recalled a high school teacher who taught her a valuable lesson about appreciating life.

This teacher lost her husband to a sudden heart attack. Soon after, she told the class, "Each of us is put here on earth to learn, share, love, appreciate and give of ourselves. None of us knows when this fantastic experience will end...From now on, on your way to school, or on your way home, find something beautiful to notice. It doesn't have to be something you see; it could be a scent, perhaps of freshly baked bread wafting out of someone's house, or it could be the sound of the breeze slightly rustling the leaves in the trees...Although it may sound trite to some, these things are the 'stuff of life.' The little things we are put here on earth to enjoy. The things we often take for granted."

Beamer said, "Every once in a while, I think of that teacher and remember what an impression she made on all of us, and I try to appreciate those things that sometimes we all overlook."

**In the end you will appreciate my words. (Sirach 31:22)**

*Open my eyes to the beauty around me, Father.*

## Death is Nothing

With inspiration from St. Augustine, Henry Scott Holland—the late Canon of Christ Church, Oxford—once wrote this reflection on death to bring comfort to those who grieve.

"Death is nothing at all. I have only slipped away into the next room. Whatsoever we were to each other, that we are still. Call me by my old familiar name, speak to me in the easy way which you always used to. Laugh as we always laughed at the little jokes we enjoyed together. Play, smile, think of me, pray for me. Let my name be the household word that it always was. Let it be spoken without effort.

"Life means all that it has ever meant. It is the same as it ever was, there is unbroken continuity. Why should I be out of your mind because I am out of your sight? I am but waiting for you, for an interval, somewhere very near, just around the corner. All is well. Nothing is past, nothing is lost. One brief moment and all will be as it was before, only better, infinitely happier and forever—we will be one together with Christ."

**Today you will be with Me in Paradise. (Luke 23:43)**

*Bless me with the comfort of knowing my lost loved ones have been embraced by You, Jesus.*

## More Than 'Just' a Taxi Driver

In conversation during a ride to the airport, a rabbi learned that his young driver had stopped being religious. "So, Rabbi, what do you say to a Jew like me who hasn't been in a synagogue since his bar mitzvah ceremony?"

The rabbi took advantage of their few minutes together to encourage the cabbie to see the honor in his labor. The rabbi said that an attentive and caring driver could facilitate many human connections.

For instance, he said, the next fare might be a woman being discharged home from the hospital. "You could be a small part of her healing process, an agent in her re-entry into the world of health," he added.

Or, the rabbi said, "You might drive someone just back from seeing a dying parent. You're one of the unseen people who make the world work as well as it does. That is holy work."

**Commit your work to the Lord, and your plans will be established. (Proverbs 16:3)**

*Every person is a part of the entire fabric of life. May we always keep that in mind, Lord.*

## Geo the Hero

Carly Riley was walking with her three young sons and eight-month old German shepherd/collie mix, Geo, in their British hometown of Clacton-On-Sea, Essex.

While waiting to cross the street, a truck careened onto the sidewalk, heading straight towards them. Geo immediately pushed ten-year-old Charlie out of harm's way, taking the brunt of the vehicle's hit himself.

The truck driver drove off, so Riley called the police. But the family's main concern was for their courageous dog. Geo sustained a broken leg, a fractured spine and numerous bruises as a result of the impact. His veterinary bills total 8,000 pounds, a sum the Rileys fully intend to pay. To this end, they even set up a Facebook page for him called "Geo the Hero," where every donation given will go towards the healing of their heroic pet.

"[The truck] could have wiped us all out," Riley told the *Daily Mail*. "If it wasn't for Geo, I am 100 percent sure it would've been Charlie... We want him [healed] no matter what it costs. He's family."

**But ask the animals...they will teach you. (Job 12:7)**

*Abba, bless all pets, guardians of our families and friends.*

## The Boy on the Wooden Box

One of the books for young people honored at the 2014 Christopher Awards was the autobiography *The Boy on the Wooden Box* by Leon Leyson.

Ten-year-old Leon's life changed forever when the Nazis invaded his homeland of Poland in 1939, bringing deprivation, persecution and evil with them. Yet this powerful memoir is actually a story of hope thanks to Leon's relationship with the man he describes as a "hero disguised as a monster."

That hero was Oskar Schindler, the industrialist and member of the Nazi party who saved over 1,000 Jews by putting them to work in his enamel factory. Leon was so short, he had to stand on a wooden box to get his job done. But that job allowed him and several members of his family to survive the war and begin new lives in America.

Though Leon passed away in 2013, this book remains as a testament to the courage of an unlikely hero—and also to Leon's own spirit, which never allowed the world's darkness to overcome its light.

**I am saved from my enemies. (2 Samuel 22:4)**

*May I be a help to those who are persecuted, Lord.*

## Low Expectations Lead to Determination

At Newark, New Jersey's University Hospital, ER doctor Hugo Razo deals with traumas, gunshot wounds, and horrific injuries on a regular basis. Throughout everything, he remains calm and compassionate. Yet few people would have predicted that Dr. Razo would pursue this life-altering responsibility.

During an interview on the documentary TV series *NY Med*, he explained, "I was always told I'm not going to amount to anything. Just look at the town where I came from. Like pretty much every other Latin teenager, no one expected much. The most people expected of me was to work at McDonald's or something of that nature. It's almost like I wanted to show all those people that they were wrong."

Dr. Razo relishes his ability to make a genuine difference in patients' lives, and could easily be a role model for inner-city youth who want to better themselves. His example teaches us that our struggles can become redemptive when we use them to build a life of service to others in need.

**I know the plans I have for you, says the Lord, plans...to give you a future with hope. (Jeremiah 29:11)**

*Don't let other people's negativity burden my heart, Lord.*

## What All Teens Want

As she travels around the country performing at churches and teen events, Christian singer Tori Harris relishes her encounters with teens and the way they respond to her music both in person and through emails and Facebook posts.

During an interview on *Christopher Closeup,* she recalled a girl coming up to her after a performance and saying, "I was here for a guy because I thought he was cute, but I experienced something here that was real and powerful and I want to know more of what that is."

In an age when more and more young people describe themselves as "nones," as following no particular religion, getting them interested in Christianity is vital.

For Harris, there's one common denominator: "What's universal to all [teens] is the desire to be accepted and feel loved. When they have those two things, then they desire to search for what is true and what is right and what is wrong when it comes to their faith and when it comes to God."

**Beloved, since God loved us so much, we also ought to love one another. (1 John 4:11)**

*Help teens experience Your love, Divine Savior.*

## When You Let the Pope Drive...

The website CatholicHumor.org recently shared the following joke. The pope flew to Chicago, and was picked up at the airport by a limousine. He admired the car and asked the driver, "I never get to drive anymore. Would you please let me?" The driver responded, "Okay, I can't say no to the pope."

The pope took the wheel, hit the gas, and started going 100 miles per hour. A policeman noticed, pulled him over, and asked the pope to roll down the window. Startled and surprised at who was driving, the officer went back to his patrol car and called headquarters. "Chief," he said, "I've got a problem. I pulled over this guy for driving way over the speed limit, but it's someone really important."

"Important like the mayor or the governor?" the chief asked. The officer responded, "No, more important than that."

"Important like the president?" asked the chief. "More important," said the cop.

"Who's more important than the president?" wondered the chief. The officer answered, "I don't know, but he's got the pope driving for him!"

**Abraham fell on his face and laughed. (Genesis 17:17)**

*Lord, instill me with a good sense of humor.*

## A Math Teacher's Secret Life

When St. Francis High School senior Pat McGoldrick attended a meeting at Children's Hospital Los Angeles for a blood drive he was heading, he was surprised to hear people tell him, "Oh, you must know Jim O'Connor. Isn't he wonderful?"

McGoldrick only knew the 70-year-old O'Connor as his tough-as-nails math teacher, but soon discovered there was a lot more to the earnest Vietnam vet. Not only was he listed on a plaque as one of the hospital's top blood donors, but he also held another distinction there. For 20 years and counting, O'Connor has volunteered at the hospital three days a week to hold, cuddle, and feed sick babies.

"I just like them and relate to them somehow. I don't want to see them alone," he told *CBS News*. Nurse Erin Schmidt says the babies feel the same way because they relax in his arms.

And what does McGoldrick now think of the man whose calculus lessons often torment him? He says, "He's the epitome of a man of service."

**I know your works—your love, faith, service. (Revelation 2:19)**

*Help me bring comfort to the lonely, Holy Spirit.*

## Prepare to Win

Tom Coughlin, the coach who led the NFL's New York Giants to two Super Bowl wins, learned at an early age that preparation is the key to success. In his book *Earn the Right to Win,* he recalled a lesson that his father John taught him after young Tom gave a poor effort in a game.

Coughlin wrote, "During my sophomore year in high school, I played varsity football. When I came home one Saturday afternoon after we'd been beaten, [my father] was waiting at the front door for me. It looked like he'd been standing there a while. All he said to me was, 'If that's the effort you're going to give, you probably ought to find something else to do with your time.' That was devastating for me to hear. His message was clear: If you're going to do something, do it to the best of your ability—or don't waste your time. It never happened again."

Giving your best effort doesn't guarantee success, but lack of effort usually guarantees failure. Give your best in all you do.

**You must make every effort to support your faith with goodness, and goodness with knowledge. (2 Peter 1:5)**

*Lord, make me untiring in developing my full potential.*

## Andy Griffith Finds Grace in Hardship

In 1983, actor Andy Griffith thought his life might be over. He couldn't find work because of his age (he was in his 50s), and he was diagnosed with an inflammatory nerve disease called Guillain-Barré syndrome. With no cure or treatment, Griffith's pain and partial paralysis became debilitating—until an old friend, psychiatrist Dr. Leonard Rosengarten, led him to California's Northridge Hospital Medical Center.

Griffith wrote in *Guideposts* that everything changed when a doctor acknowledged the severity of his condition and promised to help him through it. Simply hearing those words brought the actor hope. With medication and mental imagery techniques, his life soon improved. He even went on to shoot a pilot for the TV series *Matlock*, which then ran for nine years.

And what did Griffith learn from all this? He said, "Each of us faces pain. But I firmly believe that in every situation, no matter how difficult, God extends grace greater than the hardship, and strength and peace of mind that can lead us to a place higher than where we were before."

**My grace is sufficient for you.**
**(2 Corinthians 12:9)**

*When pain overwhelms me, Lord, send me Your grace.*

## Matthew Bears

The death of her son Matthew, while he was serving as a Marine in Afghanistan in 2009, made Lisa Freeman especially sensitive to the needs of military families who have lost loved ones in war. While preserving memories can be comforting, she thought it would be helpful if they could hold onto something more tangible as well.

That's why the Georgia mom created Matthew Bears. *The Daily News* reported, "Families of fallen service members send Freeman their loved ones' uniforms and she uses the material to hand sew teddy bears." It's a labor of love for Freeman, who said, "I kind of pray over the uniforms while I'm going."

Matthew Bears are an extension of The Matthew Freeman Project which Lisa founded to collect school supplies for children in war-torn countries, and to provide college scholarships to siblings of fallen soldiers.

Lisa believes that Matthew would be proud of her work, saying, "He's loving that something good is happening out of something so tragic."

**He has sent me...to bind up the brokenhearted. (Isaiah 61:1)**

*Savior, grant comfort to those mourning the losses of family and friends.*

## Giving Hope to the Nation

The young girls who fled to St. Monica's school in Gulu, Uganda, during that country's civil war found a guardian angel in Sister Rosemary Nyirumbe. She and her fellow sisters welcomed these children, who had been victims of kidnapping, violence, and rape.

As reported by *U.S. Catholic*, the war ended in 2006, but Sister Rosemary knew career options for women were limited in Uganda. To deter the girls from choosing lives of begging or prostitution in order to support themselves and, in many cases, their babies, she taught them "sewing, cooking, catering, and other skills." That training led many to jobs in Uganda's top hotels. The girls at the school also earn money by making purses out of aluminum can pop tops, which sell well in the U.S.

Sister Rosemary says, "These girls need support, need education. That is why I took up the skills training, to let society [know] that these women are the greatest contributing factor to the economy of the country. They are giving hope to the nation."

**Let me not be put to shame in my hope. (Psalm 119:116)**

*Bring victims of war into Your loving embrace, Savior.*

# An Anti-Semite's Shocking Revelation

Notorious for his fierce and outspoken anti-Semitism, Hungarian politician Csanad Szegedi served in the European Parliament beginning in 2009, and accused Jews of trying to take over Hungary. However, in 2012, he resigned his post after his maternal grandmother revealed a shocking fact: she was both Jewish and a Holocaust survivor.

Szegedi claims the news upended his life and worldview. He told *NPR,* "For 30 years I lived a harmful, aggressive and radical life with extreme views. Now I'm taking the time to reconsider my life and my expectations and where to go next."

Szegedi soon contacted a Hungarian rabbi to help guide him in becoming an observant Jew. *NPR* reports that he now "calls himself Dovid, wears a black skull cap, regularly attends synagogues, studies Hebrew and the Torah, and keeps kosher."

Remember, it's never too late to turn your back on prejudice and hatred.

**If the wicked turn away from all their sins... they shall surely live. (Ezekiel 18:21)**

*Lord, send Your redeeming grace to change the hearts of those mired in hatred.*

## Brooklyn Castle

If Albert Einstein were on the chess team at Brooklyn's I.S. 318 junior high, he would only be the fourth-best player, outranked by several 11-to-13 year olds. That's because the students there defy society's low expectations for children who come from below-the-poverty-line families.

The Christopher Award-winning TV documentary *POV: Brooklyn Castle* takes us inside the school's remarkable chess program run by a teacher and administrator with an infectious passion for the game.

We also meet the young people who pursue chess mastery and academic excellence while struggling with anxiety, peer pressure, and even budget cuts that threaten their beloved program.

By depicting public education at its best—and featuring young people determined to build a brighter future for themselves and their families—*POV: Brooklyn Castle* demonstrates that extracurricular programs can be at the heart of students' future success.

**O simple ones, learn prudence; acquire intelligence, you who lack it. (Proverbs 8:5)**

*May we always cherish the gift of education, Divine Teacher.*

## Writing to Your Congressman

A lesson on how to write to a congressman was given by a member of the House of Representatives. Here are some of his recommendations:

- Address the letter correctly.
- Make it clear which of the thousands of bills introduced each year that you're referring to. At least describe it if you don't know its official number.
- Be brief, even about complex subjects.
- Give your own views; specify what prompts your stand on a specific piece of legislation.
- Avoid threats.

Elected leaders depend on feedback from their constituents to guide their votes on crucial issues. Exercise your God-given right to let the person who represents you hear your voice about the running of our country.

**The mind of the wise makes their speech judicious, and adds persuasiveness to their lips. (Proverbs 16:23)**

*Father, never let me forget that good government is my responsibility as much as it is anybody's.*

# The Lawyer Who Might Have Been

When a 29-year-old Florida bandit went on trial for a bank robbery, he told his lawyer to sit down because he wanted to conduct his own defense. It didn't work out too well, so the defendant was sentenced to prison. But the U.S. District Judge who presided over the case told him:

"You know as much as most of these lawyers. You make a pretty good closing argument, and you cross-examined witnesses very well. You should have studied law. You might have made a real good lawyer instead of a robber."

Most, if not all, lawbreakers have potential for good that could make them assets to society instead of liabilities. What we may fail to realize is that all of us, each time we act against the best interests of others, could have used our abilities in a constructive way. Instead of pointing a finger at others, we should ask God to help us see ourselves as we really are so we can become the individuals that He created us to be.

**Confess your sins to one another, and pray for one another, so that you may be healed. (James 5:16)**

*Grant us the wisdom and courage to know ourselves, Lord, and to act upon that knowledge.*

## A Higher Call

In December 1943, Second Lieutenant Charlie Brown of the U.S. Air Force flew a badly damaged bomber over the war-torn skies of World War II Germany.

With half his crew either dead or wounded and the heavily fortified German coastline ahead, Brown guided his plane toward England rather than ordering a parachute drop because he knew that one of his injured men couldn't make the jump.

Suddenly, fighter pilot Franz Stigler of the German Luftwaffe pulled up alongside them. Brown and his crew were certain they would be shot down. But Stigler, a Catholic who opposed Hitler, adhered to the code of chivalry common among German flyers before the Fuhrer's rule. He saw the plane was crippled, and flew in formation on its wing to protect it from being fired upon as it passed over the coastline.

Years later, Brown tracked down Stigler and gathered with other surviving crew members from that mission. They wept in gratitude over the families that now exist because Franz Stigler chose honor and mercy that day.

**Love your enemies. (Matthew 5:44)**

*Lord, help us to practice mercy in difficult situations.*

## Worry is Like Sand in a Machine

"There are very few things as destructive to our mental health as worry. Worry is like sand in a machine. It not only hinders the working of the machine, but damages it as well."

So writes Msgr. Charles Pope from the Archdiocese of Washington, D.C. He believes we can find an antidote to worry in St. Paul's words from Philippians 4: "Do not be anxious about anything, but in everything, by prayer and petition… present your requests to God."

Msgr. Pope believes that St. Paul is reminding us "that the power of God is only a prayer away… He may not always come when you want, or handle things exactly the way you want, but when I look back over my life and think things over I can truly say that God has made a way for me. And whatever my struggles and disappointments, none of them has ever destroyed me. If anything, they have strengthened me."

Along with prayer, Msgr. Pope recommends cultivating a sense of God's presence in your life: "Ponder deeply how He has delivered you in the past, how He has made a way out of no way, and how He has drawn straight with crooked lines."

**Rejoice in the Lord always. (Philippians 4:4)**

*Help me to overcome my worries, Redeemer, with deep, fervent prayer.*

## The Komosa Phenomenon

In 1999, 17-year-old Rob Komosa was running practice drills on his high school football field in Rolling Springs, Illinois, when he broke his neck.

Though he'd always believed that God had a plan for every person, that concept now seemed empty and incomprehensible in light of his lifelong paralysis and reliance on a ventilator to breathe. But as documented by Dr. Don Grossnickle in the book *Unbreakable Resilience,* the love of his family and community started moving Komosa past his understandable self-pity.

First, a wheelchair-accessible van was donated by a local businessman. Then, the Komosa family was able to buy a home retrofitted for someone in Rob's condition with money raised by volunteers through car washes, collection jars, and dinners. Dr. Grossnickle writes, "The Chicago media [called] the fruitful community-wide rally the 'Komosa Phenomenon.'"

Komosa now counsels other paralyzed athletes and relies on role models, friends and optimism to move forward in life.

**We are God's servants, working together.**
**(1 Corinthians 3:9)**

*Nurture the spirits of people struggling with disability, Lord.*

## And Justice for All

"Catholic Social Teaching" is a term often used in conversation, but few people know the ins and outs of what it entails. Here are the basics, as summed up into seven themes by *The Catholic Spirit*, newspaper of the Archdiocese of St. Paul-Minneapolis:

- Life and dignity of the human person...because every human person is created in the image and likeness of God.
- Call to family, community and participation... because every human is not only sacred, but social.
- Solidarity...because we are one human family.
- Dignity of work...because the economy must serve people, not the other way around.
- Rights and responsibilities...because we have a fundamental right to life with decency, and with regard for others' rights.
- Option for the poor and vulnerable...because we follow the teaching of Scripture.
- Care for God's creation...because the world that God made has been entrusted to all of us.

**Be careful then how you live. (Ephesians 5:15)**

*I pray to treat others with a loving heart, Father.*

## Doing It All for Love

Sometimes the most profound wisdom is the simplest. Consider these quotes by St. Thérèse of Lisieux.

- "Miss no single opportunity of making some small sacrifice, here by a smiling look, there by a kindly word; always doing the smallest right and doing it all for love."

- "For me, prayer is a surge of the heart; it is a simple look turned toward heaven, it is a cry of recognition and of love, embracing both trial and joy."

- "I know now that true charity consists in bearing all our neighbors' defects—not being surprised at their weakness, but edified at their smallest virtues."

- "If I did not simply live from one moment to another, it would be impossible for me to be patient, but I only look at the present, I forget the past, and I take good care not to forestall the future."

- "Without love, deeds, even the most brilliant, count as nothing."

- "A word or a smile is often enough to put fresh life in a despondent soul."

**The fruit of the Spirit is love, joy, peace. (Galatians 5:22)**

*May my faith inspire loving actions, Lord.*

## The Most Challenging Job

Patheos.com blogger Billy Kangas spent one summer several years ago working as a hospital chaplain. He called it one of the most challenging jobs of his life because "chaplains are asked to escort people through death, and failure, and sorrow beyond words."

Kangas notes that the two things he did most frequently were hold people's hands and recite the Lord's prayer. Why did those two actions bring comfort?

He explains, "Holding someone's hand is like a little sacrament. It is an act of incarnational communion, filled with the mystery that each person is an icon of God. The Lord's prayer is the liturgy of the word in miniature…It is the invitation and the commission into the Kingdom of God. It joins our words with Christ and His body. It is powerful."

If you're ever called on to help a troubled soul, consider those two simple actions—holding a hand and saying the Our Father. They will make you a vessel of God's love.

**Give us this day our daily bread. (Matthew 6:11)**

*Lord of Hope, may I give witness to Your love to all those around me.*

## Shine Through Me

If you want God's light to shine through you, consider saying the following prayer by Cardinal John Henry Newman:

"Dear Lord, help me to spread Your fragrance wherever I go. Flood my soul with Your spirit and life. Penetrate and possess my whole being so utterly that all my life may only be a radiance of Yours. Shine through me, and be so in me that every soul I come in contact with may feel Your presence in my soul.

"Let them look up and see no longer me, but only You, O Lord! Stay with me, then I shall begin to shine as You; so to shine as to be a light to others. The light, O Lord, will be all from You; none of it will be mine; it will be You shining on others through me.

"Let me thus praise You in the way You love best, by shining on those around me. Let me preach You without preaching, not by words but by my example, by the catching force, the sympathetic influence of what I do, the evident fullness of the love my heart bears to You. Amen."

**Restore us, O God of hosts; let Your face shine, that we may be saved. (Psalm 80:7)**

*Abba, make me a reflection of Your goodness.*

## A Few Special Needs Here and There

Sarah, a stay-at-home mom and blogger at Wifeytini.com, wants to change the way our culture discusses disability. The reason? An ultrasound during her pregnancy revealed that her son Henry had the birth defect spina bifida, which results in physical challenges like clubbed feet and mobility issues.

Sarah writes, "We were advised to terminate, by more than one person, seemingly because a life with spina bifida is so terrible that it's better to not live it at all. Can you comprehend that? There is such a disconnect between the beautiful children I see who happen to have a disability, and the sorry, deformed, faceless nobodies that our culture makes them out to be. And the disconnect didn't hit me until right after Henry was born."

Though Henry has lots of doctor appointments, Sarah describes the 14-month-old as an "absolute joy" with "a few special needs sprinkled here and there." She concludes, "People with disabilities...are endowed by our Creator with human dignity. Yes, we should keep them. We should cherish them. We should change the way we think and talk about them."

**My life was precious in your sight.**
**(1 Samuel 26:21)**

*Help us to see the dignity of all Your children, Father.*

## Why Did Lincoln Grow a Beard?

A letter from an 11-year-old girl may have inspired Abraham Lincoln to grow a beard as a help to his presidential campaign efforts.

Grace Bedell of Westfield, New York, wrote to candidate Lincoln suggesting that "all the ladies like whiskers and they would tease their husbands to vote for you and then you would be President." She added, "You would look a great deal better for your face is so thin."

Often, hidden motives can influence our choice for those we elect to lead us. The nation was fortunate in having chosen Lincoln to steer it through the dark years of the Civil War—however much his beard may have influenced the voting.

A better way to select a President or other candidates for public office is to weigh carefully their records, their stands on issues confronting the nation, and their plans to address those issues.

**Choose for each of your tribes individuals who are wise, discerning, and reputable to be your leaders. (Deuteronomy 1:13)**

*May my actions, Holy Spirit, flow from a deep concern for the nation and the world.*

## Tim Conway Finds a Friend in Jesus

During his high school years, comedian Tim Conway suffered a back injury during a football game that left him unable to talk or move. After his team members carried him off the field, a doctor took an X-ray, found nothing broken, and put him in a neck brace for a few weeks.

Many years later, Conway visited a doctor due to back spasms. As he writes in his memoir *What's So Funny*, he was shocked when the doctor told him his "spasms were a residual effect stemming from a broken vertebra." Conway insisted he'd never broken a vertebra, then recalled the football incident.

The doctor explained that he'd likely broken his vertebra, but when his teammates picked him up, his back got stretched out and the vertebra went back into place. If Conway hadn't been moved, he may have been permanently disabled. That was a watershed moment for Conway, spiritually speaking. He writes, "Ever since that incident, which might have altered the course of my life, Jesus and I have stayed in constant touch. I never stop saying thank you."

**Give thanks in all circumstances.**
**(1 Thessalonians 5:18)**

*Thank You for the times You've helped me, Lord, without me knowing it.*

## Enjoy the Noise

"Hurry!" Matt Archbold told his wife and five kids. "We've got to get on the road so we can sit in traffic."

And sit in traffic they did during the family's road trip to Boston. To test Archbold's patience even more, the kids spent most of the ride noisily arguing, laughing, and yelling at each other while playing a game called Robot Apocalypse.

After finally arriving in Boston, the family did some sightseeing and Archbold found himself engaged in conversation with an elderly man who saw his abundance of kids. "My wife and I had seven," he told Archbold. "Enjoy them. Treasure every moment. It used to be I couldn't wait until I had some quiet in the house. And now quiet's all I got. I miss the noise."

That observation left an impression on Archbold. He wrote in *Catholic Digest*, "The next day the kids, my wife, and I got back into the van to go home. We took our time, sang, giggled, and snorted the whole way...It was a great long trip. When I parked the van in our driveway, I sat a moment and thanked God for the noise."

**O that I were as in the months of old...when my children were around me. (Job 29:2,5)**

*Help me appreciate the blessings of family, Father.*

## Salvation from the Storm

Hurricane Sandy is long gone from the New York-New Jersey metropolitan area, but the aftereffects of the storm linger on. In addition, many of its victims are still far from living a normal life, a fact reinforced by a message from the Salvation Army.

That venerable organization not only provided immediate care to victims with feeding, warming and changing stations, but followed it up with casework and Emergency Assistance Centers. In the summer and fall of 2013, as the first anniversary of Sandy approached, the Salvation Army moved into a new phase of the recovery effort, stationing case managers across New Jersey for those hardest hit by the October storm.

Brenda Beavers, director of human services, pointed to the importance of personal counseling, opportunities to socialize, and respite camp sessions that are all part of the continuing effort to help the victims of Sandy—and let them know they're not forgotten. "These special events show that The Salvation Army is what communities need it to be," she said.

**In the shadow of Your wings I will take refuge, until the destroying storms pass by. (Psalm 57:1)**

*Shelter those hurt by life's storms, Compassionate God.*

## Help, Teach, Love

The third-place winner in The Christophers' 24th Annual Poster Contest for High School Students was Payton Hale, a senior at Briar Woods High School in Ashburn, Virginia. Her poster presented three different snapshots featuring Hale herself using American Sign Language (ASL) to teach a child how to sign three different words: help, teach, and love.

We also received a letter from Hale's proud grandmother telling us the backstory of her interest in ASL. She wrote, "Payton has been studying ASL since she was a third-grader, and has decided to study this as her college major so that she can help others to come out of the silence. When Payton's dad was transferred to Virginia while she was in middle school, her first friend was a young lady whose mother was deaf. Payton was the only one of this friend's friends who could converse with her mom. This summer she will be helping a deaf student with Down syndrome from another high school in Virginia."

We applaud Payton Hale not just for her winning poster, but for her compassionate heart that inspires us all to "help, teach, and love."

**A friend loves at all times. (Proverbs 17:17)**

*Guide me in being a friend to the lonely, Divine Healer.*

## The Most Beautiful People

Psychiatrist and author Elisabeth Kübler-Ross was known for her book *On Death and Dying,* and for developing the five stages of grief. But she also offered many insights about living, not just dying. Here are just a few:

- "The most beautiful people we have known are those who have known defeat, known suffering, known struggle, known loss, and have found their way out of the depths. These persons have an appreciation, a sensitivity, and an understanding of life that fills them with compassion, gentleness, and a deep loving concern. Beautiful people do not just happen."

- "There is within each one of us a potential for goodness beyond our imagining; for giving which seeks no reward; for listening without judgment; for loving unconditionally."

- "People are like stained-glass windows. They sparkle and shine when the sun is out, but when the darkness sets in, their true beauty is revealed only if there is a light from within."

**It is You who light my lamp; the Lord, my God, lights up my darkness. (Psalm 18:28)**

*Father, take my struggles and brokenness, and make me a more compassionate, holy person.*

## Paying Respects to a Hero

Members of a college basketball team from Wisconsin were so amazed at the heroism of a nine-year-old boy who lost his life in a fire in upstate New York that they undertook an eight-hour bus trip to attend his funeral—and moved the boy's family to tears.

Tyler Doohan, a fourth-grader, was asleep when fire broke out in his grandfather's home near Rochester, New York. After saving six people he went back into the blaze to attempt to rescue two others. Tragically, he succumbed to the flames.

Inspired by Tyler's heroism, the team at Silver Lake College in Manitowoc, Wisconsin, (sponsored by the Franciscan Sisters of Christian Charity) attended the funeral with the family's approval, and met the boy's mother and father.

"How did it make you feel to put a smile for a few minutes on the faces of a family going through the worst day of their lives?" asked Coach Phil Budervik on the ride back. "One of the players said, 'It was the best feeling in the world to do that.' That's when I knew we had done the absolute right thing. We helped a family and paid our respects to a true hero."

**When will you comfort me? (Psalm 119:82)**

*Heal the hearts of the suffering, Divine Savior.*

## A Brother's Love

Eight-year-old Noah Aldrich is crazy about his six-year-old brother, Lucas. "I like everything about him, he's perfect," Noah says. "He's just like every other kid out there."

In one respect, however, Lucas is different from other children; he was born with a rare genetic condition called *lissencephaly.* "They said he'd be non-verbal…not be able to eat, and have a shortened life span," his mother Alissa told *KTVB.* "He's doing way better than we ever expected."

Lucas's overall health is in no small part due to the unfailing love of his older brother. Thanks to Noah, Lucas was even able to take part in a mini-triathlon in their Boise, Idaho, community, sponsored by the YMCA. It included a one-mile run, a three-mile bike ride and a 200-meter swim. Noah tirelessly pushed or pulled his wheelchair-bound brother in all three races. The two boys finished the triathlon in just under 54 minutes.

"They definitely have a special bond, the two of them," their father Brian concluded. "It just brings a smile to your face."

**Encourage…and build up each other.
(1 Thessalonians 5:11)**

*Abba, strengthen the bonds between families.*

## Afraid of Making Mistakes?

In a talk entitled "Hang Loose," a corporate executive offered several pieces of advice to the person who would be his successor. One of the suggestions was, "Make sure you generate a reasonable number of mistakes."

He explained, "Too many executives are so afraid of error that they rigidify their organization with checks and counterchecks, discourage innovation, and, in the end, so structure themselves that they will miss the kind of offbeat opportunity that can send a company skyrocketing."

"If you can come to the end of a year and say that you haven't made any mistakes," he cautioned, "then I say that you just haven't tried everything you should have tried."

No one wants to be wrong. But fear of mistakes can be a hindrance to creativity at home, in school, or in business. Think things through, trust in God, and act. Then, accept there will be unavoidable mistakes, and determine to use them as an opportunity to learn.

### All of us make many mistakes. (James 3:2)

*Father, don't let excessive fear of being wrong paralyze our efforts to improve the world.*

## Appreciating Our Elders

"Make sure that what you do elevates or encourages, and doesn't tear down." Martha Williamson was given that advice by her father when she told him she wanted to become a TV producer and writer. She took those words to heart when working on her shows *Touched by an Angel* and her new Hallmark Channel series *Signed, Sealed, Delivered* about postal workers who track down the recipients of long-lost mail.

Williamson incorporates her father's virtues into her stories whenever possible. She notes that he was born in 1901, always remained a gentleman, and conveyed a lot of wisdom to her. She thought of him when writing a recent storyline about a young postal worker who befriends a lonely, elderly woman at a retirement home. The goal was to share a message about how we as a society treat our elders.

Williamson said on *Christopher Closeup,* "Because my father was so much older, I not only spent time with him as an elderly person, but with his friends. The greatest mistake we can make is to discount the power of what those folks have to offer."

**Do not ignore the discourse of the aged. (Sirach 8:9)**

*Inspire us to learn from our elders, Divine Teacher.*

## A Gift of Time

In 1999, halfway through their third pregnancy, Amy Kuebelbeck and her husband learned that their unborn son, who they named Gabriel, had an incurable heart condition and wouldn't live long if he was carried to term.

Committed to their son's life from conception to natural death, they didn't find much support except from one nurse who told them they could still love and parent Gabriel, even if it was just for a brief period. Kuebelbeck took that advice to heart.

Though Gabriel lived for only two-and-a-half hours, his family found moments of beauty and peace in the otherwise heartbreaking experience.

Since then, Kuebelbeck has reached out to others facing similar diagnoses through her books *Waiting with Gabriel* and *A Gift of Time*. She also edits the website PerinatalHospice.org, which offers locations of hospice and palliative care programs in every state that has one. She says, "It's wonderful that caregivers are responding to this need and stepping up to light a candle in the darkness for these families."

**My soul melts away for sorrow; strengthen me according to Your word. (Psalm 119:28)**

*Comfort the hearts of those who've lost children, Creator.*

## Actor Sees Coach as Model of Christ

Early in his career, Jim Caviezel met veteran actor Jimmy Stewart, who gave him a piece of advice: "Young man, whatever you do, make good movies." And what qualifies as a good movie to Caviezel? During a *Christopher Closeup* interview, he said, "A story that has redemption to it, a story that has real love."

Those qualities are the reasons that Caviezel chose to play high school football coach Bob Ladouceur in the film *When the Game Stands Tall.* Ladouceur led his team—Concord, California's De La Salle Spartans—on a 151-game winning streak. But he didn't do it by obsessing about winning. Instead, he was intent on building young men of character and virtue—and on modeling those traits himself.

Caviezel explained, "Why aren't more coaches like that? It's the worst three-letter word ever: Ego. Edge God Out. When you look at the Christian life, many people go out and claim one thing, but they do another. So authenticity is very important because there was no one more authentic than Christ. Ladouceur takes that seriously. He really follows the Savior."

**Strive first for the kingdom of God. (Matthew 6:33)**

*Help me to model the principles I preach, Savior.*

## A Priest Defiant

No praying out loud, no Mass, no rosaries, no group prayers. Those were the Polish Army's rules under the communist regime in the 1970s when a young Catholic seminarian named Jerzy Popieluszko was forced to complete his military service. Though the government tried to break the spirits of these future priests so they would give up their vocations and their faith, the atheist indoctrination didn't work on Father Jerzy.

When his sergeant ordered him to stop praying the rosary while doing calisthenics, he refused and was punished by being made to stand outside in the rain and snow, sometimes barefoot, thereby damaging his health for the rest of his life.

"They couldn't dent his faith. That's the most remarkable thing about him," said Paul Hensler, who wrote and produced the Christopher Award-winning documentary *Jerzy Popieluszko: Messenger of the Truth.*

In fact, Father Jerzy went on to become a Polish human rights hero. More of his story tomorrow.

**With their mouths the godless would destroy their neighbors, but by knowledge the righteous are delivered. (Proverbs 11:9)**

*Grant me the courage and wisdom to defend my faith, Lord.*

## Messenger of the Truth

When Pope John Paul II visited Poland in 1979, he prayed to God, "Let Your Holy Spirit descend and renew the face of the earth and this land." Those in the audience, including Father Jerzy Popieluszko, took that message to mean that it was time for the people of Poland to nonviolently resist their communist oppressors who controlled every aspect of their lives.

Thousands of workers in steel mills and shipyards went on strike demanding more freedom and better treatment. Father Jerzy even entered the steel mill, which had been considered a communist fortress, and celebrated Mass for the striking workers. Eventually, the Polish government relented and gave its citizens what they wanted.

Father Jerzy's masses at Warsaw's St. Stanislaus Kostka Church attracted thousands. His homilies included messages like, "Justice and the right to know the truth require us, from this pulpit, to repeatedly demand a limit on the tyranny of censorship."

Those homilies angered the communists, and they soon took action against the brave priest. More tomorrow.

**Send out Your light and Your truth. (Psalm 43:3)**

*Grant us the grace to accept Your truth in our hearts, Lord.*

## The Fruit of His Love

"Let's ask God to make us free from revenge and hatred, to give us freedom, which is the fruit of His love," said Father Jerzy Popieluszko in one of his homilies. That message became especially relevant when Poland's communist government had the beloved 37-year-old priest murdered in 1984 because he spoke out on behalf of freedom.

Father Jerzy's call to action had always involved nonviolent resistance. Though his parishioners and Poland's citizens felt enraged about his murder, they honored Father Jerzy's life by refusing to engage in violence. A million people came to his funeral and remained peaceful.

Furthermore, says Paul Hensler, the filmmaker behind the Christopher Award-winning documentary *Jerzy Popieluszko: Messenger of the Truth*, the priest's death galvanized the people of Poland in their resistance to communism, eventually leading to its downfall.

Today, Father Jerzy's legacy lives on. His tomb remains a sacred place for both citizens and tourists—and he is likely to be declared a saint within the next few years.

**For freedom Christ has set us free.**
**(Galatians 5:1)**

*Free my heart from hatred, Holy Spirit.*

## Unreasonable Leadership

As someone who achieved business success in the grocery industry—and philanthropic success through support of Catholic Charities, Wounded Warriors, and his own education foundation—Gary Chartrand wanted to share the lessons he'd learned in his life and career with others. That's why he wrote a book called *Unreasonable Leadership*. Why that title?

During an interview on *Christopher Closeup*, he explained, "It's based on the quote from George Bernard Shaw that all progress is made from unreasonable people because reasonable people adjust to their surroundings. Unreasonable people rebel against those surroundings and produce progress."

How can the average person apply this concept to his or her life? Chartrand said, "My advice is—get out of your comfort zone. Happiness is found when you pierce through all those things that try to keep you in that reasonable, comfortable, safe place. If you move beyond your fear zone, you'll discover things about yourself that you just didn't think were possible."

**Receive a wreath for your excellent leadership. (Sirach 32:2)**

*Give me courage and wisdom to achieve progress, Lord.*

## How Long Does It Take to Be Successful?

We may think of composers like Mozart or painters like Picasso as being masters of their craft—and they are! But they weren't born that way; it took a lot of hard work. How much exactly?

That's what John Hayes, a cognitive psychology professor at Carnegie Mellon University, set out to discover. He researched the lives and work of 76 composers and how long it took them to produce their most enduring works.

In summing up Hayes' research, entrepreneur James Clear wrote on his blog, "Not a single person produced incredible work without putting in a decade of practice first. Even a genius like Mozart had to work for at least 10 years before he produced something that became popular. Professor Hayes began to refer to this period, which was filled with hard work and little recognition, as the 'ten years of silence.'" In addition, Hayes found that practice-time alone doesn't make you the best, but rather, "deliberate practice" focused on specific goals is key.

Is there a craft or art form that you want to master? If so, start chipping away at those "ten years of silence."

**Do not hate hard labor. (Sirach 7:15)**

*Instill me with perseverance and determination, Creator.*

## From Beauty to Joy

"On Easter Sunday, April 4, 1999, Pope John Paul II wrote an open letter to all artists—both Christian and secular—reminding them of their vocation to Beauty. He urged them not to waste their artistic talent but to develop it, and to put it at the service of humanity as an authentic vehicle of culture."

Those words were written by the students of John Paul the Great University in Escondido, California, who are pursuing careers in media and the arts. To celebrate the canonization of their school's patron, they created a three-minute video that summarizes the late pope's 6,000-word letter to artists.

Not every line is a direct quote, but the students highlight the heart of his message: "Society needs you artists. The world in which we live needs beauty in order not to sink into despair. Beauty, like truth, brings joy to the human heart."

**For from the greatness and beauty of created things comes a corresponding perception of their Creator. (Wisdom 13:5)**

*Holy Spirit, inspire our culture's influencers to create stories that remind us of beauty and truth.*

## We Care Bears

When Bob and Kathleen Carscadden of San Diego adopted their daughter Jessica at age five, they showered her with lots of love—and even some stuffed animals. The child, who had been abandoned at birth because of facial deformities, found comfort in her teddy bears and cherished their presence in her life.

Now age 11, Jessica is paying forward the kindness she received. As reported by *USA Weekend*, she was cleaning her room one day and decided to donate some of her stuffed animals to kids in need. That idea became the We Care Bears Project, which invites other kids (and adults) to donate as well.

On October 23rd, 2013—the 23rd annual Make a Difference Day—Jessica "oversaw donations of about 3,000 stuffed bears for police and firefighters to give to injured or frightened children while on emergency calls." Sixty volunteers [most of them children] filled about 580 bags with bears, providing every police car in San Diego with stuffed animals to offer comfort to children during scary times.

**Whoever becomes humble like this child is the greatest in the kingdom of heaven. (Matthew 18:4)**

*Bless and strengthen children performing acts of service, Holy Spirit.*

# A 24-Carrot Ring

During some heavy duty pre-Christmas baking in 1995, Lena Pahlsson put her wedding ring on the kitchen counter, only to discover later that it had disappeared. She and her husband Ola searched everywhere around their house and property in central Sweden, but they never found it—until 2011, that is.

While Lena was collecting carrots from the family vegetable patch in October, she pulled up a tiny carrot that she was going to throw away because it was so small. Then she noticed something unusual that seemed to be growing at the bottom of the carrot. Yes, it was her wedding ring, made of white gold and seven small diamonds, looking very good after all those years in the dirt. So how did it get there? Theories abound.

The Pahlssons told the newspaper *The Local* that it might have fallen into their compost bin, been spread over the vegetable patch, and just taken all these years to finally latch on to a sprouting seed. Regardless, they're happy the ring is safe.

Life is full of mysteries. Accept them and trust in God.

**Your God is...a revealer of mysteries. (Daniel 2:47)**

*Help me to appreciate—and sometimes laugh at—life's unexpected joys, Divine Creator.*

## 'Your Life Will Not Go Unnoticed'

"Your life will not go unnoticed because I will notice it. Your life will not go unwitnessed because I will be your witness." Writing in *Venture* magazine, Katie Marchetti recalls that line from an unnamed movie because it reflects the human desire to know that our lives are meaningful in someone else's eyes.

Marchetti writes, "To hold the knowledge that someone is watching your life, that you are not below their notice, that the littlest details of your existence have not escaped them...this fills a part of you, which happily overflows into your whole being."

As good as it feels when we find someone who affirms us, Marchetti concludes that we also need the comfort of knowing a higher power is watching over us too: "We upturn our faces to soak up the sunshine pouring out from the heavens, and we feel seen. We feel loved. We have the knowledge that God is watching our lives, that we are not below His notice. That the littlest details of our existence have not escaped Him. That He has mulled over our hearts when we were not looking."

**When he sees you his heart will be glad. (Exodus 4:14)**

*Holy Spirit, help me to know that I'm loved and I matter.*

## You Should Think About Being a Doctor

Sometimes, an unexpected word of encouragement or gesture of kindness can have a major impact on someone's life. That was the case with Dr. Kevin Hunt from Chicago, who wouldn't have even entered the medical field if not for the advice and support of other people.

During an interview on *Christopher Closeup*, he recalled with heartfelt emotion a formative experience from his youth: "I started working as a nurse's aide many years ago and, at that time, I wasn't considering going into the medical field. I was just working a side job while going to school. I used to work the night shift in the cancer ward, so I talked to the patients. They'd always say to me, 'You should think about being a doctor.'"

Dr. Hunt continued, "Then one patient told me, 'If you get into medical school, I'll pay for a semester of school.' She was a terminal, dying patient. I got into medical school right before she died. And she actually sent me the check for my first semester. So it was really inspiring to me."

**You guide me with Your counsel. (Psalm 73:24)**

*Holy Spirit, guide me in being a light to those I meet, to help them fulfill their God-given potential.*

# The Weight of a Glass of Water

A psychologist walked around a room while teaching Stress Management to an audience. As she raised a glass of water, everyone expected they'd be asked the "half-empty or half-full" question. Instead, with a smile on her face, she inquired, "How heavy is this glass of water?"

Answers called out ranged from 8 ounces to 20 ounces. She replied, "The absolute weight doesn't matter. It depends on how long I hold it. If I hold it for a minute, it's not a problem. If I hold it for an hour, I'll have an ache in my arm. If I hold it for a day, my arm will feel numb and paralyzed. In each case, the weight of the glass doesn't change, but the longer I hold it, the heavier it becomes.

She continued, "The stresses and worries in life are like that glass of water. Think about them for a while and nothing happens. Think about them a bit longer and they begin to hurt. Think about them all day long, and you will feel paralyzed and incapable of doing anything. Remember to put the glass down."

**My yolk is easy, and My burden is light. (Matthew 11:30)**

*Thank You for helping me bear my burdens, Jesus.*

## Band of Mercy

We don't want your kind here.

That was the examiner's message to Angieleca Hayahay, who was taking a test that would allow her to work at a call center in her homeland of the Philippines. What was the problem?

Hayahay was born with a cleft lip and palate, which she had surgically repaired as a child through the Philippine Band of Mercy program. Her facial deformity remained slightly noticeable, though, so she faced discrimination growing up—and now again as she neared adulthood. The call center had a policy which barred anyone with cleft from being hired.

Despite the roadblocks, Hayahay would not be denied a bright future. She became a registered nurse in 2009, and now works with Philippine Band of Mercy (which has become affiliated with the nonprofit Smile Train), offering hope and help to children suffering with cleft—and providing witness that life *can* get better.

**For we are what He has made us, created in Christ Jesus for good works, which God prepared beforehand to be our way of life. (Ephesians 2:10)**

*May I never reject anyone based on their appearance, Lord.*

## R-E-S-P-E-C-T

Respect is something we gain for ourselves the more we give it to other people. The word comes from the Latin root "respicere," which means "to look upon." And we define respect as "to consider worthy of esteem; to value."

If we look at others as persons created in God's holy image, we are more likely to treat them with the consideration to which all human beings have a right.

This, of course, is a tall order. It implies a refusal to lump people together in an unfavorable stereotype. It also requires that we make solid efforts to see through appearances to the real person beneath.

A resurgence of respect—both for ourselves and for other people—could work wonders in transforming many problems in our troubled world into opportunities. Take some time today to really look at each man, woman, and child you meet. See them as coming from the hand of God: honor them for what they are or can be. Respect their freedom as God respects yours.

**He endowed them with strength like His own, and made them in His own image. (Sirach 17:3)**

*Increase my sensitivity towards others, Creator.*

## Who Will be the First to Love?

As a member of the Focolare movement, which tries to create unity among people of different nations and religions, Lenny Szczesniak often put love into action. He did it in his work as an advertising executive at *Good Housekeeping* magazine—and also at home with his wife and nine children.

At Szczesniak's funeral, his children recalled what they learned from his approach to life. They said, "In our house, 'love' had nothing to do with fairy-tale princesses. Love was something you did. We fought and bickered like most siblings would, but our dad did not scold or punish us. Instead, he would challenge us: 'Who will be the first to love?' This tactic sometimes led to a battle of wills, but in the end we understood the message: in our house, loving one another was our primary responsibility. It came before anything else.

"In our father's life, it always did. As he would tell us, 'You don't have to like everyone, but you do have to love them.' This lesson, that love is an action, was one of Dad's greatest gifts to us."

**Steadfast love and faithfulness will meet. (Psalm 85:10)**

*Help me to love all people, Lord—even those I don't like.*

# Flood the Path with Light

All of us go through times of hardship and suffering, times when God is difficult to see. Even the saints endured those kinds of experiences. In response, St. Augustine composed a timeless prayer that can also help you find light in times of darkness.

He wrote, "God of our life, there are days when the burdens we carry chafe our shoulders and weigh us down; when the road seems dreary and endless, the skies gray and threatening; when our lives have no music in them, and our hearts are lonely, and our souls have lost their courage.

"Flood the path with light, run our eyes to where the skies are full of promise; tune our hearts to brave music; give us the sense of comradeship with heroes and saints of every age; and so quicken our spirits that we may be able to encourage the souls of all who journey with us on the road of life, to Your honor and glory."

**Let us not grow weary in doing what is right, for we will reap at harvest time, if we do not give up. (Galatians 6:9)**

*Give us the strength, wisdom and grace, Divine Comforter, to face life's challenges and remain focused on You.*

## The Lights of Nightfever

On All Saints Day 2013, volunteers stood outside New York City's St. Patrick's Cathedral holding unlit candles and asking passersby, "Would you like to light a candle in the cathedral?" Some 1,500 people took them up on their offer.

As reported by Juliann DosSantos in *Catholic New York,* the event, called Nightfever, originated in Germany. Mario Bruschi, director of St. Patrick's Cathedral's young adult group, said, "We are doing all this for that one soul to come back to God." Father Bob Bubel, the young adult group's spiritual director, added, "Everyone has a desire to worship God, to love God, but in most cases they don't know how or what to do. We provided them a way to satisfy that longing within their heart."

Eva Greitemann, a volunteer who traveled from Germany to Manhattan for Nightfever, wants to help others discover God's love. She notes that people left the cathedral looking more peaceful and happy than when they entered. "I know that it's not from a materialistic thing," she observed, "but because they have been in the divine presence of God."

**My soul is consumed with longing.**
**(Psalm 119:20)**

*May I seek You whenever I feel lost, Savior.*

## A Prayer for All Souls Day

Father Jonathan Morris of The Christophers shared the following All Souls Day prayer on his Facebook page:

"Lord God, You established creation and said, 'It is good.' And while we know death is a part of our reality and a part of our lives, we know that Christ has conquered death through His suffering, death and glorious resurrection.

"We pause this day to remember those who have passed on. Grant them, Lord, Your rest and Your presence. Please remember (name). May this person be counted as one of Your saints and be raised to a new life when Jesus comes again.

"We also remember those in mourning, especially those who have recently lost a friend, family member or loved one. Grant these Your peace and comfort that can only come from the loving and holy hand of Jesus.

"Finally, we pray that, at the hour of our own death, that You, Lord, will be with us and take us home to be with You, so that we may dwell in Your glory forever. Amen."

**I am the resurrection and the life. Those who believe in Me, even though they die, will live. (John 11:25)**

*May my loved ones rest in Your eternal peace, Merciful Savior.*

## The 99-Year-Old Altar Boy

You could say that Melvin Harris became an altar boy a little late in life. Actually, he was 97, which makes it a "lot late" in life. Still, it wasn't *too* late because he is now a vital part of three parish communities in the Columbus, Ohio area.

Harris was raised Baptist, but found himself impressed by the masses he saw when he worked his childhood job of delivering newspapers at St. Anthony Hospital. With the influence of a Catholic neighbor, he converted at age 12.

As reported by *The Columbus Dispatch,* Harris only became an altar server two years ago when his elderly sister couldn't handle it anymore. Father Joshua Wagner, pastor of three local parishes, relies on the 99-year-old to serve his weekday and weekend masses.

He said, "[Melvin] is one of the happiest people I have ever met. We've talked about some of the crises in his life, and I know it's his faith that has gotten him through."

Harris himself remains grounded in God's love. He said, "I believe if God made me, God has to love me because I'm part of His making."

**Gray hair is a crown of glory. (Proverbs 16:31)**

*May I take advantage of every opportunity to serve You, Father.*

## Oklahoma Justice — and Forgiveness

Jessica Eaves of Guthrie, Oklahoma, had noticed a man skulking behind her in the grocery store. When she discovered that her wallet was missing, she had a feeling that he was the perpetrator so she tracked him down in one of the aisles.

As reported by Yahoo.com, Eaves quietly confronted the robber and told him, "You can either give me my wallet and I'll forgive you right now, and I'll even take you to the front and pay for your groceries." Otherwise, she'd call the police.

The man returned her wallet and apologized numerous times, explaining, "I'm broke, I have kids, I'm embarrassed and I'm sorry." Eaves then paid $27 for his groceries.

Why did the Christian Outreach volunteer handle the situation the way she did? "Some people are critical because I didn't turn him in, but sometimes all you need is a second chance…My brother and I lost my dad to suicide when I was seven, and I remember him telling me years ago that no matter what I become in life, to always, always be kind."

**Let Your mercy come to me, that I may live; for Your law is my delight. (Psalm 119:77)**

*When I want revenge, Lord, fill me with mercy.*

## Choosing Your Coffee Cup

A group of successful alumni got together to visit one of their favorite university professors. Conversation soon turned into complaints about stress in work and life. Offering his guests coffee, the professor put out a large pot and an assortment of cups—some plain looking, some expensive. He told them to help themselves. When all the students had a cup of coffee in hand, the professor said:

"If you noticed, all the expensive cups were taken up, leaving behind the plain and cheap ones. While it's normal for you to want only the best for yourselves, that is the source of your problems and stress. Be assured that the cup itself adds no quality to the coffee. In most cases it is just more expensive."

The professor continued, "Now consider this: Life is the coffee; the jobs, money and position in society are the cups. They are just tools to hold and contain Life, and the type of cup we have doesn't define, nor change the quality of life we live. Sometimes, by concentrating only on the cup, we fail to enjoy the coffee God has provided us."

**Be content with what you have. (Hebrews 13:5)**

*Help me to look past life's superficial elements, Creator.*

## Change Begins with a Whisper

When 15-year-old Nathalie Traller discovered that only four cents of every dollar given to the National Cancer Institute goes to children's research, she felt "shocked and angry."

That shortcoming hit home because Traller herself is suffering from ASPS, a rare cancer that doesn't respond well to traditional treatments like chemotherapy and radiation. Now the teen is trying to change the medical and pharmaceutical systems to give kids like her the chance of a brighter future.

On her blog, she reveals that she's been denied use of a promising drug for her type of cancer because she's not within the age range for which the clinical trial is being run. "When it comes to children's lives," Traller writes, "I believe they should be allowed access to the few treatments available to them."

"We're fighting against a faulty system of clinical trials that needs to be rethought and adjusted," Traller concludes. And though she's just one small voice, she's determined to make a difference. "After all," she says, "change begins with a whisper."

**Rejoice in hope, be patient in suffering, persevere in prayer. (Romans 12:12)**

*Lord, guide us toward being agents of positive change.*

## Kelsey Grammer Forgives His Sister's Killer

Actor Kelsey Grammer is best-known for his comedic role as Frasier Crane on the TV series *Cheers* and *Frasier.* But the actor also has a troubled past including multiple marriages and drug abuse. In light of the tragedies in Grammer's life (the murder of his sister, the shooting death of his father), perhaps it's not surprising that he went off the rails at times. Yet a recent act of mercy displayed an enormous sense of character.

Via videoconference, the actor took part in a 2014 parole hearing for Freddie Glenn, who murdered Grammer's sister Karen in 1975. Glenn repeatedly expressed remorse for his crime—and it struck Grammer as genuine.

He told Glenn, "You could not have come to a better person in the world than me to advocate for someone who has made some bad choices. I accept your apology. I forgive you."

Though Grammer wouldn't support parole, he chose to free himself from the burden of anger and hatred—and to spiritually free Glenn from his own past.

**Then the Lord said, "I do forgive, just as you have asked." (Numbers 14:20)**

*No matter how justified our anger, grant us the courage and mercy to forgive our enemies, Redeemer.*

## Redemption Tale

Since 1998, Chris Vogt has been serving a 48-year prison sentence in Colorado's Sterling Correctional Facility for second-degree murder. He's been using that time to make some kind of cosmic amends by taking part in a program called Colorado Cell Dogs, which trains abandoned canines to work with the blind and deaf. Vogt's focus, however, is a little different.

As reported by *ABC News,* "Vogt read all he could about autism, and came up with unique training techniques for service dogs—aimed at helping autistic children overcome behavioral and emotional issues."

Zachary Tucker, age nine, used to have anxiety so bad that he often couldn't function and he refused to be touched. Desperate for help, the Tucker family started traveling 200 miles to work with Vogt and his new dog, Clyde.

Clyde learned to "nudge" Zachary whenever he sensed the boy's anxiety building, and so far the approach has worked wonders. It's worked wonders for Vogt as well. He says, "When Zach and the other kids work with me, they don't see the murderer. This has given me a chance to do something better."

**He sent redemption to His people. (Psalm 111:9)**

*Help those in prison pursue righteousness, Redeemer.*

## Career Advice: Be a People Person

Career expert Roberta Roesch suggests these pointers for developing a top job asset: consideration for others:

- **Go out of your way to do extra things for people.** Offer them a helping hand, even if you don't have to.

- **Be attentive to people both on the phone and in the office.** Listen to what they have to say.

- **Keep your cool instead of getting hot under the collar.** Let people explain actions that ordinarily make you bristle.

- **Show people you care what happens to them and to their families.** Offer support in every way possible.

Love for people is so basic that reminders would hardly seem necessary. Only, the theory doesn't fit the facts. From Moses through the prophets to Jesus, the same message keeps ringing out: Love your neighbor as yourself. One day, enough of us will try it. Wouldn't you like to be there when it happens?

> **The whole law is summed up in a single commandment, "You shall love your neighbor as yourself." (Galatians 5:14)**

> *Keep after us, Father, until we begin to act on the twofold commandment: love of You and of others.*

## Opening Your Heart to Adoption

Christina Beahan was born Maria Clara Mora in Medellin, Colombia, to a poor maid who was unable to raise her. As a result, her birth mother brought her to an orphanage run by nuns who cared for her for 14 months, until the Beahan family from Grand Rapids, Michigan, arranged to adopt her in 1983.

Knowing she was adopted never bothered Christina, who revealed on *Christopher Closeup* that she is grateful for the beautiful sacrifice her birth mother made in giving her the opportunity of life with a loving Catholic family.

Christina now gives talks on behalf of the Birthline Lifeline Ministry in the Diocese of Palm Beach, Florida, and advocates for adoption. Her message to anyone going through an unplanned pregnancy: "The child is a blessing, whether you planned it or not. It's either a blessing for you, or it's a blessing for somebody else. There's always somebody out there who is looking to adopt, that wants children to love. Open your heart up for this child or open your heart enough to give the baby up for adoption."

**Whoever welcomes one such child in My name welcomes Me. (Mark 9:37)**

*Help our culture be more open to adoption, Father.*

## Helping a Hero

While on patrol in Afghanistan searching for a terrorist bomb-making operation, Sgt. Drew Mullee saw the colored wires lying on the ground and knew an I.E.D. (Improvised Explosive Device) was nearby. Before he could find it with his metal detector, an explosion knocked him through the air, resulting in a traumatic brain injury, the loss of a leg, and other wounds.

Sgt. Mullee would have died if his determination to return to his wife Jennifer and their unborn child hadn't prompted him to call for a medic. During a painful and challenging year-and-a-half long rehabilitation at Walter Reed National Military Medical Center, Sgt. Mullee learned how to walk, eat, and simply live again. Happily, he also witnessed the birth of his son, Easton.

To help Sgt. Mullee and his family adjust to their new situation, The Patriot Charities and HelpingAHero.org joined forces to build them a home in Kannapolis, North Carolina, specially designed for wheelchair access and mobility. The Mullees received the keys to the house on June 5, 2014, and are profoundly grateful for the love and support they've been given.

**Many were wounded and fell. (1 Maccabees 9:40)**

*Bless and guide all wounded warriors, Prince of Peace.*

## Things My Parents Taught Me

Julie Drawdy Bulloch wrote the following reflection expressing gratitude to her parents: "These are a few things I am thankful for. Parents that taught me:

"...to say 'yes ma'am' and 'no ma'am' because it was expected; to say 'please' and 'thank you' because it was polite; to shake hands and make eye contact because it showed honesty; to give 110 percent and do it with a smile on your face because it showed character; to give the shirt off your back to someone in need because it showed grace; that giving my word was as good as a contract...and proved you could be trusted; that taking the garbage out, mowing the yard, and cleaning my room were chores done without an allowance because I had a roof over my head, food on the table and clothes on my back.

"I was taught that nothing in life was free, and anything worth having was worth working for. I am thankful for parents that loved the Lord and made sure I went to church. I hope and pray that when I reach my golden years, that I too can leave such a legacy."

**Train children in the right way. (Proverbs 22:6)**

*Father, bless all children with wise and loving parents.*

## Fear versus Love

All of us endure periods of worry and fear in our lives, times when we think we're not good enough or that failure is our destiny. We forget that God created us with a purpose and loves us.

On her Facebook page, singer-songwriter Sarah Hart shared the following reflection to remind us that we can choose love over fear:

"Fear says, 'You are typical.' Love says, 'You are extraordinary.'

"Fear says, 'You have nothing to offer.' Love says, 'You are creative beyond measure.'

"Fear says, 'You are less than everyone else.' Love says, 'You are more than you will ever know.'

"Fear says, 'Life will crush you.' Love says, 'I have conquered death.'

"Fear is a thief; love is a giver. May we live in love."

**God did not give us a spirit of cowardice, but rather a spirit of power and of love and of self-discipline. (2 Timothy 1:7)**

*Help me not to allow fear to overtake my life, Paraclete.*

## It Comes Down to Human Connections

As a nurse in the emergency department of New York-Presbyterian Hospital, 29-year-old Diana Costine is used to taking care of patients. But during filming of season two of the documentary TV series *NY Med*, she became a patient herself.

Costine had long endured issues caused by an irregular heartbeat, but the situation was worsening to the point that she was now passing out. Doctors recommended she have surgery to implant a pacemaker, and she reluctantly agreed.

The *NY Med* cameraman assigned to Costine had always been Isaac, so she felt comforted to have him shooting as she waited to enter the operating room. Fear got the better of her, though, and she started crying. That's when Isaac put the camera down and simply held Costine's hand to offer comfort.

Recalling that moment, Costine said, "It always comes down to human connections. We want people to be there with us, and know that we are heard, especially during times where we feel out of control or lost." Now healthy and fully recovered, she will always be grateful for Isaac's ministry of presence that day.

**He inclined His ear to me. (Psalm 116:2)**

*Lord, help me to comfort the fears of a troubled soul.*

## Love in Motion

Every Thursday during her lunch break, Kasonja Holley heads to the local Subway sandwich shop near her downtown Chicago office. But she's not getting lunch for herself. Instead, she's buying sandwiches to distribute to hungry and homeless people on the street.

Holley believes that God originally put the idea in her heart, though she was also influenced by her love of feeding people and her grandmother's work running a homeless shelter.

When Holley's co-workers found out what she was doing, they joined in and found the experience life-changing because of the way recipients would respond to these acts of kindness.

Holley grew her mission even more by putting together bags of toiletries to hand out as well. Today, her outreach has an official name—Love in Motion—and accepts donations from the public so more hungry people can be fed. She hopes the concept spreads around the country, and says, "I don't look for any reward. I just do it because it's a good thing to do."

**Contribute to the needs of the saints; extend hospitality to strangers. (Romans 12:13)**

*Holy Spirit, guide me in putting love into action.*

## The Baby Girl in the Rain

In 1955, 14-year-old Dave Hickman and his grandfather were hunting in the woods in Wayne County, Indiana, when the teen heard a strange cooing sound nearby. He went to investigate and found a cold, drenched-from-the-rain baby girl on the ground.

The abandoned child was taken in by the local government, given the name Roseann Wayne, and eventually placed for adoption. Before beginning life with her new family, however, two nurses brought her to Dave for one last goodbye.

Though Hickman went on to marry and start a family of his own, he never forgot Baby Roseann and yearned to reconnect with her. With the investigative skills of retired Wayne County Sheriff John Catey, that dream came true.

In December 2013, Hickman learned that Baby Roseann had become Mary Ellen Suey and now lived in California. She was thrilled to hear from the man who had given her a second chance at life. Though Suey called him a hero, Hickman denied it, saying, "I'm just very fortunate I was there. I found her because God allowed me to save her life."

**You will hear and save. (2 Chronicles 20:9)**

*Lead me, Lord, to those who need my help.*

# A Clutch Shooter Scores Big

In February 2014, 18-year-old Kevin Grow from Bensalem, Pennsylvania, became an Internet phenomenon when video of him scoring four three-pointers in the final two minutes of a high school basketball game went viral.

One month later, the sports-loving teen, who was born with Down syndrome, took his moment in the sun even farther when he was invited to play with the Harlem Globetrotters at the Wells Fargo Center in Philadelphia. The team and crowd welcomed Grow with shouts of support and plenty of applause.

In addition, the NBA's Philadelphia 76ers signed Grow to a two-day contract in recognition of his efforts, and even had him practice with the team. Grow became the only person, other than Wilt Chamberlain, to ever play for both the Globetrotters and the 76ers.

What does Grow's mother say about all this? "Kids with special needs have a lot of abilities that you don't even know. Don't undersell them. Challenge them. Make sure they can reach their full potential."

**God will accomplish something through you, and my Lord will not fail to achieve His purposes. (Judith 11:6)**

*Help me use my talents and fulfill my potential, Creator.*

## Harry Connick Jr. in Dad Mode

When 18-year-old contestant Emily Piriz sang a sexually suggestive song during the 2014 season of *American Idol*, judge Harry Connick Jr., who is the father of three daughters, kicked into dad mode. Prior to her performance, Piriz said she chose the song for its female empowerment feel, not because of the lyrics.

After she finished, Connick congratulated her on a good performance, then asked her to speak the song's first two lines because he wanted to verify that she understood their sexual message. He then said, "I know you said you're not interested in the storyline, but you're a singer. This is your choice now. Is that really what you want to be singing about?" Flustered, Piriz repeated that she liked the song's sense of female empowerment.

Some websites criticized Connick for "shaming" Piriz, but that's not what happened. He just challenged her to consider who she wants to be because he knows young people can get lost in the lure of money and fame. That's a testament to the fact that he cares about her. It's something any good dad would do.

**The tongue of the wise dispenses knowledge. (Proverbs 15:2)**

*Help me choose my words wisely, Heavenly Father.*

## The Baby on the Highway

Can a man who served 10 years in prison for manufacturing cocaine turn his life around and become a hero? Based on Bryant Collins' story, the answer is yes.

After getting out of prison five years ago, Collins gave up drugs and got a job as an auto repairman. On June 16, 2014, the Madison County, Georgia resident was driving on Highway 72 when he thought he saw a baby crawling on the side of the road. He stopped his car to check and, sure enough, it was a 15-month-old girl with a few bumps and bruises.

Collins called 911 and played the child gospel music on his cell phone to try and stop her crying. The police determined that the baby, who had been left unattended at her nearby home, crawled 300 yards through the woods, fell down an embankment, and wound up on the highway. The sheriff, who arrested the child's father, said it was "almost a miracle" she wasn't killed.

Collins felt grateful for the opportunity to save a life. He told *WXIA TV,* "It made me feel good, that I could be in society and do good."

**He shall save my people. (1 Samuel 9:16)**

*Save me from my sins so I can live a good life, Redeemer.*

## Thinking Creatively

Want to sharpen your ability to think creatively? Here's a four-point program designed to help:

- **Be receptive to new ideas.** Creative thinking requires an open mind, not one that freezes into a negative position when confronted by the unusual.

- **Keep your information reservoir full.** A creative mind never stops acquiring facts, figures, and opinions.

- **Train yourself to capture stray thoughts.** Too many people have good ideas, then forget them. Learn to jot down your ideas before they evaporate.

- **Think an idea through in concrete terms.** This involves self-discipline. It means working out the implementation of an idea step-by-step in your head, on paper, or on a computer screen.

Surrounded by a world full of question marks, each of us needs creativity. By toning up our intelligence, which is why God gave it to us, we can tackle some issues that need constructive action.

**The mind of one who has understanding seeks knowledge. (Proverbs 15:14)**

*Lead me towards both intellectual and spiritual wisdom, Divine Word.*

# Ten-Year-Old's Hunch Saves Senior's Life

It was a frigid January night in Howell, New Jersey, when ten-year-old Danny DiPietro and his father were driving home from a hockey game. As they passed a condominium with an open garage door, Danny thought he spotted a dog out of the corner of his eye. "It was late at night and super cold out and something just didn't feel right," he told *WXYZ 7 Action News*.

Even after he arrived home, Danny couldn't shake his uneasiness and asked his mother, Dawn, to go check on the dwelling, which wasn't far from their own.

When she arrived, Dawn saw, not a dog, but a person on the ground frantically waving for help. It was 80-year-old Kathleen St. Onge, who had fallen down nearly two hours earlier. Unable to get back up, she had just about abandoned any hope of rescue.

Thanks to Danny's uncanny instincts, St. Onge was soon transported to a hospital to receive the care she needed, and is expected to make a full recovery. Both St. Onge and her daughter, Sandy, call Danny their "hero."

**Do not be weary in doing what is right.
(2 Thessalonians 3:13)**

*Christ, may we never hesitate to help someone in need.*

## Time is Precious and Limited

When his high school friend Monique unexpectedly passed away from a rare immune disorder called HLH, Rocco Recce, age 18, felt devastated. The experience left him with an acute awareness of the fragility of life.

Recce wrote on Facebook, "In *Our Town* by Thornton Wilder, the main character, Emily, goes back in time after her own passing to relive one day in her life. That day was nothing special, but even still, she was heartbroken, because she realized how little she took the time to look at her family and friends before it was too late."

Recce concluded, "In this life, we often fail to realize that our time here is precious and limited. So, make the most of it. Once you've finished reading this, find the people that you love and just enjoy being in their presence. Look at them. Take in every detail of their appearance and their persona. Tell them how much you care about them. You never know when the time will come that this will no longer be possible to do."

**This slight momentary affliction is preparing us for an eternal weight of glory. (2 Corinthians 4:17)**

*Open my eyes to the extraordinary in the ordinary, Lord.*

## The Antidote to Anxiety

"The antidote to fear isn't courage. The antidote to worry isn't faith. The antidote to anxiety isn't a devil-may-care attitude. Rather, the antidote, I believe, is gratitude. It's thanksgiving."

That idea might seem to defy conventional wisdom, but Patheos blogger David R. Henson makes a compelling case.

He continues, "Something profound and transformative happens when we give thanks and live our lives in gratitude to God and to one another. And if we make a lifelong practice of it, it fundamentally shifts the way we view the world. Worry and anxiety are rooted in fear, scarcity and isolation. Gratitude is rooted in love, abundance and connection."

Henson then notes that the word Eucharist literally means "Thanksgiving," and "Thanksgiving is a sacrament, an outward sign of an inward grace. Each week there is a table set and a feast of love and thanksgiving which we share with each other... It is the ultimate reminder that we are not alone in this world or in our struggles. It is the ultimate reminder not to worry or to fear not. For God is with us—and with us through this community."

**Sing to the Lord with thanksgiving. (Psalm 147:7)**

*May I ground my life in gratitude, Divine Giver.*

## Grateful for a Smile

Nineteen-year-old Iraqi native Noor Khafaji was born with a facial deformity that kept one side of her face from developing correctly, thereby leaving her embarrassed and self-conscious. She said, "Always, I have been the girl who stays at home doing nothing."

That's all changing, however, thanks to the Little Baby Face Foundation, which offers free reconstructive surgeries to those who can't afford them.

The teen and her mother were flown to New York City where Dr. Thomas Romo—the director of Facial, Plastic, and Reconstructive Surgery at New York's Lenox Hill Hospital—will perform surgery free of charge. The *Daily News* reports, "The complex procedure will require rebuilding the teen's nose, ear, jawbone and cheekbone."

Noor is looking forward to her new life, while her mother, Shatha Hassan, expresses eternal gratitude. She said, "No one has ever cared like Dr. Romo. As long as I'm alive, I'm going to pray for him. I'm so thankful to him and to everyone who has helped us make [Noor] smile."

**I am grateful to God. (2 Timothy 1:3)**

*May I always show kindness to strangers, Father.*

# Thanksgiving Day Prayer

*The Catholic Times* of the Diocese of Columbus, Ohio, shared this heartfelt prayer of gratitude that you can say with your family and friends before eating Thanksgiving dinner:

"Father, all of Creation rightly owes You thanks and praise. Your justice, love and mercy abound. We thank You this day for all that You have given us. For the Passion and Death of Your Divine Son, we thank You, Father. Through the Cross, He redeemed the world.

"For loving spouses, we thank You, Father. Together we seek You. For the gift of children, we thank You, Father. They are Your precious gifts to us and to the world. For the gift of our families, loved ones, and good friends, we thank You, Father. Through them we see the reflection of Your Son.

"For jobs, our homes, and all that we have, we thank You, Father. Give us only that which we need, as we seek Your kingdom. For the bounty we are about to eat, we thank You through Christ our Lord. Amen."

**Every generous act of giving...is from above. (James 1:17)**

*Messiah, we always give You thanks for the miracle of life.*

# A Nation Says 'Thank You'

In 1789, President George Washington issued the first Thanksgiving Proclamation. Here are some excerpts:

"Now, therefore, I do recommend and assign Thursday, the 26th day of November next, to be devoted by the people of these States to the service of that great and glorious Being who is the beneficent author of all the good that was, that is, or that will be; that we may then all unite in rendering unto Him our sincere and humble thanks for His kind care and protection of the people of this country…"

"And also that we may then unite in most humbly offering our prayers and supplications to the great Lord and Ruler of Nations, and beseech Him to pardon our national and other trangressions; to enable us all, whether in public or private stations, to perform our several and relative duties properly and punctually…to promote the knowledge and practice of true religion and virtue, and the increase of science among them and us; and, generally, to grant unto all mankind such a degree of temporal prosperity as He alone knows to be best."

**I will magnify Him with thanksgiving.
(Psalm 69:30)**

*Today I ask for nothing, Lord. I simply say, "Thank You."*

## A Black Friday Challenge

When Brian Bagnall of Franklin Park, Illinois, saw the mobs of people on TV pushing and shoving each other to get bargains on Black Friday, he decided that he wanted to "encourage some human kindness." Though he had planned on selling everything in his house before moving to a new furnished home in Virginia, he decided to give it all away for free instead.

Bagnall posted his initiative on Craigslist and noted some ground rules, which included no pushing, shoving, or acting rude. As reported by *NBC Chicago*, approximately 200 people showed up and calmly cleaned out his three-bedroom home of everything from couches and tools to ladders and shelves.

After it was all over, Bagnall observed, "There were a lot of smiles today. People need happiness more than ever right now and Black Friday shows it."

This year, try to avoid getting too wrapped up in the materialistic aspect of the holiday season. Instead, pursue the type of happiness that money can't buy.

**Strive first for the kingdom of God.
(Matthew 6:33)**

*As I buy gifts for my family and friends this year, Lord, remind me to respect the dignity of all Your children.*

## The Condition of our Hearts

"Fear and faith have one thing in common: they both ask you to believe in something that hasn't happened yet." Singer-songwriter Danny Gokey lived those words after his wife Sophia died due to a congenital heart defect during their fourth year of marriage. Though raised in a Christian church, Gokey couldn't move beyond his bitterness at God for allowing this to happen.

Eventually, Gokey realized that he had to make a choice: anger or hope. Hope, he realized, was an act of the will, not an emotion. During a *Christopher Closeup* interview, he said:

"The toxic emotions—the injustice, the bitterness, the questions of, 'Why? I don't understand, it's not fair!'—those emotions just drained once that plug was pulled out. I started realizing how the condition of our hearts affects the way we see. If your heart is full of bitterness, anger and resentment, you're going to look at this world as a very evil place. That's exactly what I was doing. Once I let that go, I found this beautiful place. The sky was bluer, the grass was greener. I don't know how to explain it. It's powerful to have a pure heart."

**Put away from you all bitterness.
(Ephesians 4:31)**

*When my world is dark, Lord, help me to choose the splendor of Your light.*

## The Currency of Heaven

Former *American Idol* contestant Danny Gokey wanted to memorialize his late wife Sophia in a meaningful way. After receiving a $39,000 death benefit from her insurance plan, he founded a nonprofit called Sophia's Heart to help homeless families in Nashville create better futures for themselves.

It was a pure-hearted intention that drew others to help him as well. Gokey said, "When I put my brokenness in the hands of the Creator, He made something out of it. In 2010, a man came up to me and gave me a 77,000-square-foot facility for free. It was worth several million dollars. We take in homeless families now. We don't just provide food, clothing and shelter. We create programs that help them design their future."

Gokey also shares with them the lesson he learned himself: "Most of our struggles come from thinking, 'God doesn't like me, He wants to see me suffer.' If that's our mentality, we open the door to a lot of negative things. But when you understand that God wants the best for you, you start utilizing faith—and faith is the currency that heaven responds to."

**The faithful will abide with Him in love. (Wisdom 3:9)**

*Holy Spirit, diminish my doubts and increase my faith.*

## Denzel Washington Reminds You to Pray

"I pray that you all put your shoes way under the bed at night so that you gotta get on your knees in the morning to find them. And while you're down there, thank God for grace and mercy and understanding."

That was a piece of advice Denzel Washington gave in a speech to young actors getting started in show business. He encouraged them to build the foundation of their lives on faith.

The Academy Award winner revealed that the cast of the Broadway show in which he was appearing at the time, *A Raisin in the Sun*, gathers for prayer before each performance. Led by child actor Bryce Clyde Jenkins, they pray that they're able to touch someone in the audience that night.

Washington also acknowledged the need to share your financial blessings with others. No matter how much money anyone makes, he noted, "you'll never see a U-Haul behind a hearse...I can't take it with me and neither can you. It's not how much you have, but what you do with what you have."

**Give thanks in all circumstances; for this is the will of God in Christ Jesus for you.**
**(1 Thessalonians 5:18)**

*Lord, I pray that those in show business find their way to You.*

## The Path to Grumpiness

"You don't just get grumpy. You've got to work at it. It takes time. Like making a fine wine."

That line from actor Bruce Dern playing a gruff-but-lovable grandfather in the film *Pete's Christmas* is meant to elicit a laugh. But there's truth inside the humor.

Dern's character had a negative attitude for so long that he wound up alienating his son. Now that he's older, he wants to restore the relationship, but finds it difficult to admit that his bitterness over life's hardships has pushed his son away.

We too can drive a wedge between ourselves and other people when we allow bitterness and self-pity to rule our minds and hearts. At first, these emotions may seem like an understandable reaction to a bad situation, but if we allow them to fester, they can develop into our dominant personality trait.

The Christmas season is the perfect time to welcome light back into our lives: the light of Jesus Christ, who brings faith, hope, and love. Make the choice to open your heart to Him and leave your past "grumpiness" behind.

**Give light to my eyes. (Psalm 13:3)**

*When negativity overpowers me, send me Your light, Lord.*

## Back to School

For Tom Brady and Shannon Coughlin, Room 301 in their old high school not only represents the past, but the beginning of their future.

As reported by the *Rhode Island Catholic,* Brady and Coughlin met as freshmen in Providence, Rhode Island's LaSalle Academy. They began dating their junior year, and their relationship even endured being apart during their college years.

Though they both currently live in California—Brady works as a television writer, while Coughlin is working on her doctorate in physical therapy—they returned home for Christmas 2013. That's when Brady surprised Coughlin by proposing to her in LaSalle's Room 301, site of their first class together.

Coughlin highlighted the role of God in their relationship. She said, "Faith is so important, especially during the time we were apart for college. Our faith made us stronger because we had to trust each other and trust that God had a plan for our relationship. It got us through it."

**None of those who put their trust in Him will lack strength. (1 Maccabees 2:61)**

*Increase my trust in You during times of struggle, Lord.*

## The Family That Eats Together

Chef John Besh's culinary interests began as a nine-year-old after a drunk driver paralyzed his fighter-pilot father. Besh wasn't prepared for his new cooking responsibilities, notes Peter Finney in *St. Anthony Messenger,* but he soon learned how "just throwing things together for (Dad) would make him so happy. I connected right then that food equals happiness."

Today a successful restaurateur at age 45, Besh faced early professional challenges, but was always buoyed by his parents' courageous example and his Catholic faith.

Both those inspirations were necessary when Hurricane Katrina dealt a blow to the Louisiana native's first restaurant and made him re-evaluate life goals. He decided that even if his business was to be lost, he would still use his talents "to make a better world"—by establishing soup kitchens, for instance.

To this day, the restaurateur relishes family meals and models positive values for his children. He says, "The family table in the home is the altar. That's the place that ties us together."

**Whether you eat or drink...do everything for the glory of God. (1 Corinthians 10:31)**

*Dear God, may families create stronger bonds by sharing meals together.*

## Family Stories Unite Generations

Do your kids know significant family facts and events? You might fortify them and future generations by sharing stories both contemporary and ancestral.

"If you want a happier family," writes Bruce Feiler in the *New York Times*, "create, refine, and retell your family's best moments and your relations' ability to bounce back from the difficult ones."

Some research indicates that children become more resilient and self-confident if they grow up hearing narratives about earlier generations.

Emory University's Marshall Duke and Robyn Fivush created a "Do You Know?" testing scale. When youngsters knew, for instance, where their grandparents grew up or how older generations dealt with a tragedy, they had a "stronger sense of control over their lives."

The academics said the most self-confident kids have "a strong intergenerational self. They know they belong to something bigger than themselves."

**Remember His covenant forever...for a thousand generations. (1 Chronicles 16:15)**

*Lord, may we value the lives of our ancestors.*

## Creating Calm Amid Christmas Chaos

Although Christmas is supposed to be a time of joy and reflection on God's love for us, we often find ourselves getting overly stressed. Writer Mary DeTurris Poust offers five ways to relax during the holidays in her book *Everyday Divine: A Catholic Guide to Active Spirituality:*

- **Stop multitasking now.** Doing too many things at once can diminish the beauty of the simple pleasures of life

- **Seek silence daily.** In today's technology-filled world, make room for moments of complete solitude, for it is often in silence that God speaks to us most clearly.

- **Find the divine in the mundane.** Strive to make even the most tedious chore an act of prayer.

- **Create everyday rituals.** Catholic Church services are steeped in ritual. May we instill similar religious practices into our own day-to-day routines.

- **Practice daily self-examination.** At the end of the day, take stock of all of your thoughts and actions, the good and the bad, and look for ways to improve yourself.

**Cast all your anxiety on Him, because He cares for you. (1 Peter 5:7)**

*Messiah, may we seek the gift of Your divine peace.*

## The Modern Heir to St. Nicholas

Father Joseph Marquis comes at his job as a priest with a thorough knowledge of Christmas, which isn't all that surprising. But he has an equally thorough knowledge of Santa Claus too, learned first-hand. He's been a department-store Santa and collected awards for the way he played the role. He didn't stop there. He appeared in parades as Santa, wrote a book about him, and even made the Santa Claus Hall of Fame.

Father Marquis, then a layman, became a hospital chaplain and grew more interested in the church. After studies he was ordained a priest and today, at 63, is pastor of Sacred Heart Byzantine Catholic Church in Livonia, Michigan.

His interest in Santa is as strong as ever, and two years ago he began an institute that provided professional Santa Claus training—using the example about "the real Santa Claus," St. Nicholas of Myra. He tells his students of how St. Nicholas left a legacy of love, and emphasizes the importance of this ministry to children.

"They get all choked up," he said. "It's funny how St. Nicholas can read into the hearts of people."

**Let the little children come to Me.
(Matthew 19:14)**

*Instill me with St. Nicholas's generous spirit, Savior.*

## Why Pray Daily?

Isaac Bashevis Singer, the storyteller whose tales of Polish ghettos and immigrant Jews in America charmed readers for several generations, once explained his belief in the importance of prayer.

He said, "Whenever I'm in trouble, I pray. And since I'm always in trouble, there is not a day when I don't pray. The belief that man can do what he wants, without God, is as far from me as the North Pole."

Frequent prayer is to be recommended—and not only when we're in trouble. We have to keep our priorities in order, to remind ourselves that life is bigger than we are—and to gain a better grasp of our mission in life. We need to ask for what we need for ourselves and others, to adore the Absolute, to be thankful for our blessings, and to say we're sorry.

After all, with a support system as strong as God, why *wouldn't* we call on Him as much as possible?

**Confess your sins to one another, and pray for one another, so that you may be healed. (James 5:16)**

*May my prayers lead me closer to You, O Lord.*

## Full of Grace

Theologian Dr. Edward Sri knows we're all familiar with the Christmas story, but he also thinks we can be so familiar with it that we miss a lot of its important points. That's why he wrote a book called *The Advent of Christ*.

During a *Christopher Closeup* interview, he reflected on the words "full of grace," which the angel Gabriel uses to greet Mary. Dr. Sri explained, "The word in Greek for 'full of grace' describes an action that began in the past and continues to have its effects in the present. It describes the life of God, the work of redemption, and forgiveness of sins. It's as if the angel is saying, 'You who have been and continue to be graced.'"

Dr. Sri continued, "I certainly think it points to the doctrine of Mary's Immaculate Conception because the angel doesn't say, 'Hail, you who are going to be graced when you conceive this child'—or 'Hail, you who have grace right now in my presence.' The angel is pointing out that Mary already has the life of grace in her, before Gabriel ever came to her."

More about what we can learn from Mary tomorrow.

**You have found favor with God. (Luke 1:30)**

*Send me Your grace to guide me, Lord Jesus.*

## Lord, What Are You Teaching Me?

In the New Testament, Mary faces many challenging circumstances, from conceiving a child by the Holy Spirit, to giving birth in poor conditions, to hearing Simeon say that a sword will pierce her soul. How does she handle these situations? Luke 2:19 states, "Mary kept all these things and pondered them in her heart."

Dr. Edward Sri suggests that Mary's response should teach us something. He says, "She's turning inward and prayerfully reflecting, 'Lord, what are You trying to teach me?' That's a great model for us because when life takes an unexpected turn, we often panic or get discouraged or complain. But we want to be like Mary, prayerfully turning to the Lord and saying, 'Lord, what are You trying to show me? This is hard, but I believe there's some good You can bring out of this for me.'"

Dr. Sri concludes, "Mary trusts that God's hand is in this. She may not fully understand what's happening, but she surrenders to the mystery—and that's what we need to do."

**Here am I, the servant of the Lord; let it be with me according to Your word. (Luke 1:38)**

*Guide me with Your grace, O Lord, to be more like Mary.*

## Diamond in the Rough

Kansas City homeless man Billy Ray Harris usually gets spare change and dollar bills in his donation cup, but 2013 marked the first time he ever found an engagement ring there.

Sarah Darling had taken off both her wedding and engagement rings because they were "bothering her" and placed them into her purse. When she grabbed some coins from her purse to give to Harris, the engagement ring accidentally fell into his paper cup as well. Harris briefly debated selling the ring, but ultimately decided to keep it safe until Darling returned to claim it, which she did, three days later.

In honor of Harris's honesty, Sarah and her husband, Bill Krejc, created a fundraising website page on GiveForward.com to help him out. To date, monetary contributions for Harris total over $190,000. These donations have enabled him to purchase his own car, as well as put a down payment on a house. He has also since reunited with long-lost family members whom he hadn't seen in 20 years. "It just makes you realize, there are good people out there," Sarah Darling told *KCTV*.

**You see that a person is justified by works. (James 2:24)**

*Jesus, may I try to do good without thought of repayment.*

## The Worrier Warrior

In life, we often allow our worries to fill our hearts, leaving no room for God. Former hypochondriac Gary Zimak knows this from experience. For over 30 years, he gave himself over to his anxiety, seeking no refuge in his Christian faith.

Only by consciously choosing to turn his fears over to Jesus was Zimak able to take the first steps towards becoming the "Worrier Warrior" he is known as today. Now a traveling Catholic evangelist and author of the aptly named *Worrier's Guide to the Bible,* Zimak presents his audiences with five ways to fight worry:

- **Prepare.** Do as much as you can, physically and mentally, to lessen the stresses in your life.
- **Present.** Worry is in the future, peace is in the now.
- **Pray.** Do not hesitate to ask for divine help.
- **Participate.** Be active in your faith.
- **Prize.** Remember that eternal, not earthly glory is your ultimate goal above all else.

**The peace of God will guard your hearts. (Philippians 4:7)**

*Master, release us from the weight of our many anxieties.*

## The Blessing of Carols

Robyn Lee, the Managing Editor of CatholicMatch.com, cites caroling with her family in their Connecticut neighborhood as one of her favorite Christmas traditions. "Most people," she writes, "are happy for the visit and offer us...chocolate, warm cookies and even an invitation to sit in front of a blazing fire."

One visit in particular stands out in Lee's mind. A young woman came to the door, visibly upset while talking on the phone. Lee recalls, "We sang 'Hark, the Herald Angels Sing.' She didn't hang up the phone, but gazed at us. I remember trying to smile my brightest, as I saw tears streaking her face. When we finished singing, she asked, 'What charity are you from?' We told her that we aren't raising money, but just family and friends out caroling together. Tears filled her eyes again as she thanked us: 'You don't know what this means to me.'"

Lee felt grateful to be a messenger of joy that Christmas. She hopes that as she continues her caroling tradition, it will "bring a glimmer of peace and joy" to others in need of God's love and beauty.

**Awake, awake, utter a song! (Judges 5:12)**

*Jesus, help me bring Your joy to others this Christmas.*

## Love, Hope and Forgiveness

There is an iconic picture from the Vietnam War taken by *Associated Press* photographer Nick Ut in 1972. It depicts three screaming children running from their bombed village. The young girl in the center is emaciated and naked, her clothes scorched off from napalm, a substance used in bombs.

That nine-year-old girl, now a woman, Kim Phuc Phan Thi, has survived to tell her harrowing tale of love, hope and above all, forgiveness. Only after Thi forgave the attackers of her village was she able to move above and beyond her pain. She even befriended U.S. Army Capt. John Plummer, who helped plan the bombing of her village—much to his deep regret, especially as their intended target was an enemy bunker.

Today, Thi is head of the Kim International Foundation, a nonprofit that provides medical care for child victims of war. She lives in Canada with her family, but travels throughout the U.S., spreading her message of reconciliation. "I came from war, and now I value peace," Thi told *The Tablet* writer Nichole Golden. "I am blessed to be here."

**Blessed are the merciful. (Matthew 5:7)**

*God, teach us to forgive our enemies.*

# A Christmas Prayer for the Grieving

Father Austin Fleming, the pastor of Holy Family parish in Concord, Massachusetts, wrote a prayer for those who are grieving the loss of a loved one at Christmas. Here is an excerpt:

"Dear God, There is an empty chair near the tree, an ache in our hearts and tears on our faces. We may try to shield one another from the grief we bear but we cannot hide it from You.

"We pray for (name) whose presence we miss so much in these days of peace and joy. Open our hearts and minds to the healing...light of Your presence. We pray, Lord, and we trust that those we miss have found the place You prepared for them, their home within Your heart. Open our hearts, Lord, to joyful memories of love shared with those who have gone before us.

"Teach us to lean on You, Lord, and on each other, for the strength we need to walk through these difficult days...Help us to trust that one day we shall be with those we love when Your mercy gathers us together in the joy of the life You promise us. This is the Christmas You have made, Lord: help us to rejoice in it and in the blessings of Your peace. Amen."

**May their memory be blessed. (Sirach 46:11)**

*Replace heavy hearts with joyful memories, Divine Savior.*

## Ten Ways to be a Christopher

Many years ago, Maryknoll Father James Keller, founder of The Christophers, wrote out 10 reminders that he hoped fellow Christophers would always remember. They're simple but effective points, written in such a way that all people can use them as a guide to fulfill their God-given mission in life. Here they are:

1. Depend more on God, less on self. 2. Share the truth, don't hoard it. 3. Be world-minded, not just local-minded.

4. Go among people, don't avoid them. 5. Be a doer, not just a talker. 6. Offer ideas, don't impose them. 7. Aim to serve, not to be served.

8. Inspire confidence, don't dishearten. 9. Disagree without being disagreeable. 10. Keep first things first.

Simple as these concepts are, they can be profound in the way they help shape the world for the better. And they're just as valid today as they were when Father Keller first set them down!

**They are to do good, to be rich in good works, generous, and ready to share. (1 Timothy 6:18)**

*Holy Spirit, encourage and guide us to walk in the ways the Lord has prepared for us.*

## Papal Problem Solver

Leave it to Pope Francis—he certainly has a knack for saying the right thing. Take the simple issue of problem-solving, for example. He was speaking specifically about problems within the church, but his words apply to conflicts of any sort.

"Problems cannot be resolved," the pope says, "by pretending they don't exist." His suggestion: "Confronting one another, discussing and praying" about it. If a solution exists, he continues, that's the best way to find it.

The pope recently addressed a group of pilgrims in Rome about the day's readings, which described rising tensions among early Christians. By facing these problems head-on, as well as talking and praying about them, they were able to eventually reach a consensus.

In the church or outside it, big problems or small, that sounds like good solid advice. Try following it the next time a problem arises at work or within the family—and if anyone asks you about it, just say that the idea comes from the pope himself.

**Live in harmony with one another.
(Romans 12:16)**

*Christ, may we seek to promote peace rather than incite disputes.*

## A Faithful Shepherd

Maria Margherita Lochi of San Donaci, Italy, welcomed several stray dogs into her home over the years, but Ciccio was her favorite. The German shepherd even accompanied her to Mass every day at Santa Maria Assunta Church.

When Lochi died in November 2012, the devoted Ciccio followed her coffin into the church. According to the British newspapers *The Telegraph* and the *Daily Mail,* his devotion is expressed in another way too: when the church bells ring each afternoon, Ciccio attends Mass just like he did when his owner was alive. Father Donato Panna said, "He's very well behaved. He doesn't make a sound."

Ciccio's faithfulness has tugged at the heartstrings of villagers who give him food and water, and let him make his home "in a covered area outside the church." Father Panna hopes to find Ciccio a permanent home and owner.

Faithfulness is an admirable quality. May we be as devoted to our heavenly Father as Ciccio is to his owner.

**He exhorted them all to remain faithful to the Lord with steadfast devotion. (Acts 11:23)**

*Creator, guide us toward seeking You always.*

## Jobs for People with Autism

"How in the world is Matt going to support himself when he's finished high school?" Chicago businessman David Friedman wondered about his son with autism. Studies show that 90 percent of young adults with the disorder can't get jobs.

With a background in advertising and marketing, Friedman started thinking of business ideas that would accommodate people like his son. While working at Sears Holding, which produces 90 million advertising circulars a year, he realized that many factory workers found their work repetitive and boring. Writing in *Ad Age,* Friedman observed, "Yet, to any number of people with autism spectrum disorder, the order and consistency of doing tasks requiring laser focus on the tiniest of details over and over again is not tedium but comfort."

As a result, Friedman created AutonomyWorks, which offers marketing agencies a pool of workers to perform "highly-detailed, repetitive, technology-based process tasks." The innovative firm currently employs 11 people with disabilities, and hopes to expand so that other parents can feel secure knowing their special children will be able to earn a living.

**He has filled them with skill. (Exodus 35:35)**

*Help me solve problems through innovation, Creator.*

## Holiday Eve?

Nick and Rose are an elderly couple featured in Rick Detorie's comic strip *One Big Happy*—and in 2013, they lightheartedly addressed the topic of keeping Christ in Christmas.

Nick and Rose run into their friend Blanche while they're out for a walk. She hands them an invitation to her "holiday" party, which she's holding on December 24th, "holiday eve." Rose responds, "You mean Christmas Eve, Blanche."

"I know," says Blanche, "but these days everyone's so sensitive about the 'C' word."

Rose explains, "It's the name of the holiday, as in Holy Day. It's Christmas. Blanche, you named your son Christopher. Do you go around calling him Holidaypher so as not to offend anyone? I doubt it."

Blanche gets the point and invites Nick and Rose to her "Christmas" party. They happily accept. After Blanche walks away, Nick smiles and comments, "My wife, the Christmas activist."

To which Rose responds, "And proud of it, baby!"

**Thanks be to God through Jesus Christ. (Romans 7:25)**

*I honor Your name, Jesus, and I praise You.*

## Imagine That God is Speaking to You

An anonymous author once penned these words imagining God's personal advice to each of us:

"You do not have to be clever to please Me; all you have to do is desire My love. Talk to Me as you would a dear friend.

"Are you afraid of anything? Trust your fears to Me. I will not leave you. Tell Me the things you feel guilty about and I will forgive you. Do not be ashamed of your past, there are many saints in heaven who had the same faults as you. They prayed and, gradually, their faults were corrected.

"Has anyone caused you pain? Tell Me about it, and if you add that you will forgive them, I will send a special gift of healing.

"Never hesitate to ask for blessings for your body and mind; for health and success. I can give everything you need. Remember to tell Me of your love and gratitude. Go along now with work or play. Come back soon and bring Me a devoted heart. Tomorrow I shall have more blessings for you."

**He whom God has sent speaks the words of God, for He gives the Spirit without measure. (John 3:34)**

*Lord, teach me to pray with reverence and love.*

# Full House Star Lives Christmas Spirit

Actress Candace Cameron Bure, who grew up on television playing D.J. Tanner on the sitcom *Full House,* knows first-hand that you can create a Christ-centered Christmas for kids, while still enjoying Santa Claus and the commercial aspects of the holiday. She learned to integrate the two while growing up, and now does the same with her own three children.

During an interview on *Christopher Closeup,* Bure explained that her kids understand that Jesus is the greatest gift we can receive. Therefore, she and her family live out their Christmas spirit by helping the less fortunate.

The *Dancing with the Stars* finalist said, "We wake up at about 5 a.m. on Christmas morning and, with some other family members and friends, we go to a local shelter that has about 40 or 50 people staying there. We bring breakfast, cook it there for them, and then we sit down and eat. We share stories and listen to them and encourage them. For us it's about giving back first, and then coming home and having the traditional Christmas dinner with all of our relatives."

**I was hungry and you gave Me food. (Matthew 25:35)**

*Nourish the bodies and souls of the hungry, Jesus.*

## A Christmas Lesson from Penn Station

Christmas 2013 prompted Elizabeth Scalia to reflect on the holiday through the lens of her son's encounter with a homeless woman at New York's Penn Station. Writing on the *National Review* website, Scalia said:

"[The woman] said she was hungry and wondered if he might spare some change. Instead, he walked with her to a food stand and bought her a hamburger and fries and a drink. As she ate, he sat with her, and they chatted pleasantly. When I asked him why he didn't simply hand her a few dollars and keep walking, which is what I would have done, he said that would have seemed 'dismissive'—that the woman was as deserving as anyone else of being seen, and heard, and known."

"In the noise of the world and our harried distractions and self-absorption, we lose track of the mystery and message of Christmas: that we are meant to be an Incarnational people, a people of intention, consenting to be aware of each other, fully present to each other, alive to each other, affirming each other, for God's sake."

**Love your neighbor as yourself. (Matthew 19:19)**

*Remind me that Your light shines inside everyone, Lord.*

## Every Child Has Greatness

If Julie and Rusty Bulloch were innkeepers in Bethlehem 2,000 years ago, they would have found an indoor room for Mary and Joseph, and maybe even redecorated it to make it more homey. That life-affirming spirit was evident in season two of their *UP TV* reality show *Bulloch Family Ranch*, during which they invited an unwed pregnant mother named Ciara to live with them so she has the support she needs during her difficult time.

The Bullochs, who have been taking in troubled teens and young adults for the last 15 years, had befriended Ciara years ago when she was the girlfriend of one of their "ranch kids," as they call them. When Ciara revealed that she decided to move forward with the pregnancy, Julie applauded her decision.

This isn't a sentiment that's always aired so publicly, but Julie explained during a *Christopher Closeup* interview, "There are circumstances where the conception of the child may have been a mistake or not planned. It still happened. But I believe that every child that is born is a gift. Every child has greatness, and it's up to us to nurture that and bring that greatness out."

**They are ever giving liberally. (Psalm 37:26)**

*Bless and guide mothers through crisis pregnancies, Lord.*

## When the Spirit of Christmas Prevailed

It involved only one house and a few soldiers, but there was a Christmas truce in 1944, at the height of World War II.

*The Week* magazine told the little-known story, which began when a German woman named Elisabeth Vincken opened the door of her cabin on the Belgian-German border to find three lost American soldiers. Moved with pity, she invited them in to join her in a Christmas dinner. Soon after, four German soldiers knocked on the same door. Aware of the severe penalty for harboring the enemy, she took a deep breath and told them that three Americans were inside. She invited the Germans to join them, but then laid down the law: "It is the Holy Night and there will be no shooting here."

The atmosphere was tense at first, but gradually, aided by dinner and wine, tensions eased, and before everyone left a German soldier gave the GIs directions back to their lines. Soon all involved were fighting again, and it would be another several months before a permanent peace took hold. But in that one cabin, for a few hours, the Spirit of Christmas prevailed.

**I will grant peace in the land. (Leviticus 26:6)**

*May we honor Your Son's birth with peace, Father.*

## Peace on Earth

The inspirational newsletter *Apple Seeds* reprinted the following prayer, written by Saint John XXIII in his encyclical letter *Pacem in Terris,* which means "Peace on Earth:"

"May [Jesus] banish from the hearts of all men and women whatever might endanger peace. May He transform them into witnesses of truth, justice and love.

"May He enkindle the rulers of peoples so that in addition to their solicitude for the proper welfare of their citizens, they may guarantee and defend the great gift of peace.

"May He enkindle the wills of all so that they may overcome the barriers that divide, cherish the bonds of mutual charity, understand others, and pardon those who have done them wrong.

"May all peoples of the earth become as brothers and sisters, and may the most longed-for peace blossom forth and reign always among men and women."

**Let me hear what God the Lord will speak, for He will speak peace to His people, to His faithful, to those who turn to Him in their hearts. (Psalm 85:8)**

*May peace in our hearts lead to peace in the world, Jesus.*

## What Awaits You in the New Year?

The start of any new year is a great time for making predictions, and here's a list of a few that are bound to come true. This came our way via the Internet, and we thought enough of it to pass it along to our readers.

- The Bible will still have all the answers.
- Prayer will still be the most powerful thing on earth.
- God will still pour out blessings upon His people.
- Jesus will still save the lost when they come to Him.
- Jesus will still love you.

The listing concludes with these words:

Isn't it great to remember who is really in control? Remember also that "the Word of the Lord endures forever."

**Do not work for the food that perishes, but for the food that endures for eternal life, which the Son of Man will give you. For it is on Him that God the Father has set His seal. (John 6:27)**

*As we move into a new year, Father, help me to move beyond needless worry and instead rest secure in the knowledge of Your love.*

## Too Many Choices

In today's world, we're faced with a wide array of choices when it comes to what products to buy, what websites to visit, or how to spend our free time. But an overabundance of choices can actually be a bad thing because it results in what entrepreneur James Clear calls "decision fatigue."

"Making decisions over and over again will drain your willpower," writes Clear, thereby making it hard to maintain good habits. "When we place a constraint on ourselves, it can become much easier to get something done. This is especially true if it is a constraint that forces us to start small."

If you want to start exercising, for instance, Clear recommends limiting yourself to five minutes a day initially because it's a small enough amount of time that you'll stick with it. You can always increase slowly after several weeks.

Clear concludes, "We often think that we want an open road and the ability to choose any direction for ourselves. But sometimes, what we need is a tunnel that can reduce our choices and send us in a focused direction."

**Choose this day whom you will serve. (Joshua 24:15)**

*Holy Spirit, guide me in making wise choices.*

## Diapers and Good Deeds

Katie Kanefke went to her local Walmart in Sioux Falls, South Dakota, because she needed to buy four large boxes of diapers for her son Marcus. They were more expensive than she had expected, so she asked the cashier if they would match the lower price of the diapers at a different store. When Walmart would only price match one box, Kanefke prepared to return the other boxes...until a stranger, Carol Flynn, got involved.

Flynn told Kanefke that she would pay for the extra diapers. All she asked in return was that Kanefke perform a random act of kindness for somebody else someday. The grateful mom happily agreed.

Unbeknownst to both women, another shopper, Jason Yoshino, saw the whole exchange and recorded it with his phone. After posting the video on Facebook, it gained national media attention. Kanefke told local TV station *KSFY,* "If you ever needed a sign that God's there for you in the hardships and the struggles, this is it. It's pretty awesome."

**You will be enriched...for your great generosity, which will produce thanksgiving to God. (2 Corinthians 9:11)**

*Increase my willingness to show kindness to others, Savior.*

## Distressed? You Can Still Help Others

When you're feeling overwhelmed by problems, you might conclude you have nothing to offer since your energy and emotional strength are limited. But facing struggles adds to your humanity and need not stop you from sharing another's burdens.

When you've known pain, your insight can help you to become more selfless and better able to rally to the aid of someone with troubles worse than your own.

"We may be sitting alone, lost in self-doubt or self-pity when the phone rings with a call from a friend who's *really* depressed. Instinctively, we come out of ourselves, just to be there with her and say a few reassuring words," write Ram Dass and Paul Gorman in *How Can I Help?*

"When we're done, and a little comfort's been shared, we put down the phone and feel a little more at home with ourselves. We're reminded of who we really are and what we have to offer one another."

**Let each of you look not to your own interests, but to the interests of others. (Philippians 2:4)**

*Holy Spirit, inspire us to be generous even if we feel we have nothing more to give.*

## The Origins of a Bottle of Bubbly

If you plan on buying champagne for New Year's Eve, you know you've got Benedictine monks to thank for it, right?

As Frank Weathers documented on his Patheos blog, the first ever sparkling wine, called Blanquette de Limoux, was invented by Benedictine monks in France's Abbey of Saint Hilaire in 1531. According to Wikipedia, "They achieved this by bottling the wine before the initial fermentation had ended."

They're not the ones who perfected the process, however. That honor goes to a different Benedictine monk: Dom Pierre Pérignon. He spent 47 years at the Abbey of Saint Pierre d'Hautvillers, near the Champagne region of France, working to get the creation of sparkling wine just right. He achieved his goal in 1670, and his legacy lives on today.

Whenever you pop the cork on a bottle of bubbly, remember that you're not just drinking something that tastes good. It's also a testament to the years of hard work it can take to make something great that will stand the test of time.

**In all toil there is profit, but mere talk leads only to poverty. (Proverbs 14:23)**

*May I not lose patience when hard work is called for, Lord.*

## New Year's Eve Reflections

For many people, New Year's Eve means a party. But author Bill Vaughan's take on the holiday also rings true.

He once wrote, "Youth is when you're allowed to stay up late on New Year's Eve. Middle age is when you're forced to."

For a more traditional New Year's wish, consider the words of the late advice columnist Ann Landers, who wrote:

"Let this coming year be better than all the others. Vow to do some of the things you've always wanted to do but couldn't find the time. Call up a forgotten friend. Drop an old grudge, and replace it with some pleasant memories. Vow not to make a promise you don't think you can keep. Walk tall, and smile more. You'll look ten years younger. Don't be afraid to say, 'I love you.' Say it again. They are the sweetest words in the world."

Finally, reflect on these words from author Vern McLellan: "What the New Year brings to you will depend a great deal on what you bring to the New Year."

**Now begin the work, and the Lord be with you. (1 Chronicles 22:16)**

*Lord, guide me through the year ahead.*

# Also Available

We hope that you have enjoyed *Three Minutes a Day, Volume 49*. These other Christopher offerings may interest you:

- **News Notes** are published 10 times a year on a variety of topics of current interest. Single copies are free; quantity orders available.

- **Appointment Calendars** are suitable for wall or desk and provide an inspirational message for each day of the year.

- **DVDs** include classic Christopher films, clay-animated Christmas stories, and Father John Catoir's reflections on making prayer simple and joyful.

- **Website—www.christophers.org**—has *Christopher Closeup* radio programs; links to our blog, Facebook and Twitter pages; a monthly *What's New* update; and much more.

For more information about The Christophers or to receive News Notes, please contact us:

> The Christophers
> 5 Hanover Square
> New York, NY 10004
>
> Phone: 212-759-4050/888-298-4050
> E-mail: mail@christophers.org
> Website: www.christophers.org

The Christophers is a non-profit media organization founded in 1945 by Father James Keller, M.M. We share the message of personal responsibility and service to God and humanity with people of all faiths and no particular faith. Gifts are welcome and tax-deductible. Our legal title for wills is The Christophers, Inc.